# making meaning with texts

# making meaning with texts

## louise rosenblatt

### selected essays

HEINEMANN
Portsmouth, NH

**Heinemann**
A division of Reed Elsevier Inc.
361 Hanover Street
Portsmouth, NH 03801–3912
www.heinemann.com

*Offices and agents throughout the world*

The author and publisher wish to thank those who have generously given permission to reprint borrowed material:

"Theory and Practice: An Interview with Louise M. Rosenblatt" from *Language Arts*, 77.2, November 1999 by Nicholas J. Karolides. Copyright © 1999 by the National Council of Teachers of English. Reprinted with permission.

"The Transactional Theory of Reading and Writing" by Louise Rosenblatt from *Theoretical Models and Processes of Reading*, 5/e edited by Robert B. Ruddell and Norman J. Unrau. Published by the International Reading Association. Reprinted by permission of the publisher.

"Toward a Cultural Approach to Literature" by Louise Rosenblatt from *College English*, 7.8 (1946). Copyright © 1946 by the National Council of Teachers of English. Reprinted with permission.

"Viewpoints: Transaction Versus Interaction—A Terminological Rescue Operation" by Louise Rosenblatt from *Research in the Teaching of English*, 19.1 (1985). Copyright © 1985 by the National Council of Teachers of English. Reprinted with permission.

"Foreword" by Louise Rosenblatt from *English Journal*, 35.6 (1946). Copyright © 1946 by the National Council of Teachers of English. Reprinted with permission.

*(Credits continue on p. vi)*

**Library of Congress Cataloging-in-Publication Data**
Rosenblatt, Louise M. (Louise Michelle)
    Making meaning with texts : selected essays / Louise Rosenblatt.
        p. cm.
    Includes bibliographical references.
    ISBN 0-325-00768-3 (alk. paper)
    1. Literacy—Philosophy.   2. Literature—Study and teaching.   3. Criticism.
4. Psycholinguistics.   5. Sociolinguistics.   I. Title.
LC149.R67 2005
809—dc22                                                    2004025566

*Editor:* Lisa Luedeke
*Production:* Lynne Costa
*Cover design:* Lisa Fowler
*Cover illustration:* Richard Combes, *Young Woman Reading*, oil on canvas, 18×24 inches.
              Courtesy of Mark Murray, Fine Paintings, New York.
*Typesetter:* TechBooks
*Manufacturing:* Steve Bernier

Printed in the United States of America on acid-free paper
09 08 07 06     EB     2 3 4 5

To Jonathan and Anna

# Contents

## Part 3  Practice: Criticism

# To My Readers

I write this preface to directly address you who hold this book in your hands. I have selected these essays on the teaching of reading and literature because they seem to me to have present-day significance. I began teaching in the nineteen-thirties, a time when our democratic way of life was being subjected to external threats from antidemocratic, totalitarian forces, which were in turn being made the excuse for internal practices limiting our democratic freedoms. Traditional teaching methods, passed on from generation to generation, were, I felt, producing shallow and unquestioning readers who passively accepted the authority of the printed word. In my own classroom, I had developed collaborative methods of teaching reading of all types, fiction and nonfiction, scientific and aesthetic, based on a theory of the reading process. It seemed that students could be helped to develop the ability to read independently, purposively and critically. Such an approach was very different from their passively receiving indoctrination from a biased reading list. Fostering a critical approach to all writings, no matter what their point of view, would in itself, I believed, serve their advancement of democracy.

I have constantly been energized by the tacit belief that language engages the whole person and can enable us to reach out beyond ourselves as we make the choices that compose our lives. To jump out of the way of an oncoming car—life as against death—is easy. In settled times, most choices can be made just as automatically, according to values absorbed from family, peer group, the media, school, or community. In our tumultuous, changing world, beset by poverty, pollution, and war, unthinking, ready-made responses are dangerous. Sometimes we must choose between alternative positive values, such as security and freedom of speech. How much should we give up of one or the other, in order to have both? There must be a weighing of priorities.

Many of our ideas are so deeply rooted that they have become habitual, taken for granted, automatic. Usually an author can assume that he and his contemporary readers share such fixed ideas about the world, and can tacitly build his message on these common assumptions. This, however, was not entirely true for me. The foundation of my theory of reading embodied/ included some new ways of thinking about the relation of human beings to the world around them. I was sometimes asking my readers to give up mental habits and ideas traditionally taken for granted. New meanings, new uses, had to be developed for familiar words—for example, reading, text, word, poem.

When I finally wrote a tentative theoretical statement of the theory of reading and writing that grounded my teaching practices, I adopted the term *transaction* that the Pragmatist philosopher, John Dewey, had worked out for this new approach. The term *interaction*, he pointed out, is usually associated with a one-way process in which separate, static things are involved: one predefined unchanging thing acts on another. For example, Newtonian physics is interactional: it considers as suitable for scientific experiments only problems that deal with factors that can be held constant. In contrast, in Einstein's physics, the observer as well as the things being studied are taken into account. They are in a reciprocal, transactional relationship, continuously changing, shaping and being shaped by one another in relation to changing time and space.

Thus, from the transactional point of view, *reading* always implies both a reader and a text in a reciprocal relationship. A *text* by itself is simply a set of marks or squiggles on a page. These become a sequence of *signs* as they meet the eyes of a reader. He/she engages in a dynamic, fluid, reciprocal, to-and-fro, back-and-forth process of choosing at each moment meanings that can be merged to make tentative sense of the text. A *reader* implies someone whose past experience enables him or her to make meaning in collaboration with a text. Even if the reader immediately rereads the same text, a new relationship exists, because the reader has changed, now bringing her memory of the first encounter with that text and perhaps new preoccupations. The text may now yield a different sense or may confirm the first reading. A *text* implies squiggles or signs whose potential meaning changes with changes in the reader, the time or the place. *Meaning—whether scientific or aesthetic, whether a poem or a scientific report—happens during the interplay between particular signs and a particular reader at a particular time and place.*

Although a sign, e.g., *dog,* automatically brings up its socially produced commonly used literal referent or denotation, that response is never completely without connotations. The reader usually has conscious and subconscious memories of meeting that sign in particular social contexts such as the family or school. Usually, someone was pointing to a real dog or to a picture or description of a dog. The literal meaning is registered, but it will always also carry some feeling, perhaps pleasant for a sleek greyhound or a fluffy cuddly poodle, or fearful for a threatening, snarling bulldog. However, in different contexts some signs may acquire different, e.g., slang, meanings: "He has to stand on his dogs [feet] all day." or "She is a dog [unattractive]." Hence each reader's memory will have a unique accumulation of various past encounters with the sign carrying different mixtures of ideas and feelings, denotations and connotations.

In any reading, many personal, textual, and contextual factors will at any moment influence which of these aspects a reader will pay attention to. A reading event is like a journey. Some reader—perhaps a student who faces a true-false test about it—may be focusing mainly on what he is to remember after the reading journey is over. Another may be focused on just enjoying the journey itself, mainly paying attention to the ideas, scenes, characters, and feelings lived through during the actual reading. Another, without a clear purpose, may end with a blurred, shallow impression.

My essays are very often concerned with the fact that a text may be read with different proportions of attention to the literal, denotational aspect, and the felt, connotational aspect. The two aspects are always present, fused, in any reading. When our purpose is to read a Shakespeare sonnet as a poem, we pay attention mainly to the personal ideas and feelings aroused during the reading, but the feelings are always about something, the more or less ignored literal, cognitive, aspect. Or we can read the sonnet with attention geared to focus cognitively on the factual examples of Elizabethan grammatical usage, and we pay little attention to the linked personal, affective aspect. I term readings that focus attention more on the literal denotation *mainly efferent* reading, and those that focus more on felt connotation *mainly aesthetic* reading.

Fortunately, steadily growing numbers of teachers have freed themselves from entrenched ideas and have adopted the transactional way of thinking. Yet the interactional efferent way of thought has remained dominant in our schools, as in our society. Students have to submit to the often confusing, mainly efferently oriented demands of the traditional teacher-centered classroom, especially in the universities. Recall that my essays were not originally written to be read in a collection. Each was addressed to a specific audience at a particular time. Year after year, I often addressed my essays to those who have been taught to read all texts with the same undifferentiated approach, without a clear purpose. So year after year, I stressed what I thought they needed most, counterbalancing their learned overemphasis on the text by emphasis on the reader's selective role. Such repetition should not be dualistically misunderstood as implying that the reader alone determines the text. Since the aesthetic approach was most generally ignored, I repeatedly emphasized it, but that required also differentiating it from the efferent approach. Different does not mean contradictory. The intellectual and the affective are equally essential in both approaches, though in different proportions.

The title of this book, *Making Meaning with Texts*, should be read transactionally. The essays are grouped under two major interrelated emphases: Theory and Practice. Any classroom activities are based on a set of conscious and unconscious theoretical beliefs, and every abstract theoretical statement requires translation into actual practical behavior. Practice has been further grouped under the interrelated headings "Practice: Education" and "Practice: Criticism." Those who are meeting me for the first time probably should start with essays under "Practice: Education."

I look forward to transacting with you through the squiggles on the following pages.

*Arlington, Virginia*
*September 15, 2004*

# Acknowledgments

I thank Gordon Pradl, the first to urge an essay collection, Nicholas Karolides, Robert Probst, Edward Farrell, James Squire, Julie Cheville, Steven Mailloux, and others who have supported my theories and helped them survive through their writings and teaching. I have been expertly led through the publication process by Lisa Luedeke, Executive Editor, and Lynne Costa, Production Editor. Melissa Wood, Editorial Assistant, compiled the essays, based on the bibliography listed by my late husband, Sidney Ratner. Essential, too, over the decades, was the transaction with students, teachers, and prospective teachers in my classes, workshops, and professional conferences. The thoughtful care and stimulating companionship of my son, Jonathan Ratner, and my granddaughter, Anna, is the reason for my still being here to tell the tale.

# Theory and Practice: An Interview with Louise M. Rosenblatt

*In this* Language Arts *article, Nicholas Karolides has a conversation with distinguished educator Louise Rosenblatt, this year's Outstanding Educator in the Language Arts. Recipients of this annual award are selected by members of the Elementary Section of the National Council of Teachers of English.*

Long recognized as a preeminent leader in our profession, Louise M. Rosenblatt has been chosen to receive the fourth NCTE Award for Outstanding Educator in the Language Arts. Her presence in our field and her influence can be measured by the frequency with which she is cited, not only in NCTE periodicals, but also in the texts of our discipline and others. As a writer and speaker, as a creative thinker, Rosenblatt's energetic and dedicated espousal of a theoretical doctrine and its application in our classrooms has indeed been massively influential since *Literature as Exploration* burst upon the language arts scene in 1938.

In "Reaffirmations," her epilogue to the fifth edition of *Literature as Exploration* (1995), Louise reveals features of her background that prepared her for developing her transactional theory. She highlights, first, her family's role. Intellectually influenced by antiauthoritarian, European writers and such Americans as Emerson and Thoreau, she was "saved from acquiring lingering Victorian attitudes—especially about gender, class, and ethnic differences." Peter Kropotkin's ideas about "mutual aid" supplanted the struggle-for-survival ideas of social Darwinism.

Rosenblatt's undergraduate experience at Barnard, the women's college at Columbia University in New York, was not conventional. An "honor student" during her last two years, she did not follow the traditional liberal arts English program but instead read, mainly on her own, intensively in English and American literature and widely in the social sciences. Upon graduation, she accepted a graduate fellowship at the University of Grenoble. In the following years, she was accepted as a doctoral candidate in Comparative Literature at the Sorbonne, the faculty of letters of the University of Paris. She received her doctorate in 1931; her dissertation, written in French, *L'Idée de l'art pour l'art dans la littérature anglaise pendant la période victorienne,* was published the same year. Subsequently, while teaching at Barnard College, Rosenblatt undertook graduate studies in anthropology with Professors Franz Boas, the great founder of American anthropology, and Ruth Benedict.

During her Barnard affiliation, Rosenblatt's combined training in literature, anthropology, and the other social sciences led, in 1935, to her appointment to the Commission on Human Relations of the Progressive Education Association. An independent outgrowth of her work with the commission was the writing of her *Literature as Exploration* (first published in 1938, reissued in 1968, 1976, 1983, and 1995). Her contacts with education specialists and her visits to schools where innovative ideas had been introduced supported the decision to write this text, as did her own teaching experiences in introductory courses. In these courses she had begun to develop insights about the nature of the reading experience as well as discussion strategies in contrast to the traditional teacher-dominated lecture which was oriented toward future English majors.

Louise Rosenblatt has been teaching and actively engaged in advancing reforms in education for six decades, starting in 1927 with her first decade of teaching experience at Barnard College. After twenty years in liberal arts departments at Columbia University (Barnard) and Brooklyn College, she taught at New York University's School of Education from 1948 to 1972, after which she reached mandatory retirement age. (It was my great good fortune to have been both her student and her doctoral candidate during this period.) She has also taught, after 1972, at Rutgers University, Michigan State University, University of Pennsylvania, and others. For the past several winters, she has been lecturing and working with doctoral candidates at the University of Miami, Coral Gables, Florida.

During World War II, Louise took a leave of absence from Brooklyn College to become Associate Chief of the Western European section and Chief of the Central Reports section of the Bureau of Overseas Intelligence of the Office of War Information. Thus, from 1943 to 1945, she was immersed in information gathering and propaganda analysis of radio texts and published documents (e.g., newspapers) that had been smuggled out of occupied countries.

Louise Rosenblatt's name is well known among teachers of English language arts, chiefly because of *Literature as Exploration*. Indeed, its immediate positive reception propelled her toward her first major presentation for NCTE, addressing 3,000 teachers in the Manhattan Opera House at the 1939 annual convention in New York. Secondary and elementary school teachers persisted in their interest in her approach during the post-WWII years, although New Criticism gained dominance among college and university faculties. A resurgence of attention occurred in the 1970s, steadily increasing since then, encompassing all levels of instruction.

Many presentations and publications have established, in the words of Wayne Booth, Rosenblatt's "powerful influence" and her theory has proven to be "relevant to decade after decade of critical and pedagogical revolution" (as cited in Rosenblatt, 1995, p. vii). Chief among these publications, *The Reader, the Text, the Poem: The Transactional Theory of the Literary Work* (1978, revised paperback edition 1994) expresses her theoretical vision as does "The

Transactional Theory of Reading and Writing" (1994). (A selection of her publications follows the interview.)

Louise Rosenblatt has served the profession in other ways as well. She was appointed to the Commission on English of the College Entrance Examination Board as well as the Commission on the English Curriculum of the National Council of Teachers of English. For the latter, she was chair of the committee on the first two years of college; she contributed to the five-volume set of texts that emerged from the commission's work. She has also served as a member of the Executive Committee of the Conference on College Composition and Communication. Additionally, she has been a consultant for state boards of education.

Among the many honors that Rosenblatt has received are the Franco-American Exchange Fellow, 1925–1926; Guggenheim Fellow, 1942–1943; NYU Great Teacher Award, 1972; NCTE Distinguished Research, 1980; Leland Jacobs Award for Literature, 1981; the Assembly on Adolescent Literature Award, 1984; and the IRA Reading Hall of Fame, 1992. The Society for the Advancement of American Philosophy devoted a plenary session to her work at its 1997 national convention.

All of this is on the record. I want to add to the record a few words about Louise M. Rosenblatt, the teacher. Intense. Her classes were invariably intense, whether they focused on literary works, criticism, or theory. Louise herself was engaging and receptive; she encouraged response, asking reflective and stimulating questions. She managed to create a classroom ambiance that was both welcoming and demanding. Certainly, she practiced what she preached. Wayne Booth's judgment applies here, too: she has been a "powerful influence" on her students!

I interviewed Louise M. Rosenblatt at her home in Princeton, New Jersey, in May of 1999.

*Nicholas*: Congratulations on the Outstanding Educator in the Language Arts award, additional evidence of the widespread influence of your work.

*Louise*: I am tremendously pleased at being given this award. Although my own teaching experience has been in college and university, I have thought that if I could start all over again, I would again choose the noble profession of teacher, but for the earliest years. As for the acceptance of this approach in many classrooms and schools, I know that many people have contributed to the changes over the years. And I must admit, my tendency, as always, is to dwell, not so much on rewards for past efforts, no matter how much appreciated, as on what remains to be done, on current problems and controversies.

*Nicholas*: As you look back, can you discern any generative ideas that brought you to write *Literature as Exploration*?

*Louise*: I like your phrase "generative ideas"—it helps me to link up different strands in my thinking. I have been interested in turn-of-the-millennium talk about the changes that have come about in this century. There have been great changes in science, in the physical sciences, for example, after Einstein, with tremendous effect on technology and our practical life. The way we think of our relation to our world has changed. There has been the emergence of the social sciences. The sufferings of a great Depression earned us its legacy of acceptance of government's responsibility for the economy and the welfare of its citizens. There have been terrible wars, totalitarian threats to democracy, whether from the left or the right. And there still continue to be conflicts over alternatives to democracy. There has been great diversification in the ethnic background of American citizens.

Somehow, I've always been so involved in the future that only recently have I actually realized that I have lived through almost the whole span of the century. It helps me to see that in my little corner of the picture I was trying to deal with some of the repercussions of those changes in the way we look at the world, and with the recurrent threats to democracy.

Within that context, I would say the truly "generative" ideas have been the value of democracy for human beings, and the importance of preserving and improving our democratic way of life. This is what colored my thinking about literature and led to my becoming involved with education, with trying to understand how schools can contribute to the growth of people able to preserve and carry into greater fulfillment the democratic society, imperfect as it may be, that we are now benefiting from.

*Nicholas*: Would you elaborate on your remarks about changing ways of looking at the world?

*Louise*: The traditional way assumed that the "self," the observer, was completely separate from nature. This produced the Newtonian stimulus-response paradigm, which still has its uses, and which studies an "interaction" between things viewed as distinct and self-contained. Einsteinian theory brought about a challenge to this. It opened the way to increasing recognition that the observer must always be taken into account in any observation, that human beings are the mediators in the perception of their world. They have come to be seen as constantly in mutual interplay with their physical and human environment.

John Dewey and other Pragmatist philosophers had developed this approach early in the century. In 1949 John Dewey and Arthur F. Bentley suggested that the term "interaction" was too much involved with the older stimulus-and-response approach. They suggested "transaction" for the idea of a continuing to-and-fro, back and forth, give-and-take reciprocal or spiral relationship in which each conditions the other. "Transaction" has implications for all aspects of life. Ecology offers an easily understood illustration of the transactional relationship between human beings and their natural environment. "Transaction" also applies to individuals' relations to one another, whether we think of them in the family, the classroom, the school or in the broader society and culture.

This approach had been an important part of my thinking, so that I welcomed the term transaction, to emphasize that the meaning is being built up through the back-and-forth relationship between reader and text during a reading event.

*Nicholas*: You are often said to be at least 30 years ahead of your time in your response to the changes. Can you explain how that happened?

*Louise*: I was fortunate, I guess. You know the saying about the right place at the right time. It's hard for me to weigh all the influences—family (which was extremely important), education, friends—that converged to make me receptive to the new ideas in the exciting intellectual environment of the 20s and 30s. I was fortunate in being at Barnard, the women's college at Columbia University in New York City, both for my undergraduate years and, after taking my doctorate at the Sorbonne, as an instructor in the Barnard English department. Those were the years when while teaching composition and literature, I was studying linguistics and ethnography in the graduate anthropology department. I was encountering the most innovative thinking in the arts, philosophy, and the social sciences, as well as in education. Those were the years also when I was a member of a philosophical conference organized by John Dewey, Horace Kallen and other Pragmatist philosophers, and I read some of their writings and those of C. S. Peirce.

*Nicholas*: What were the circumstances that brought you to the writing of *Literature as Exploration?*

*Louise*: In the course of my undergraduate years at Barnard, I found myself very much interested in literature, but also discovering the social sciences, especially anthropology. When I approached graduation, I was torn between doing graduate work in literature or anthropology. I chose literature. But, in order to satisfy my anthropological interest in different cultures, I chose to go abroad to a country with a different language. Even after I had my doctorate in Comparative Literature and had started to teach in the Barnard College English Department, I did two years of graduate work in anthropology.

And because I could draw on both literature and the social sciences, in 1935 I was appointed to a Commission on Human Relations. Its purpose was to publish a group of books about such topics as family relations, human development, and psychology for late high school or early college readers. My function was to help plan the books. Others, skilled in popular writing, were to do the actual writing. That gave me my first contact with the schools.

When my part of the work was done, I reflected on the difference between reading about human relations in these books and the discussions of human relations in my classes after the reading of literary works of art.

I had great respect for the impersonal, scientific approach of the books we had planned. In contrast, the class discussions of problems in human relations arose out of what the readers had thought and felt in reading the text, and were efforts to think rationally about such topics in an emotionally colored context. It seemed to me that the resulting insights might be more personally felt, perhaps more lasting. Both approaches seemed to me to be needed. There was no provision for any Commission book on the teaching of literature. But I felt impelled to express these ideas. I went out to the country with a secretary and dictated most of the book. Recall that this was in the 30s, when both Nazism and Stalinism were powerful. I was motivated to relate all of these concerns to their role in a democracy. My work for the Commission gave me the opportunity to organize my ideas about the relation of literary experience to thinking about human relations.

*Nicholas*: What had gone on in your classes that brought these things to the surface of your thinking?

*Louise*: I recall a moment early in my teaching. I found myself in a classroom in which I had taken an undergraduate class in 18th century literature. It was taught by a tall Englishman in a three-piece suit, who spoke rather formally, with occasionally a slight catch in his speech. Standing at the same podium, holding forth, I suddenly heard a little catch in my speech! I realized that I was subconsciously imitating my professors' lectures—that it was not me talking! It's natural to teach the way we've been taught. I understand how much we are dominated by what we have assimilated from our environment—that even after we accept new ideas, it's not easy to develop new patterns of behavior.

Although the Barnard department was mainly traditional, there was some experimentation, mostly imitative of the British universities. In addition to the usual courses, I was given the opportunity to meet students in small groups. These evidently were supposed simply to fulfill the usual traditional teacher-dominated functions. However, I was free to carry on my classes in my own way, and gradually over about a decade I had arrived at the ideas expressed in my book. Actually, many of the examples in the book came from my own classes, yet I was always very much aware of how much I failed to achieve.

I recall discussions in my classes about relations between the generations in *Romeo and Juliet*. Or a student who declared that she did not consider the play a tragedy, because Romeo and Juliet would certainly be reunited in heaven. Or about the lively arguments about *A Doll's House* concerning the tension between Nora's need to become an independent person and her responsibilities as a mother.

Such interchanges demonstrated to me how much what readers make of their interplay with a text depends on what they bring to it, in linguistic and life experiences, in assumptions about the world, and in personal preoccupations. I was amazed at the differences in the actual works the readers lived through as well as in their reactions to them. I couldn't ignore the fact that each brought different personal experiences and sometimes very different assumptions about people and society to the reading. I couldn't simply be handing out neat little definitions of tragedy and comedy or asking students to analyze and classify the technique of a supposedly already made literary work.

I learned the most from the small-group discussions and from spontaneous written responses, although l welcome any kind of effective classroom practice or combination of lecture and discussion methods, so long as it is productive of interchanges with the teacher and among the students. Reflecting on and discussing what they had lived through in reading could, under proper conditions, I decided, lead to self-criticism and to growth in reading ability. It could also lead to more lasting insights into human relations than would more impersonal scientific presentations, important though they were.

*Nicholas*: Some might have been satisfied simply to settle for advocating a change in teaching methods, for more small-group discussions. How did your teaching experience lead to the development of a whole literary theory?

*Louise*: My work for the doctorate had already involved me in theory. However, my thinking about the nature of the literary work and the social role of literature had been primarily from the point of view of the creative process carried on by the author, the poet or novelist. My literature classes gave me the opportunity to observe and reflect on the relationships between readers and texts.

I saw ways in which teaching should be changed. My hope was above all to influence actual teaching. But I felt that this could happen only if I explained the theoretical basis for my ideas. The traditional approaches were based on assumptions, not only about education but about language and literature, that I questioned. Hence the chapter on the nature of the literary experience. John Dewey had published *Art as Experience* in 1934, and, as I stated in my book, his influence is obvious. However, it is hard to be very specific about this. I think I have already spoken at various times of how so many influences converged and reinforced one another in those years.

I dictated most of the book away from libraries, and there were no boxes of notes and quotations such as had been the preparation for writing my dissertation. The book was a distillation, rather, of all the reading and reflection of those years.

*Nicholas*: You earlier mentioned the philosopher Charles Sanders Peirce as an influence. As I recall, you quote his definition of science in *Literature as Exploration,* but later mention him mainly in connection with your views on language.

*Louise*:  Nowadays, Peirce is being cited as a founder of what he called semi-ology, and is now called semiotics. In the early 30s, my husband and I had read his letters to a fellow semiotics pioneer (who should be more often remembered), Lady Welby, in which he sets forth his triadic concept of language. Although I didn't write about it until later, his triadic view of language already permeated my thinking.

Then—as, alas, for many, even now—the traditional either/or notions about language prevailed. Meaning was somehow assumed to be already there "in" the text, like the kernel of a nut waiting to be pried out. The sig-nifier and what it signified were treated as a dual, self-contained system apart from its human context.

I was immune to this, because I had assimilated Peirce's triadic concept of language— sign, object, interpretant—a sign and its object linked by a mental association. A sign is simply squiggles on a page or vibrations in the air until an idea in somebody's mind links the sign with what it points to. The triadic view of language explains why we can't just concentrate on the words and their meaning apart from particular linguistic events. This firmly grounds literature in its human context.

Both Peirce and Dewey reinforced my recognition that, before there can be a scientific report or a novel or poem, there must be both a text, a set of signs, and a reader (if only the author) who will transact with it to make meaning. Meaning happens during the reading. When we talk about the interpretation or the work, we are talking about what is evoked during the reading event.

There is always a personal and a social context within which the read-ing event occurs. The individual internalizes, draws on, a socially pro-duced language presented by the family and society. We have not only a particular moment in the personal life of the reader, but also a particular social and cultural environment. Hence my insistence from the beginning on reading as a unique event in time.

*Nicholas*:  Nevertheless, students often assume that the text alone determines whether the reading produces a literary work or a scientific report. They point to *Hamlet* in a collection entitled *Tragedies* and the general assump-tion that it should be read as poetry.

*Louise*:  That's the kind of confusion remaining from traditional conceptions of language. When we speak of Shakespeare's tragedies, I believe we mean that he probably intended that the text should be read (or listened to) in a certain way and should produce certain effects called "tragedy." But there is not absolute agreement even about that. For instance, should a cer-tain text be classified as history play or tragedy? New evidence may lead us to modify our ideas about how the texts were regarded by author and readers.

*Nicholas*:  But how about inculcating respect for the author's intention?

*Louise*:  We can inculcate respect for the author's intention without inculcating confusing assumptions about how language works. We should talk about the author's *probable* intention, since we can never enter into the author's mind. That doesn't mean there can be no responsible reading. Usually, we try to find a coherent organization for what the signs on the page stir up in our consciousness. We look for clues that may reflect the intention that guided the actual writing process. We may look for external "background" information that will suggest or confirm the internal.

However, even if we have clues as to the writer's intention, perhaps even statements by the author, we can't just argue "That's what the author says is the intention, so that's what the text 'says'." We still have to decide whether the particular signs on the pages permit us to fulfill that intention.

Moreover, readers may find various possible interpretations different from the author's and different from each other. While we were talking about Shakespeare, I was reminded of when I was a graduate student and was asked to help someone who was doing research on Shakespeare's metaphors as a possible source of clues to Shakespeare's biography. I was supposed to help classify and count the metaphors—metaphors derived from nature, law, food, clothing, medicine, etc. If I had done this, I certainly would not have been reading *Hamlet* as a tragedy or as poetry. I would not have been sharing his experiences. I would have had potential categories such as nature or law in mind. I would have been scanning the pages for items to classify and record—in other words, with a mindset akin to that of a scientist recording data.

Important as the text may be, you can't explain these differences by simply looking at the text. The pattern of signs on the page remains the same; the difference is in the reader's activity in relation to those signs.

My interpretation of the text of *Hamlet* in the light of today's world, I recognize, must be different from that of a contemporary of Shakespeare. And it may be different from yours. That's all right, so long as we recognize that different transactions between readers and texts at different times under different circumstances and for different purposes may produce different interpretations, different "works."

*Nicholas*:  When I present this point of view to my class, their immediate deduction is that anything goes. What is your reaction to that?

*Louise*:  I don't blame them for that misconception. Actually, some postmodernists or deconstructionists and their disciples have made exactly that leap from "No single, absolute, 'correct' interpretation" to "All interpretations are equally acceptable." The narrow view of "comprehension" fostered by the notions of "correct" or "incorrect" interpretation of a static meaning hidden in the text has led to a pendulum, either/or, swing to extreme relativism. That is not a necessary, unavoidable conclusion.

Although there isn't a single "correct" interpretation of any text for all circumstances, that doesn't necessarily rule out responsible reading. We can consider some interpretations better or poorer than others. Or we can find that readers bringing different knowledge and assumptions or in different social and historical contexts may have equally defensible interpretations.

*Nicholas*: Once you speak of "better" or "poorer," you are, of course, consciously or unconsciously assuming some criteria or standards by which you are judging the interpretations.

*Louise*: Exactly. For example, for me, as an adult, the interpretation that takes into account more of the text would have more weight than one that ignores parts of the text—such as an interpretation of a sentence that ignored an important word, or an interpretation of *Hamlet* that ignores the scene between him and his mother. Or, I would not accept an interpretation, or parts of an interpretation, for which no basis can be found in the text. Or, I might prefer an interpretation that organizes, relates, the elements or ideas in a more plausible or more mature or more discriminating way. We might find two different interpretations equally justifiable according to such criteria. Unlike those deconstructionists, most experienced readers accept and apply such broad basic requirements, although they may disagree about others.

*Nicholas*: I believe that someone has argued that that takes us back to the traditional view of the text as dominant.

*Louise*: No, I might speak of returning to the text, but that is because the signs on the page are the only observable, empirical aspect shared by readers. Meaning "happens" during the interplay between the text and a reader. Actually, as soon as we start to say what a text means, we are reporting and analyzing the transaction we have just engaged in. We return to the text to see how, drawing on a personal reservoir to transact with the text, we arrived at our particular interpretation. Comparison of our interpretations and the application of criteria such as I have suggested can lead to self-criticism and increased reading ability. That's what should be going on when we "return to the text."

Although I emphasize the importance of the personal aspect, because it had been taken for granted and largely ignored, *Literature as Exploration* and my other publications devote many pages to the assumptions and beliefs involved in such reflection on the transaction.

*Nicholas*: That leads back to the question: How did your general view of transaction lead to the detailed model of the reading process set forth in *The Reader, the Text, the Poem* and later publications?

*Louise*: William James and Lev Vygotsky gave me formulations for the psychological processes or strategies involved. For the triadic linkage of sign and object, Vygotsky says that the meaning of a sign—I can quote exactly—is "the sum of all the psychological events aroused in our consciousness by that word." The sign is not only linked to a referent, but this is embedded in a complex web of associations, sensations, feelings, and ideas. Encountering a printed sign, for example, c-a-t, the readers have to draw on, select from, the residue of experiences of that linguistic sign in their individual, past life-situations—a unique mix of referent, associations, feelings, sensations, ideas, and attitudes in which the sign is embedded.

William James—I don't recall when I read his *Principles of Psychology*—William James's ideas about "the stream of consciousness" as a "choosing activity" were wondrously helpful. It became possible to show that the text stirred up, brought into the stream, a complex welter of sensations, thoughts, and feelings. "Selective attention" brings some elements into the center of attention and pushes others into the background or ignores them.

"Selective attention" was very important in explaining my transactional view of reading as a dynamic, fluid process in time. It helped to show that reading is a selecting, organizing, synthesizing activity. It helped to explain the back-and-forth, spiraling influence of the reader and the text on the emerging meaning: the creation of tentative meanings, their influence on the possibilities to be considered for the following signs, the modification as new signs enter the focus of attention. Sometimes, as signs emerge that can't be fitted into what we have constructed, we have to look back and revise. "Selective attention" was also important in explaining the difference between a reading that produced a scientific report and a reading that produced a poem.

*Nicholas*: But why the new terminology? Why "efferent" and "aesthetic" instead of a choice between simply "scientific" or "poetic" stances? Why the other special terminology—public, private, etc.?

*Louise*: A theory, since it will be tested, needs precise terminology. I suppose that it is more important to someone doing research, whereas the teacher needs it mainly to understand the reasons for the pedagogical implications of the model. That's why I believe that one doesn't have to worry about the terminology, once the general approach is assimilated. One develops habits of selection. The terminology was necessary for thinking about the reading process without being hampered by old unexamined assumptions. For example, the difference between the two ways of reading is implicitly recognized by many contrasting terms—science/art, nonliterary/literary, prose/poetry, expository/imaginative, etc. These classify the result, *the kind of meaning produced,* whereas I was concerned with the *process* that goes on during the actual reading event. Moreover, I had to counteract the either/or misconception that throughout any reading event, attention is given *completely* to one or the other aspect. It's easy to forget that a transaction is an event over time, and that there is always a mix of kinds of attention to different aspects of meaning. Attention may shift back and forth many times during any reading. The very absorption in a powerful feeling may lead to a shift to reflection about it or about the author's technique, before returning to the narrative. I had to have a vocabulary for talking about where the attention was mainly directed, about proportions.

Vygotsky, if I recall correctly, speaks of "intellectual and affective" aspects of meaning. Some of the other terms applied to these two aspects are denotation/connotation, cognitive/affective, empirical/qualitative, impersonal/personal. None of these, I found, could be used to cover all such paired possibilities, so for general terms, I settled on "public" and "private" aspects of meaning or sense. Then it was possible to talk about the two major kinds of activity that produce a scientific report or a poetic experience.

*Nicholas*: The distinction between scientific and poetic seems especially hard to define.

*Louise*: Yes, if we look in the text for words or syntax content that are exclusively either scientific or poetic, we are lost. Instead, we should be thinking about different psychological processes. Hence, I looked at what readers *do* in those two kinds of reading transactions.

I decided that the *proportion* or mix of selective attention to the "public" and "private" aspects of language determined whether it would be an efferent or an aesthetic reading.

I looked for particular reading acts that would illuminate the difference between the two kinds of selective activity. A favorite illustration has been the mother whose child had swallowed a poisonous liquid and who was frantically reading the label to discover what to do. She would be transacting with the signs, of course, but with attention focused on learning what to do after the reading was over. The word "water" might appear. She would pay attention to what it pointed to, its referent, its public aspect. She would not pay attention to her many associations with the word, from sensations of refreshing coolness to "water, water everywhere" and other oft-repeated lines of verse. She would push these into the fringes of attention. She would ignore her own emotional state, even though she might recall it later. Her attention would be centered on the most abstract referential aspects of meaning—what objects to reach for, what actions to perform *after* the reading ends.

I call this the "efferent" approach or "stance" in the selective process, from the Latin *efferre,* to carry away. In efferent reading, a greater proportion of attention is centered on the public, generally shared meanings, and less on the privately felt aspects. This is the kind of meaning the scientist aspires to—impersonal, repeatable, verifiable. I say, "aspires to," because we postmoderns know that the observer cannot be completely banished from the observation.

As for the poetic readings, instead of attention mainly to facts and ideas abstracted for use afterwards, the reader of, say, a lyric by Keats would focus on what was being lived through during the reading, on the ideas as they are embodied in the images, the sensations, the feelings, the changing moods. Attention would be given to the public, referential aspect, but mainly to the aura of feelings and attitudes surrounding it. I called this *aesthetic* reading.

The tendency in the teaching of literature has been to turn the student's attention away from the actual experience, and to focus on presenting a "correct," traditional interpretation, and on knowledge about technical devices or biographical or historical background.

*Nicholas*: That explains the difference between the two stances, but why do you emphasize the idea of an efferent/aesthetic *continuum*?

*Louise*: Again, because of the pedagogical implications. I am emphasizing the range of possible stances between the efferent and the aesthetic poles. Between the two poles, there is a sequence of possible proportions of attention to public and private aspects of sense. I have been citing reading events whose selective attention clearly placed them at one or the other end of the continuum. But there are many, perhaps most, reading events with the proportion falling nearer the middle. Thinking of different reading transactions as places on a continuum solves the problem most theorists have about such texts as Emerson's essays, or *The Book of Isaiah,* or Lincoln's Gettysburg Address.

*Nicholas*: That reminds me of your use of the wave metaphors in your IRA essay to illustrate the idea of the efferent/aesthetic continuum.

*Louise*: I can recall the metaphors. A scientific reading of "the wave theory of light" clearly falls near the efferent end of the continuum. And it's easy to place near the aesthetic end of the continuum a reading of Shakespeare's, "Like as the wave makes toward the pebbled shore, / So do our minutes hasten to their end." But how about an author who says of fascism, "There is no fighting the wave of the future, any more than as a child you could fight the gigantic roller that loomed up ahead of you."

This is a powerful aesthetic metaphor, meriting attention to vivid images and feelings. However, since the author's purpose is political analysis and persuasion, the reading, though near the middle of the continuum, should be efferent. Attention to factual and logical aspects should remain dominant, to judge whether they support this appeal to submission. I might have used *Silent Spring* by Rachel Carson as a middle-of-the-continuum illustration, with a more positive answer to such reflection.

Much of our reading falls into this middle area—from newspapers, political speeches, writings about social problems, advertisements—many kinds of writing with a strong affective appeal, but where the predominate stance should be efferent. We have to help students learn to handle the affective as well as cognitive aspects of meaning during every reading event. This applies to the teaching of reading across the whole scientific/literary spectrum. And it's the middle of the continuum that creates the main teaching problem. How do we help students develop the ability to adopt the appropriate stance?

*Nicholas*:  You mention teaching. Could we look more closely at the application of theory to practice?

*Louise*:  Students don't need theory. It's the teacher who needs to assimilate the theory in order to act on it. Once the transactional approach is assimilated, its pedagogical implications are not complex. Theory should help us provide the conditions, the contexts, that will foster growth toward competent reading. Most important, theory should help us to avoid methods and strategies that may satisfy short-term goals but obstruct growth.

I'll repeat a story that I've told many times. When my son was in the third grade, he brought home a workbook. From across the table, I saw the broad margins and uneven lines of text that led me to exclaim, "At last, your class is reading a poem!" Then I read the question that prefaced it: "What facts does this poem teach you?"

The question implicitly told the students that you read a poem in the same way you would read a railroad timetable. It happened to be a description of a scene with cows standing in a brook. Would the students have paid more attention to details such as the number of cows or to the feelings of calm and quiet that would create a mood? A question, like all methods and strategies, also implicitly teaches and reflects its underlying, often unacknowledged, unexamined theoretical base. This anecdote exemplifies, perhaps in rather blatant form, the failure to do justice to this matter of adoption of an appropriate stance.

What would be more influential in setting the reader's stance, for example: the teacher's statement that expression of "personal response" would be welcomed, or her addition that there would be a five-minute quiz before such discussion, "just to test whether the work had actually been read." The general reliance on mechanistic, multiple-choice testing reinforces the implicit pressure to treat literature as a body of knowledge rather than of potential experiences. Failure to take this matter of stance into account and to give a clear sense of purpose, or the giving of mixed or contradictory signals, produces, in general, shallow, unproductive readings, and uncritical acceptance of emotional appeals or unsound analogies.

Not only the teacher, but the total school environment, the types of teaching strategies, and the types of assessment influence the student by their tacit "messages" about what is really important. The transactional approach provides the basis for thinking about both the direct and the indirect, tacit effects.

*Nicholas*: Is that why you prefer "transactional theory" to "reader response theory"?

*Louise*: Precisely. I recall first formally using "transactional theory" in an article in 1969. In the reaction against the New Criticism in the 70s and 80s, the term "reader response" came to be applied to a wide range of theories that actually differed in their treatment of the reader/text relationship. Some, such as the psychoanalytic critics, were mainly subjectivist, reader-oriented. The structuralists and deconstructionists were ultimately, like the New Critics, mainly text-oriented, treating language as autonomous, without reference to author or reader. Text-oriented theories are least likely to challenge the traditional pedagogy.

When I published *The Reader, the Text, the Poem,* I called my theory "transactional" to differentiate it from both of these approaches and to emphasize the reciprocal importance of both reader and text. I keep on insisting on this point because of its pedagogical implications.

*Nicholas*: We've already talked about some pedagogical implications, such as the value of students' expression of personal reflections on their reading. Could you elaborate further?

*Louise*: I'm reminded of a college instructor in a freshman course who indignantly told me, "Your theory doesn't work. I assigned a story and told my class to interpret it personally, that they could speak freely, but the class was a failure. No one spoke up, they waited for me to interpret for them." I recall this episode because it illustrates my fears, first, that people will think of the transactional approach without concern for the total picture and the students' readiness, and, second, that they will think of the transactional approach too much in terms of a specific pedagogical strategy.

This well-meaning teacher didn't understand that probably these students had, for twelve years, been led to be insecure readers—not to respect their own thought processes. Moreover, they had probably been reading in order to answer multiple-choice factual questions on literature; they had learned to treat literature as a body of knowledge rather than potential experience. Or perhaps some of their teachers had invited personal interpretations, then spent the rest of the class period demonstrating their inadequacy in comparison with the teacher's interpretation. That college instructor needed first of all to understand what his students were bringing to the transaction with him as well as with texts. He needed to create the environment for transition to this approach.

I gather that, increasingly, students are coming to college accustomed to reading freely. But my second fear remains, concerning a narrow emphasis on the personal as a pedagogical strategy, rather than on the general approach. Sometimes, even those teachers who respect the students as readers may make a narrow view of personal response an end in itself. If the reading transaction leads students to talk and write about specifically personal matters, that is probably a good sign, especially early in the transition to this approach. But in these days of what seems, in print and TV, almost a confessional mania, the danger is to think that the job is done, that that is the final goal.

Personal response, to my mind, has to do with the entire process of response to the text. Students don't need necessarily to write about Uncle Bob, they need to be free to draw on ideas, expectations, attitudes that are the residue of having known Uncle Bob. That's what the importance of the personal aspect adds up to—freely drawing on what the signs stir up in the reservoir of past experience in order to make personally significant new meanings. That's simply basic to all aspects of evoking and reflecting on meaning—such as the choice of stance, reflection on the evoked experience from a broader perspective, recognition of personal bias—basic for growth.

*Nicholas*: Along these lines, what is your view of the literature-based curriculum?

*Louise*: "Literature" seems to be a rather vague term— that's why the concept of the aesthetic/efferent continuum had to be developed. Some people seem to think simply of using complete works, rather than anthologized snippets. Others who espouse this program assume works written primarily to be experienced, to be read aesthetically. At any rate, therein lies the source of potential problems, and therein lies the need for at least setting up some danger signals.

As I have for years felt that the aesthetic was neglected or underemphasized in our society, my first impulse is to welcome what seems to be a pendulum-swing effort to do justice to the aesthetic. But my next thought is of the importance of providing, as early as possible and as consistently as possible, a sense of alternative ways of transacting with texts.

If the literary work is used simply to sweeten the teaching of skills, if traditional methods of teaching and testing are continued, the whole value of the emphasis on so-called literature is negated. It will lead as usual to the feeling that, in school, the really important things are the skills to be acquired and demonstrated. The value of the text seen as a source either of information or experience is lost through its use primarily as the basis for teaching skills.

The either/or response is the ridiculous assumption that this constitutes a denial that skills are essential. It's a question of how they are to be acquired. So many youngsters acquire them automatically that it is wasteful to put everyone through dead-end drills, instead of providing them at the proper time for those who need the more systematic drill. The important thing is that the reading be learned as a means of making meaning, either predominately efferent or predominately aesthetic, and that skills be acquired as tools in a really meaningful activity. The problem, then, is to create a situation in which students from the beginning and throughout their education, see reading as a purposive activity.

People in the primary years have often been extraordinarily successful at this. Habits and skills are built up through meaningful reading experiences and opportunity to express reactions and reflect freely, verbally or otherwise. Some texts have been written to incorporate drill in a skill, but they provide really meaningful experiences. Long before the fourth grade, the students understand that reading is a matter of inferring, creating meaning.

*Nicholas*: Despite your reluctance to encourage formulaic methods, you have addressed teachers about instruction at different academic levels, for example, in their professional journals.

*Louise*: Your comment leads me to think back. It seems to me that I tried to suggest a whole new way of thinking, that I was concerned with indicating the concepts about language, about the process of making meaning, about the processes of reading and writing—understandings that would enable the teacher to choose among possible patterns of instruction, possible paths that would enable their particular students to advance toward increased ability to transact with texts. That usually involved changes in the teacher's assumptions and attitudes, as well as changes in classroom procedures. But it left the implementation, the specific strategies, to be worked out by people working at the different levels; primary, elementary, secondary, college, and university.

I have greatly admired the many books and articles that have shared the experience of implementing such an approach at specific levels, whether the first grade, the high school, or college, sometimes in year-long, day-by-day detail.

*Nicholas*: We have been talking about reading, but in recent articles and presentations you have dealt with reading and writing.

*Louise*: Yes, I have always been interested in the processes involved in creating, as well as reading a text. Also, I was usually teaching both reading and writing. My transactional view of language applies to all modes of language behavior. A speaker assumes a listener, and a reader assumes a writer, and vice versa.

At first, I wrote almost exclusively about reading, because that is what I was asked to do. Fortunately, many composition teachers didn't have to be addressed directly, and they were very receptive from the very beginning.

In the late 80s, when reading and writing experts organized a conference on the connections among the various language activities, I was delighted to be asked to contribute. After that, I decided that I could no longer write about reading without also dealing more fully with writing. Perhaps I should add that the reverse also holds: I find I can't deal with writing without talking about reading.

Both writer and reader transact with texts, both compose meanings. That is why all the transactional concepts hold for both. But there are differences that should be kept in mind. The reader starts with the author's text and tries to build a meaning consonant with it. The writer starts with a blank page; as the text emerges on the page, its author is its first reader. Reading is part of the writing process.

Actually, I find there are two kinds of authorial reading—first, expression-oriented, when the writer is testing the emerging text in the light of a more or less clear intention; and second, reception-oriented, when the writer reads the text in the light of whether it assumes knowledge or experience potential readers may not bring to it.

Both types of authorial reading may bring revisions. The more experienced the writer, the more likely these two types of reading will occur throughout the writing process, and the more automatically they will alternate. Sometimes the writer may have to decide between words that are personally more satisfying, more expressive, and words that will be more effective links with the linguistic and life experience of prospective readers. A word might be too technical, or a metaphor based on the game of chess might not be understood by many potential readers.

The traditional preoccupation with reading in the early years seems to be waning as more and more schools recognize the importance of writing. The opportunity to engage purposefully in these parallel linguistic activities should reinforce habits that are important for both writing and reading.

*Nicholas*: What are you working on now?

*Louise*: Actually, I'm having a problem about priorities. I should be finishing an essay on the relation between writing and reading for an IRA handbook. But I may not meet the deadline, because I feel that more important than anything else right now is the political situation. As a teacher and as a citizen, I feel guilty about using my energy on other matters so long as I can do anything, slight as it may be, to influence what's happening in the political arena right now.

Lately, my time at the computer has been spent writing letters to legislators and drafting suggestions to officers of our professional organizations about ways of increasing our political clout.

My belief in the importance of the schools in a democracy has not only evolved but also increased over the years. In 1938, democracy was being threatened by forces and ideologies from outside. Today, I believe it is again seriously threatened, this time mainly by converging forces from within. From local schools to state standards to Supreme Court cases, education has become an arena for this ideological struggle. Special interest groups have been organized to achieve domination of local school boards; topics such as methods of teaching reading or allocation of funds to research have become political issues at all levels.

At the risk of sounding pompous, I have said that my efforts to expound my theory have been fueled by the belief that it serves the purpose of education for democracy. Ultimately, if I have been concerned about methods of teaching literature, about ensuring that it should indeed be personally experienced, it is because, as Shelley said, it helps readers develop the imaginative capacity to put themselves in the place of others—a capacity essential in a democracy, where we need to rise above narrow self-interest and envision the broader human consequences of political decisions. If I have been involved with development of the ability to read critically across the whole intellectual spectrum, it is because such abilities are particularly important for citizens in a democracy.

Of course, the schools cannot do the whole job, but they are essential. We are already overburdened as teachers, yet as citizens we need to promote and defend the social, economic, and political conditions that make it possible for us to carry on our democratic tasks in the classroom.

## Selected Bibliography of Louise M. Rosenblatt

*L'Idée de l'art pour l'art dans la littérature anglaise pendant la période victorienne.* (1931). Paris: Champion; New York: AMS Press, 1976.

*Literature as Exploration.* (1938). New York: Appleton-Century; (1968; rev. ed.). New York: Noble and Noble; (1970; 2nd ed). London: Heinemann; (1976; 3rd ed.). New York: Noble and Noble; (1983; 4th ed.). New York: Modern Language Association; (1995; 5th ed.). New York: Modern Language Association.

"The Acid Test for Literature Teaching." (1956). *English Journal, 45*(2), 66–74.

"Toward a Cultural Approach to Literature." (1946). *College English, 7*(8), 459–66.

Guest Editor, Intercultural relations issue. (1946) *English Journal, 35*(6).

"Literature: The Reader's Role." (1960). *English Journal, 49*(5), 304–10, 315. (Rpt. in *Education Synopsis, 12*(2), 196. 1–6.)

"The Poem as Event." (1964). *College English, 26*(2), 123–28.

"Literature and the Invisible Reader." (1970). In (Eds. unknown), *The Promise of English: 1970 Distinguished Lectures* (pp. 1–26). Champaign, IL: National Council of Teachers of English.

*The Reader, the Text, the Poem: The Transactional Theory of the Literary Work.* (1978; Rev. ed., 1994). Carbondale, IL: Southern Illinois University Press.

"Whitman's 'Democratic Vistas' and the New 'Ethnicity.'" (1978). *Yale Review, 67,* 187–204.

"What Facts Does This Poem Teach You?" (1980). *Language Arts, 57*(4), 386–94.

"Act I, Scene 1; Enter the Reader." (1981). *Literature in Performance, 1*(2), 13–23.

*The Journey Itself.* (1981). Leland B. Jacobs Lecture. New York: School of Library Service, Columbia University.

"The Literary Transaction: Evocation and Response." (1982). *Theory into Practice, 21*(4), 268–77.

"On the Aesthetic as the Basic Model of the Reading Process." (1981). *Theories of Reading, Looking, and Listening* (H. R. Garvin, Ed.). *Bucknell Review, 26*(1), 17–32.

"The Reading Transaction: 'What for?'" (1983). In R.P. Parker & F.A. Davis (Eds.), *Developing Literacy* (pp. 118–135). Newark, DE: International Reading Association.

"Viewpoints: Transaction versus Interaction, a Terminological Rescue Operation." (1985). *Research in the Teaching of English, 19*(1), 96–107.

"Language, Literature, and Values." (1985). In S.N. Tchudi (Ed.), *Language, Schooling, and Society* (pp. 64–80). Proceedings of the International Federation of Teachers of English. Portsmouth, NH: Boynton/Cook.

"The Transactional Theory of the Literary Work: Implications for Research." (1985.) In C.R. Cooper (Ed.), *Researching Response to Literature and the Teaching of English* (pp. 33–53). Norwood, NJ: Ablex.

"The Literary Transaction." (1986). In P. Demers (Ed.), *The Creating Word* (pp. 66–85). London: Macmillan; Edmonton, AB, Canada: University of Alberta Press. (Papers from an international conference on the teaching of English in the 1980s.)

"The Aesthetic Transaction." (1986). *Journal of Aesthetic Education, 20*(4), 122–28.

"Literary Theory." (1991, 2002). In J.R. Squire (Ed.), *Handbook of Research on Teaching the English Language Arts* (pp. 57–62). Boston: Macmillan.

"Literature—S. O. S.!" (1991). *Language Arts, 68,* 12–16.

"The Transactional Theory: Against Dualism." (1993). *College English, 55*(4), 377–86.

"The Transactional Theory of Reading and Writing." (1994). In R.R. Ruddell, M.R. Ruddell, & H. Singer (Eds.), *Theoretical Models and Processes of Reading* (4th ed.) (pp. 1057–92). Newark, DE: International Reading Association.

"Readers, Texts, Authors." (1998). *Transactions of the Charles S. Peirce Society, 34*(4), 885–921.

*Nicholas J. Karolides is a professor of English and Associate Dean at the College of Arts and Sciences at the University of Wisconsin-River Falls, where he teaches literature, composition, and methods of teaching English. His publications include* Reader Response in Elementary Classrooms *(1996) and* Banned Books: Literature Suppressed on Political Grounds *(1998).*

## Chapter One

# The Transactional Theory
# of Reading and Writing

*Terms such as* the reader *are somewhat misleading, though conven-
ient, fictions. There is no such thing as a generic reader or a generic
literary work; there are in reality only the potential millions of individual readers of individual literary works. . . . The reading of any
work of literature is, of necessity, an individual and unique occurrence involving the mind and emotions of some particular reader.*
(Rosenblatt, 1938/1983)

That statement, first published in *Literature as Exploration* in 1938, seems especially important to reiterate at the beginning of a presentation of a "theoretical
model" of the reading process. A theoretical model by definition is an abstraction, or a generalized pattern devised in order to think about a subject. Hence, it
is essential to recognize that, as I concluded, we may generalize about similarities among such events, but we cannot evade the realization that there are actually only innumerable separate transactions between readers and texts.

As I sought to understand how we make the meanings called novels,
poems, or plays, I discovered that I had developed a theoretical model that
covers all modes of reading. Ten years of teaching courses in literature and
composition had preceded the writing of that statement. This had made possible
observation of readers encountering a wide range of "literary" and "nonliterary"
texts, discussing them, keeping journals while reading them, and writing spontaneous reactions and reflective essays. And decades more of such observation
preceded the publication of *The Reader, the Text, the Poem* (Rosenblatt, 1978),
the fullest presentation of the theory and its implications for criticism.

From Ruddell, R.B., Ruddell, M.R., & Singer, H. (Eds.), *Theoretical Models and Processes of
Reading* (4th ed., pp. 1057–1092). Copyright © 1994 by the International Reading
Association.

Thus, the theory emerges from a process highly appropriate to the pragmatist philosophy it embodies. The problem arose in the context of a practical classroom situation. Observations of relevant episodes led to the hypotheses that constitute the theory of the reading process, and these have in turn been applied, tested, confirmed, or revised in the light of further observation.

Fortunately, while specializing in English and comparative literature, I was in touch with the thinking on the forefront of various disciplines. The interpretation of these observations of readers' reading drew on a number of different perspectives—literary and social history, philosophy, aesthetics, linguistics, psychology, and sociology. Training in anthropology provided an especially important point of view. Ideas were developed that in some instances have only recently become established. It seems necessary, therefore, to begin by setting forth some of the basic assumptions and concepts that undergird the transactional theory of the reading process. This in turn will involve presentation of the transactional view of the writing process and the relationship between author and reader.

## The Transactional Paradigm

### *Transaction*

The terms *transaction* and *transactional* are consonant with a philosophic position increasingly accepted in the 20th century. A new paradigm in science (Kuhn, 1970) has required a change in our habits of thinking about our relationship to the world around us. For 300 years, Descartes' dualistic view of the self as distinct from nature sufficed, for example, for the Newtonian paradigm in physics. The self, or "subject," was separate from the "object" perceived. "Objective" facts, completely free of subjectivity, were sought, and a direct, immediate perception of "reality" was deemed possible. Einstein's theory and the developments in subatomic physics revealed the need to acknowledge that, as Neils Bohr (1959) explained, the observer is part of the observation— human beings are part of nature. Even the physicists' facts depend to some extent on the interests, hypotheses, and technologies of the observer. The human organism, it became apparent, is ultimately the mediator in any perception of the world or any sense of "reality."

John Dewey's pragmatist epistemology fitted the new paradigm. Hence, Dewey joined with Arthur F. Bentley to work out a new terminology in *Knowing and the Known* (1949). They believed the term *interaction* was too much associated with the old positivistic paradigm, with each element or unit being predefined as separate, as "thing balanced against thing," and their "interaction" studied. Instead, they chose *transaction* to imply "unfractured observation" of the whole situation. Systems of description and naming "are employed to deal with aspects and phases of action, without final attribution to 'elements' or presumptively detachable or independent 'entities,' 'essences,' or 'realities'"

(p. 108). The knower, the knowing, and the known are seen as aspects of "one process." Each element conditions and is conditioned by the other in a mutually constituted situation (cf. Rosenblatt, 1985b).

The new paradigm requires a break with entrenched habits of thinking. The old stimulus–response, subject–object, individual–social dualisms give way to recognition of transactional relationships. The human being is seen as part of nature, continuously in transaction with an environment—each one conditions the other. The transactional mode of thinking has perhaps been most clearly assimilated in ecology. Human activities and relationships are seen as transactions in which the individual and social elements fuse with cultural and natural elements. Many current philosophy writers may differ on metaphysical implications but find it necessary to come to terms with the new paradigm.[1]

## Language

The transactional concept has profound implications for understanding language. Traditionally, language has been viewed as primarily a self-contained system or code, a set of arbitrary rules and conventions that is manipulated as a tool by speakers and writers or imprints itself on the minds of listeners and readers. Even when the transactional approach has been accepted, this deeply ingrained way of thinking continues to function, tacitly or explicitly, in much theory, research, and teaching involving texts.[2]

The view of language basic to the transactional model of reading owes much to the philosopher John Dewey but even more to his contemporary Charles Sanders Peirce, who is recognized as the U.S. founder of the field of semiotics or semiology, the study of verbal and nonverbal signs. Peirce provided concepts that differentiate the transactional view of language and reading from structuralist and poststructuralist (especially deconstructionist) theories. These reflect the influence of another great semiotician, the French linguist Ferdinand de Saussure (Culler, 1982).

Saussure (1972) differentiated actual speech (*parole*) from the abstractions of the linguists (*langue*), but he stressed the arbitrary nature of signs and minimized the referential aspect. Even more important was his dyadic formulation of the relationship between "signifier and signified," or between words and concept. These emphases fostered a view of language as an autonomous, self-contained system (Rosenblatt, 1993).

In contrast, Peirce (1933, 1935) offered a triadic formulation. "A sign," Peirce wrote, "is in conjoint relation to the thing denoted and to the mind. . . ." The "sign is related to its object only in consequence of a mental association, and depends on habit" (Vol. 3, para. 360). The triad constitutes a symbol. Peirce repeatedly refers to the human context of meaning. Because he evidently did not want to reinforce the notion of "mind" as an entity, he typically phrased the "conjoint" linkage as among sign, object, and "interpretant," which should be understood as a mental operation rather than an entity (6.347). Peirce's triadic model firmly grounds language in the transactions of individual human beings with their world.

Recent descriptions of the working of the brain by neurologists and other scientists seem very Peircean. Although they are dealing with a level not essential to our theoretical purposes, they provide an interesting reinforcement. "Many leading scientists, including Dr. Francis Crick, think that the brain creates unified circuits by oscillating distant components at a shared frequency" (Appenzeller, 1990, pp. 6–7). Neurologists speak of "a third-party convergence zone [which seems to be a neurological term for Peirce's interpretant] that mediates between word and concept convergence zones" (Damasio, 1989, pp. 123–132). Studies of children's acquisition of language support the Peircean triad, concluding that a vocalization or sign becomes a word, a verbal symbol, when the sign and its object or referent are linked with the same "organismic state" (Werner & Kaplan, 1962, p. 18).

Though language is usually defined as a socially generated system of communication—the very bloodstream of any society—the triadic concept reminds us that language is always internalized by a human being transacting with a particular environment. Vygotsky's recognition of the social context did not prevent his affirming the individual's role: The "sense of a word" is

> the sum of all the psychological events aroused in our consciousness by the word. It is a dynamic, fluid, complex whole, which has several zones of unequal stability. Meaning [i.e., reference] is only one of the zones of sense, the most stable and precise zone. A word acquires its sense from the context in which it appears; in different contexts, it changes its sense. (1962, p. 46)

Vygotsky postulated "the existence of a dynamic system of meaning, in which the affective and the intellectual unite." The earliest utterances of children evidently represent a fusion of "processes which later will branch off into referential, emotive, and associative part processes" (Rommetveit, 1968, pp. 147, 167). The child learns to sort out the various aspects of "sense" associated with a sign, decontextualize it, and recognize the public aspect of language, the collective language system. This does not, however, eliminate the other dimensions of sense. A language act cannot be thought of as totally affective or cognitive, or as totally public or private (Bates, 1979, pp. 65–66).

Bates provides the useful metaphor of an iceberg for the total sense of a word to its user: The visible tip represents what I term the public aspect of meaning, resting on the submerged base of private meaning. *Public* designates usages or meanings that dictionaries list. Multiple meanings indicated for the same word reflect the fact that the same sign takes on different meanings at different times and in different linguistic or different personal, cultural, or social contexts. In short, *public* refers to usages that some groups of people have developed and that the individual shares.

Note that *public* and *private* are not synonymous with *cognitive* and *affective*. Words may have publicly shared affective connotations. The individual's private associations with a word may or may not agree with its connotations for the group, although these connotations must also be individually acquired. Words necessarily involve for each person a mix of both public and private elements, the base as well as the tip of the semantic iceberg.

For the individual, then, the language is that part, or set of features, of the public system that has been internalized through that person's experiences with words in life situations. "Lexical concepts must be shared by speakers of a common language . . . yet there is room for considerable individual difference in the details of any concept" (Miller & Johnson-Laird, 1976, p. 700). The residue of the individual's past transactions—in particular natural and social contexts—constitutes what can be termed a linguistic–experiential reservoir. William James especially suggests the presence of such a cumulative experiential aura of language.

Embodying funded assumptions, attitudes, and expectations about language and about the world, this inner capital is all that each of us has to draw on in speaking, listening, writing, or reading. We "make sense" of a new situation or transaction and make new meanings by applying, reorganizing, revising, or extending public and private elements selected from our personal linguistic–experiential reservoirs.

## Linguistic Transactions

Face-to-face communication—such as a conversation in which a speaker is explaining something to another person—can provide a simplified example of the transactional nature of all linguistic activities. A conversation is a temporal activity, a back-and-forth process. Each person has come to the transaction with an individual history, manifested in what has been termed a linguistic–experiential reservoir. The verbal signs are the vibrations in the air caused by a speaker. Both speaker and addressee contribute throughout to the spoken text (even if the listener remains silent) and to the interpretations that it calls forth as it progresses. Each must construct some sense of the other person. Each draws on a particular linguistic–experiential reservoir. The specific situation, which may be social and personal, and the setting and occasion for the conversation in themselves provide clues or limitations as to the general subject or framework and hence to the references and implications of the verbal signs. The speaker and addressee both produce further delimiting cues through facial expressions, tones of voice, and gestures. In addition to such nonverbal indications of an ongoing mutual interpretation of the text, the listener may offer questions and comments. The speaker thus is constantly being helped to gauge and to confirm, revise, or expand the text. Hence, the text is shaped transactionally by both speaker and addressee.

The opening words of a conversation, far from being static, by the end of the interchange may have taken on a different meaning. And the attitudes, the state of mind, even the manifest personality traits, may have undergone change. Moreover, the spoken text may be interpreted differently by each of the conversationalists.

But how can we apply the conversation model of transaction to the relationship between writers and readers, when so many of the elements that contribute to the spoken transaction are missing—physical presence, timing, actual setting, nonverbal behaviors, tones of voice, and so on? The signs on the page are all that the writer and the reader have to make up for the absence of these other elements. The reader focuses attention on and transacts with an element in the environment, namely the signs on the page, the text.

Despite all the important differences noted above, speech, writing, and reading share the same basic process—transacting through a text. In any linguistic event, speakers and listeners and writers and readers have only their linguistic–experiential reservoirs as the basis for interpretation. Any interpretations or new meanings are restructurings or extensions of the stock of experiences of language, spoken and written, brought to the task. In Peircean terms, past linkages of sign, object, and interpretant must provide the basis for new linkages, or new structures of meaning. Instead of an interaction, such as billiard balls colliding, there has been a transaction, thought of rather in terms of reverberations, rapid oscillations, blendings, and mutual conditionings.

### Selective Attention

William James's concept of "selective attention" provides an important insight into this process. During the first half of this century, a combination of behaviorism and positivism led to neglect of the concept, but since the 1970s psychologists have reasserted its importance (Blumenthal, 1977; Myers, 1986). James (1890) tells us that we are constantly engaged in a "choosing activity," which he terms "selective attention" (I.284). We are constantly selecting out of the stream, or field, of consciousness "by the reinforcing and inhibiting agency of attention" (I.288). This activity is sometimes termed "the cocktail party phenomenon": In a crowded room where many conversations are in progress, we focus our attention on only one of them at a time, and the others become a background hum. We can turn our selective attention toward a broader or narrower area of the field. Thus, while language activity implies an intermingled kinesthetic, cognitive, affective, associational matrix, what is pushed into the background or suppressed and what is brought into awareness and organized into meaning depend on where selective attention is focused.

The transactional concept will prevent our falling into the error of envisaging selective attention as a mechanical choosing among an array of fixed entities rather than as a dynamic centering on areas or aspects of the contents of consciousness. The linguistic reservoir should not be seen as encompassing verbal signs linked to fixed meanings, but as a fluid pool of potential triadic symbolizations. Such residual linkages of sign, signifier, and organic state, it will be seen, become actual symbolizations as selective attention functions under the shaping influence of particular times and circumstances.

In the linguistic event, any process also will be affected by the physical and emotional state of the individual, for example, by fatigue or stress. Attention may be controlled or wandering, intense or superficial. In the discussion that follows, it will be assumed that such factors enter into the transaction and affect the quality of the process under consideration.

The paradoxical situation is that the reader has only the black marks on the page as the means of arriving at a meaning—and that meaning can be constructed only by drawing on the reader's own personal linguistic and life experiences. Because a text must be produced by a writer before it can be read, logic might seem to dictate beginning with a discussion of the writing process. It is true that the writer seeks to express something, but the purpose is to communicate with a reader (even if it is only the writer wishing to preserve some thought or experience for future reference). Typically, the text is intended for others. Some sense of a reader or at least of the fact that the text will function in a reading process thus is implicit in the writing process. Hence, I shall discuss the reading process first, then the writing process. Then, I shall broach the problems of communication and validity of interpretation before considering implications for teaching and research.

## The Reading Process

### Transacting with the Text

The concepts of transaction, the transactional nature of language, and selective attention now can be applied to analysis of the reading process. Every reading act is an event, or a transaction involving a particular reader and a particular pattern of signs, a text, and occurring at a particular time in a particular context. Instead of two fixed entities acting on one another, the reader and the text are two aspects of a total dynamic situation. The "meaning" does not reside ready-made "in" the text or "in" the reader but happens or comes into being during the transaction between reader and text.

The term *text* in this analysis denotes, then, a set of signs capable of being interpreted as verbal symbols. Far from already possessing a meaning that can be imposed on all readers, the text actually remains simply marks on paper, an object in the environment, until some reader transacts with it. The term *reader* implies a transaction with a text; the term *text* implies a transaction with a reader. "Meaning" is what happens during the transaction; hence, the fallacy of thinking of them as separate and distinct entities instead of factors in a total situation.

The notion that the marks in themselves possess meaning is hard to dispel. For example, *pain* for a French reader will link up with the concept of bread and for an English reader with the concept of bodily or mental suffering. A sentence that Noam Chomsky (1968, p. 27) made famous can help us realize that not even the syntax is inherent in the signs of the text but depends on the results of particular transactions: *Flying planes can be dangerous.*

Actually, only after we have selected a meaning can we infer a syntax from it. Usually, factors entering into the total transaction, such as the context and reader's purpose, will determine the reader's choice of meaning. Even if the reader recognizes the alternative syntactic possibilities, these factors still prevail. This casts doubt on the belief that the syntactical level, because it is lower or less complex, necessarily always precedes the semantic in the reading process. The transactional situation suggests that meaning implies syntax and that a reciprocal process is going on in which the broader aspects guiding choices are actively involved.

Here we see the difference between the physical text, defined as a pattern of signs, and what is usually called "the text," a syntactically patterned set of verbal symbols. This actually comes into being during the transaction with the signs on the page.

When we see a set of such marks on a page, we believe that it should give rise to some more or less coherent meaning. We bring our funded experience to bear. Multiple inner alternatives resonate to the signs. Not only the triadic linkages with the signs but also certain organismic states, or certain ranges of feeling, are stirred up in the linguistic–experiential reservoir. From these activated areas, selective attention—conditioned, as we have seen, by multiple physical, personal, social, and cultural factors entering into the situation—picks out elements that will be organized and synthesized into what constitutes "meaning." Choices have in effect probably been made simultaneously, as the various "levels" transact, conditioning one another, so to speak.

Reading is, to use James's phrase, a "choosing activity." From the very beginning, and often even before, some expectation, some tentative feeling, idea, or purpose, no matter how vague at first, starts the reading process and develops into the constantly self-revising impulse that guides selection, synthesis, and organization. The linguistic–experiential reservoir reflects the reader's cultural, social, and personal history. Past experience with language and with texts provides expectations. Other factors are the reader's present situation and interests. Perusing the unfolding text in the light of past syntactic and semantic experience, the reader seeks cues on which to base expectations about what is forthcoming. The text as a verbal pattern, we have seen, is part of what is being constructed. Possibilities open up concerning the general kind of meaning that may be developing, affecting choices in diction, syntax, and linguistic and literary conventions.

As the reader's eyes move along the page, the newly evoked symbolizations are tested for whether they can be fitted into the tentative meanings already constructed for the preceding portion of the text. Each additional choice will signal certain options and exclude others, so that even as the meaning evolves, the selecting, synthesizing impulse is itself constantly shaped and tested. If the marks on the page evoke elements that cannot be assimilated into the emerging synthesis, the guiding principle or framework is revised; if necessary, it is discarded and a complete rereading occurs. New tentative guidelines, new bases for a hypothetical structure, may then present themselves. Reader and text are involved in a complex, nonlinear, recursive, self-correcting transaction. The arousal and fulfillment—or frustration and revision—of expectations contribute to the construction of a cumulative meaning. From a to-and-fro interplay between reader, text, and context emerges a synthesis or organization, more or less coherent and complete. This meaning, this "evocation," is felt to correspond to the text.

Precisely because for experienced readers so much of the reading process is, or should be, automatic, aspects of the reading process tend to be described in impersonal, mechanistic terms. Psychologists are rightfully concerned with learning as much as possible about what goes on between the reader's first visual contact with the marks on the page and the completion of what is considered an interpretation of them. A number of different levels, systems, and strategies have been analytically designated, and research has been directed at clarifying their nature. These can be useful, but from a transactional point of view, it is important to recognize their potentialities and their limitations. A mechanistic analogy or metaphor lends itself especially to analyses of literal reading of simple texts. Results need to be cautiously interpreted. Recognizing the essential nature of both reader and text, the transactional theory requires an underlying metaphor of organic activity and reciprocity.

The optical studies of Adelbert Ames (1955) and the Ames–Cantril "transactional psychology" (Cantril & Livingston, 1963), which also derived its name from Dewey and Bentley's *Knowing and the Known* (1949), deserve first mention in this regard. These experiments demonstrated that perception depends much on the viewer's selection and organization of visual cues according to past experience, expectations, needs, and interests. The perception may be revised through continued transactions between the perceiver and the perceived object.

F.C. Bartlett's theory of *Remembering* (1932) (which I regret having discovered even later than did his fellow scientists) and his term *schema* are often called on to explain psychological processes even broader than his special field. It is not clear, however, that those who so readily invoke his schema concept are heeding his fears about a narrow, static usage of the term. Rejecting the image of a warehouse of unchanging items as the metaphor for schemata, he emphasized rather "active, developing patterns"—"constituents of living, momentary settings belonging to the organism" (Bartlett, 1932, p. 201). His description of the "constructive character of remembering," his rejection of a simple mechanical linear process, and his concepts of the development and continuing revision of schemata all have parallels in the transactional theory of linguistic events. His recognition of the influence of both the interests of the individual and the social context on all levels of the process also seems decidedly transactional.

## The Reader's Stance

The broad outline of the reading process sketched thus far requires further elaboration. An important distinction must be made between the operations that produce the meaning, say, of a scientific report and the operations that evoke a literary work of art. Neither contemporary reading theory nor literary theory has done justice to such readings, nor to the fact that they are to be understood as representing a continuum rather than an opposition. The tendency generally has been to assume that such a distinction depends entirely on the texts involved. The character of the "work" has been held to inhere entirely in the text. But we cannot look simply at the text and predict the nature of the work. We cannot assume, for instance, that a poem rather than an argument about fences will be evoked from the text of Frost's *Mending Wall* or that a novel rather than sociological facts about Victorian England will be evoked from Dickens's *Great Expectations*. Advertisements and newspaper reports have been read as poems. Each alternative represents a different kind of selective activity, a different kind of relationship, between the reader and the text.

Essential to any reading is the reader's adoption, conscious or unconscious, of what I have termed a *stance* guiding the "choosing activity" in the stream of consciousness. Recall that any linguistic event carries both public and private aspects. As the transaction with the printed text stirs up elements of the linguistic–experiential reservoir, the reader adopts a selective attitude or stance, bringing certain aspects into the center of attention and pushing others into the fringes of consciousness. A stance reflects the reader's purpose. The situation, the purpose, and the linguistic–experiential equipment of the reader as well as the signs on the page enter into the transaction and affect the extent to which public and private meanings and associations will be attended to.

## The Efferent–Aesthetic Continuum

The reading event must fall somewhere in a continuum, determined by whether the reader adopts what I term a *predominantly aesthetic* stance or a *predominantly efferent* stance. A particular stance determines the proportion or mix of public and private elements of sense that fall within the scope of the reader's selective attention. Or, to recall Bates's metaphor, a stance results from the degree and scope of attention paid respectively to the tip and to the base of the iceberg. Such differences can be represented only by a continuum, which I term the *efferent–aesthetic continuum*.

## The Efferent Stance

The term *efferent* (from the Latin *efferre*, to carry away) designates the kind of reading in which attention is centered predominantly on what is to be extracted and retained after the reading event. An extreme example is a man who has accidentally swallowed a poisonous liquid and is rapidly reading the label on the bottle to learn the antidote. Here, surely, we see an illustration of James's point about selective attention and our capacity to push into the periphery of awareness or ignore those elements that do not serve our present interests. The man's attention is focused on learning what is to be done as soon as the reading ends. He concentrates on what the words point to, ignoring anything other than their barest public referents, constructing as quickly as possible the directions for future action. These structured ideas are the evocation felt to correspond to the text.

Reading a newspaper, textbook, or legal brief would usually provide a similar, though less extreme, instance of the predominantly efferent stance. In efferent reading, then, we focus attention mainly on the public "tip of the iceberg" of sense. Meaning results from abstracting out and analytically structuring the ideas, information, directions, or conclusions to be retained, used, or acted on after the reading event.

## The Aesthetic Stance

The predominantly aesthetic stance covers the other half of the continuum. In this kind of reading, the reader adopts an attitude of readiness to focus attention on what is being lived through during the reading event. The term *aesthetic* was chosen because its Greek source suggested perception through the senses, feelings, and intuitions. Welcomed into awareness are not only the public referents of the verbal signs but also the private part of the "iceberg" of meaning: the sensations, images, feelings, and ideas that are the residue of past psychological events involving those words and their referents. Attention may include the sounds and rhythms of the words themselves, heard in "the inner ear" as the signs are perceived.

The aesthetic reader pays attention to—savors—the qualities of the feelings, ideas, situations, scenes, personalities, and emotions that are called forth and participates in the tensions, conflicts, and resolutions of the images, ideas, and scenes as they unfold. The lived-through meaning is felt to correspond to the text. This meaning, shaped and experienced during the aesthetic transaction, constitutes "the literary work," the poem, story, or play. This "evocation," and not the text, is the object of the reader's "response" and "interpretation," both during and after the reading event.

Confusion about the matter of stance results from the entrenched habit of thinking of the *text* as efferent or aesthetic, expository or poetic, literary or nonliterary, and so on. Those who apply these terms to texts should realize that they actually are reporting their interpretation of the writer's intention as to what kind of reading the text should be given. The reader is free, however, to adopt either predominant stance toward any text. *Efferent* and *aesthetic* apply, then, to the writer's and the reader's selective attitude toward their own streams of consciousness during their respective linguistic events.

To recognize the essential nature of stance does not minimize the importance of the text in the transaction. Various verbal elements—metaphor, stylistic conventions or divergence from linguistic or semantic norms, even certain kinds of content—have been said to constitute the "poeticity" or "literariness" of a text. Such verbal elements, actually, do often serve as cues to the experienced reader to adopt an aesthetic stance. Yet it is possible to cite acknowledged literary works that lack one or all of these elements. Neither reading theorists nor literary theorists have given due credit to the fact that none of these or any other arrangements of words could make their "literary" or "poetic" contribution without the reader's prior shift of attention toward mainly the qualitative or experiential contents of consciousness, namely, the aesthetic stance.

## The Continuum

The metaphorical nature of the term the *stream of consciousness* can be called on further to clarify the efferent–aesthetic continuum. We can image consciousness as a stream flowing through the darkness. Stance, then, can be represented as a mechanism lighting up—directing the attention to—different parts of the stream, selecting out objects that have floated to the surface in those areas and leaving the rest in shadow. Stance, in other words, provides the guiding orientation toward activating particular areas and elements of consciousness, that is, particular proportions of public and private aspects of meaning, leaving the rest at the dim periphery of attention. Some such play of attention over the contents of what emerges into consciousness must be involved in the reader's multifold choices from the linguistic–experiential reservoir.

Efferent and aesthetic reflect the two main ways of looking at the world, often summed up as "scientific" and "artistic." My redundant usage of "predominantly" aesthetic or efferent underlines rejection of the traditional, binary, either- or tendency to see them as in opposition. The efferent stance pays more attention to the cognitive, the referential, the factual, the analytic, the logical, the quantitative aspects of meaning. And the aesthetic stance pays more attention to the sensuous, the affective, the emotive, the qualitative. But nowhere can we find on the one hand the purely public and on the other hand the purely private. Both of these aspects of meaning are attended to in different proportions in any linguistic event. One of the earliest and most important steps in any reading event, therefore, is the selection of either a predominantly efferent or a predominantly aesthetic stance toward the transaction with a text. Figure 1 indicates different readings by the same reader of the same text at different

**Figure 1.** The Efferent–Aesthetic Continuum

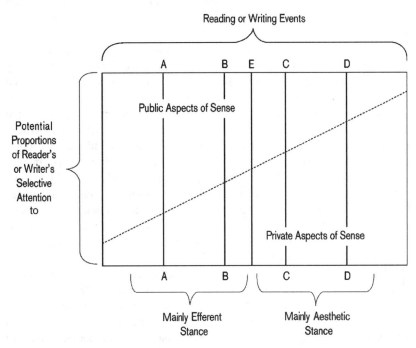

Any linguistic activity has both public (lexical, analytic, abstracting) and private (experiential, affective, associational) components. Stance is determined by the proportion of each component admitted into the scope of selective attention. The efferent stance draws mainly on the public aspect of sense; the aesthetic stance includes proportionally more of the experiential, private aspect.

Reading or writing events A and B fall into the efferent part of the continuum, with B admitting more private elements. Reading or writing events C and D both represent the aesthetic stance, with C according a higher proportion of attention to the public aspects of sense. Because the reader gives the efferent and aesthetic aspects about equal attention in E, he may adopt a stance not appropriate to his purpose, e.g., an aesthetic attitude toward a discussion of economics.

points on the efferent–aesthetic continuum. Other readers would probably produce readings that fall at other points on the continuum.

Although many readings may fall near the extremes, many others, perhaps most, may fall nearer the center of the continuum where both parts of the iceberg of meaning are more evenly balanced. Here, confusion as to dominant stance is more likely and more counterproductive. It is possible to read efferently and assume one has evoked a poem, or to read aesthetically and assume one is arriving at logical conclusions to an argument.

Also, it is necessary to emphasize that a predominant stance does not rule out fluctuations. Within a particular aesthetic reading, attention may at times turn from the experiential synthesis to efferent analysis, as the reader recognizes some technical strategy or passes a critical judgment. Similarly, in an efferent reading, a general idea may be illustrated or reinforced by an aesthetically lived-through illustration or example. Despite the mix of private and public aspects of meaning in each stance, the two dominant stances are clearly distinguishable. No two readings, even by the same person, are identical. Still, someone else can read a text efferently and paraphrase it for us in such a way as to satisfy our efferent purpose. But no one else can read aesthetically—that is, experience the evocation of—a literary work of art for us.

Because each reading is an event in particular circumstances, the same text may be read either efferently or aesthetically. The experienced reader usually approaches a text alert to cues offered by the text and, unless another purpose intervenes, automatically adopts the appropriate predominant stance. Sometimes the title suffices as a cue. Probably one of the most obvious cues is the arrangement of broad margins and uneven lines that signals that the reader should adopt the aesthetic stance and undertake to make a poem. The opening lines of any text are especially important from this point of view, for their signaling of tone, attitude, and conventional indications of stance to be adopted.

Of course, the reader may overlook or misconstrue the cues, or they may be confusing. And the reader's own purpose, or schooling that indoctrinates the same undifferentiated approach to all texts, may dictate a different stance from the one the writer intended. For example, the student reading *A Tale of Two Cities* who knows that there will be a test on facts about characters and plot may be led to adopt a predominantly efferent stance, screening out all but the factual data. Similarly, readings of an article on zoology could range from analytic abstracting of factual content to an aesthetic savoring of the ordered structure of ideas, the rhythm of the sentences, and the images of animal life brought into consciousness.

## Evocation, Response, Interpretation

The tendency to reify words is frequently represented by discussions centering on a title, say, *Invisible Man* or *The Bill of Rights*. These titles may refer to the text, as we have been using the word, that is, to the pattern of inscribed signs to be found in physical written or printed form. More often, however, the intended reference is to "the work." But the work—ideas and experiences linked with the text—can be found only in individual readers' reflections on the reading event, the evocation and responses to it during and after the reading event.

### Evocation

Thus far, we have focused on the aspects of the reading process centered on organizing a structure of elements of consciousness construed as the meaning of the text. I term this *the evocation* to cover both efferent and aesthetic transactions. The evocation, the work, is not a physical "object," but, given another sense of that word, the evocation can be an object of thought.

## The Second Stream of Response

We must recognize during the reading event a concurrent stream of reactions to, and transactions with, the emerging evocation. Even as we are generating the evocation, we are reacting to it; this may in turn affect our choices as we proceed with the reading. Such responses may be momentary, peripheral, or felt simply as a general state, for example, an ambiance of acceptance or perhaps of confirmation of ideas and attitudes brought to the reading. Sometimes something unexpected or contrary to prior knowledge or assumptions may trigger conscious reflection. Something not prepared for by the preceding organization of elements may cause a rereading. The attention may shift from the evocation to the formal or technical traits of the text. The range of potential reactions and the gamut of degrees of intensity and articulateness depend on the interplay among the character of the signs on the page (the text), what the individual reader brings to it, and the circumstances of the transaction.

The various strands of response, especially in the middle ranges of the efferent–aesthetic continuum, are sometimes simultaneous, interacting, and interwoven. They may seem actually woven into the texture of the evocation itself. Hence, one of the problems of critical reading is differentiation of the evocation corresponding to the text from the concurrent responses, which may be projections from the reader's a priori assumptions. Drawing the line between them is easier in theory than in the practice of any actual reading. The reader needs to learn to handle such elements of the reading experience. The problem takes on different forms in efferent and aesthetic reading.

## Expressed Response

"Response" to the evocation often is designed as subsequent to the reading event. Actually, the basis is laid during the reading, in the concurrent second stream of reactions. The reader may recapture the general effect of this after the event and may seek to express it and to recall what in the evocation led to the response. Reflection on "the meaning" of even a simple text involves the recall, the reactivation of some aspects of the process carried on during the reading. "Interpretation" tends to be a continuation of this effort to clarify the evocation.

The account of the reading process thus far has indicated an organizing, synthesizing activity, the creation of tentative meanings, and their modification as new elements enter into the focus of attention. In some instances, the reader at some point simply registers a sense of having completed a sequential activity and moves on to other concerns. Sometimes a sense of the whole structure crystallizes by the close of the reading.

### Expressed Interpretation

Actually, the process of interpretation that includes arriving at a sense of the whole has not been given enough attention in theories of reading, perhaps because reading research has typically dealt with simple reading events. For the term *interpret*, dictionaries list, among others, several relevant meanings. One is "to set forth the meaning of; to elucidate, to explain." Another is "to construe, or understand in a particular way." A third is "to bring out the meaning of by performance (as in music)." These tend to reflect the traditional notion of "the meaning" as inherent in the text.

The transactional theory requires that we draw on all three of these usages to cover the way in which the term should be applied to the reading process. The evocation of meaning in transaction with a text is indeed interpretation in the sense of performance, and transactional theory merges this with the idea of interpretation as individual construal. The evocation then becomes the object of interpretation in the sense of elucidating or explaining. The expressed interpretation draws on all these aspects of the total transaction.

Interpretation can be understood as the effort to report, analyze, and explain the evocation. The reader recalls the sensed, felt, thought evocation while at the same time applying some frame of reference or method of abstracting in order to characterize it, to find the assumptions or organizing ideas that relate the parts to the whole. The second stream of reactions will be recalled, and the reasons for them sought, in the evoked work or in prior assumptions and knowledge. The evocation and the concurrent streams of reaction may be related through stressing, for example, the logic of the structure of ideas in an efferent evocation or the assumptions about people or society underlying the lived through experience of the aesthetic reading.

Usually, interpretation is expressed in the efferent mode, stressing underlying general ideas that link the signs of the text. Interpretation can take an aesthetic form, however, such as a poem, a painting, music, dramatization, or dance.

Interpretation brings with it the question of whether the reader has produced a meaning that is consonant with the author's probable intention. Here we find ourselves moving from the reader–text transaction to the relationship between author and reader. The process that produces the text will be considered before dealing with such matters as communication, validity of interpretation, and the implications of the transactional theory for teaching and research.

## The Writing Process

### The Writing Transaction

Writers facing a blank page, like readers approaching a text, have only their individual linguistic capital to draw on. For the writer, too, the residue of past experiences of language in particular situations provides the material from which the text will be constructed. As with the reader, any new meanings are restructurings or extensions of the stock of experiences the writer brings to the task. There is a continuing to-and-fro or transactional process as the writer looks at the page and adds to the text in the light of what has been written thus far.

An important difference between readers and writers should not be minimized, however. In the triadic sign–object–interpretant relationship, the reader has the physical pattern of signs to which to relate the symbolizations. The writer facing a blank page may start with only an organismic state, vague feelings and ideas that require further triadic definition before a symbolic configuration—a verbal text—can take shape.

Writing is always an event in time, occurring at a particular moment in the writer's biography, in particular circumstances, under particular external as well as internal pressures. In short, the writer is always transacting with a personal, social, and cultural environment. Thus, the writing process must be seen as always embodying both personal and social, or individual and environmental, factors.

Given the Peircean triadic view of the verbal symbol, the more accessible the fund of organismically linked words and referents, the more fluent the writing. This helps us place in perspective an activity such as free writing. Instead of treating it as a prescriptive "stage" of the writing process, as some seem to do, it should be seen as a technique for tapping the linguistic reservoir without being hampered by anxieties about acceptability of subject, sequence, or mechanics. Especially for those inhibited by unfortunate past writing experiences, this can be liberating, a warm-up exercise for starting the juices flowing, so to speak, and permitting elements of the experiential stream, verbal components of memory, and present concerns to rise to consciousness. The essential point is that the individual linguistic reservoir must be activated.

No matter how free and uninhibited the writing may be, the stream of images, ideas, memories, and words is not entirely random; William James reminds us that the "choosing activity" of selective attention operates to some degree. Like the reader, the writer needs to bring the selective process actively into play, to move toward a sense of some tentative focus for choice and synthesis (Emig, 1983).

This directedness will be fostered by the writer's awareness of the transactional situation: the context that initiates the need to write and the potential reader or readers to whom the text will presumably be addressed. Often in trial-and-error fashion, and through various freely flowing drafts, the writer's sensitivity to such factors translates itself into an increasingly clear impulse that guides selective attention and integration. For the experienced writer, the habit of such awareness, monitoring the multifold decisions or choices that make up the writing event, is more important than any explicit preliminary statement of goals or purpose.

## *The Writer's Stance*

The concept of stance presented earlier in relation to reading is equally important for writing. A major aspect of the delimitation of purpose in writing is the
adoption of a stance that falls at some point in the efferent–aesthetic continuum. The attitude toward what is activated in the linguistic–experiential reservoir manifests itself in the range and character of the verbal symbols that will
"come to mind," and to which the writer will apply selective attention. The
dominant stance determines the proportion of public and private aspects of
sense that will be included in the scope of the writer's attention (Figure 1, p. 13).

In actual life, the selection of a predominant stance is not arbitrary but is a
function of the circumstances, the writer's motives, the subject, and the relation
between writer and prospective reader or readers. For example, someone who
had been involved in an automobile collision would need to adopt very different
stances in writing an account of the event for an insurance company and in
describing it in a letter to a friend. The first would activate an efferent selective
process, bringing into the center of consciousness and onto the page the public
aspects, such as statements that could be verified by witnesses or by investigation of the terrain. In the letter to the friend, the purpose would be to share an
experience. An aesthetic stance would bring within the scope of the writer's
attention the same basic facts, together with feelings, sensations, tensions,
images, and sounds lived through during this brush with death. The selective
process would favor words that matched the writer's inner sense of the felt event
and that also would activate in the prospective reader symbolic linkages evoking a similar experience. Given different purposes, other accounts might fall at
other points of the efferent–aesthetic continuum.

Purpose or intention should emerge from, or be capable of constructively
engaging, the writer's actual experiential and linguistic resources. Past experience need not be the limit of the writer's scope, but the writer faced with a blank
page needs "live" ideas—that is, ideas having a strongly energizing linkage with
the linguistic–experiential reservoir. Purposes or ideas that lack the capacity to
connect with the writer's funded experience and present concerns cannot fully
activate the linguistic reservoir and provide an impetus to thinking and writing.

A personally grounded purpose develops and impels movement forward.
Live ideas growing out of situations, activities, discussions, problems, or needs
provide the basis for an actively selective and synthesizing process of making
meaning. The quickened fund of images, ideas, emotions, attitudes, and tendencies to act offers the means of making new connections, for discovering
new facets of the world of objects and events, in short, for thinking and writing
creatively.

## *Writing About Texts*

When a reader describes, responds to, or interprets a work—that is, speaks or
writes about a transaction with a text—a new text is being produced. The
implications of this fact in terms of process should be more fully understood.

When the reader becomes a writer about a work, the starting point is no longer the physical text, the marks on the page, but the meaning or the state of mind felt to correspond to that text. The reader may return to the original text to recapture how it entered into the transaction but must "find words" for explaining the evocation and the interpretation.

The reader-turned-writer must once again face the problem of choice of stance. In general, the choice seems to be the efferent stance. The purpose is mainly to explain, analyze, summarize, and categorize the evocation. This is usually true even when the reading has been predominantly aesthetic and a literary work of art is being discussed. However, the aesthetic stance might be adopted in order to communicate an experience expressing the response or the interpretation. An efferent reading of, for example, the U.S. Declaration of Independence might lead to a poem or a story. An aesthetic reading of the text of a poem might also lead, not to an efferently written critical essay, but to another poem, a painting, or a musical composition.

The translator of a poem is a clear example of the reader-turned-writer, being first a reader who evokes an experience through a transaction in one language and then a writer who seeks to express that experience through a writing transaction in another language. The experiential qualities generated in a transaction with one language must now be communicated to—evoked by—readers who have a different linguistic–experiential reservoir, acquired in a different culture.

## Authorial Reading

Thus far, we have been developing parallels between the ways in which readers and writers select and synthesize elements from the personal linguistic reservoir, adopt stances that guide selective attention, and build a developing selective purpose. Emphasis has fallen mainly on similarities in composing structures of meaning related to texts. If readers are in that sense also writers, it is equally—and perhaps more obviously—true that writers also must be readers. At this point, however, some differences within the parallelisms begin to appear.

The writer, it is generally recognized, is the first reader of the text. Note an obvious, though neglected, difference: While readers transact with a writer's finished text, writers first read the text as it is being inscribed. Because both reading and writing are recursive processes carried on over a period of time, their very real similarities have masked a basic difference. The writer will often reread the total finished text, but, perhaps more important, the writer first reads and carries on a spiral, transactional relationship with the very text emerging on the page. This is a different kind of reading. It is authorial—a writer's reading. It should be seen as an integral part of the composing process. In fact, it is necessary to see that writing, or composing, a text involves two kinds of authorial reading, which I term *expression oriented* and *reception oriented*.

## Expression-Oriented Authorial Reading

As a reader's eyes move along a printed text, the reader develops an organizing principle or framework. The newly evoked symbolizations are tested for whether they can be fitted into the tentative meanings already constructed for the preceding portion of the text. If the new signs create a problem, this may lead to a revision of the framework or even to a complete rereading of the text and restructuring of the attributed meaning.

The writer, like readers of another's text, peruses the succession of verbal signs being inscribed on the page to see whether the new words fit the preceding text. But this is a different, expression-oriented reading, which should be seen as an integral part of the composing process. As the new words appear on the page, they must be tested, not simply for how they make sense with the preceding text but also against an inner gauge—the intention, or purpose. The emerging meaning, even if it makes sense, must be judged as to whether it serves or hinders the purpose, however nebulous and inarticulate, that is the motive power in the writing. Expression-oriented authorial reading leads to revision even during the earlier phases of the writing process.

## The Inner Gauge

Most writers will recall a situation that may illustrate the operation of an "inner gauge." A word comes to mind or flows from the pen and, even if it makes sense, is felt not to be right. One word after another may be brought into consciousness and still not satisfy. Sometimes the writer understands what is wrong with the word on the page—perhaps that it is ambiguous or does not suit the tone. But often the writer cannot articulate the reason for dissatisfaction. The tension simply disappears when "the right word" presents itself. When it does, a match between inner state and verbal sign has happened.

Such an episode manifests the process of testing against an inner touchstone. The French writer Gustave Flaubert with his search for *le mot juste*, the exact word, offers the analogy of the violinist who tries to make his fingers "reproduce precisely those sounds of which he has the inward sense" (1926, pp. 11, 47). The inner gauge may be an organic state, a mood, an idea, perhaps even a consciously constituted set of guidelines.

For the experienced writer, this kind of completely inner-oriented reading, which is integral to the composing process, depends on and nourishes an increasingly clear though often tacit sense of purpose, whether efferent or aesthetic. The writer tries to satisfy a personal conception while also refining it. Such transactional reading and revision can go on throughout the writing event. There are indeed times when this is the *only* reading component—when one writes for oneself alone, to express or record an experience in a diary or journal, or perhaps to analyze a situation or the pros and cons of a decision.

*Reception-Oriented Authorial Reading*

Usually, however, writing is felt to be part of a potential transaction with other readers. At some point, the writer dissociates from the text and reads it through the eyes of potential readers; the writer tries to judge the meaning they would make in transaction with that pattern of signs. But the writer does not simply adopt the "eyes" of the potential reader. Again, a twofold operation is involved. The emerging text is read to sense what others might make of it. But this hypothetical interpretation must also be checked against the writer's own inner sense of purpose.

The tendency has been to focus on writing with an eye on the anticipated reader. My concern is to show the interplay between the two kinds of authorial reading and the need, consciously or automatically, to decide the degree of emphasis on one or the other. The problem always is to find verbal signs likely to activate linkages in prospective readers' linguistic reservoirs matching those of the writer. A poet may be faced with the choice between a personally savored exotic metaphor and one more likely to be within the experience of prospective readers. Or a science writer may have to decide whether highly detailed precision may be too complex for the general reader.

Writers must already have some hold on the first, expression-oriented kind of inner awareness if they are to benefit from the second reading through the eyes of others. The first becomes a criterion for the second. The experienced writer will probably engage in a synthesis, or rapid alternation, of the two kinds of authorial reading to guide the selective attention that filters out the verbal elements coming to mind. When communication is the aim, revision should be based on such double criteria in the rereading of the text.

## Communication Between Author and Readers

The reader's to-and-fro process of building an interpretation becomes a form of transaction with an author persona sensed through and behind the text. The implied relationship is sometimes even termed "a contract" with the author. The closer their linguistic–experiential equipment, the more likely the reader's interpretation will fulfill the writer's intention. Sharing at least versions of the same language is so basic that it often is simply assumed. Other positive factors affecting communication are contemporary membership in the same social and cultural group, the same educational level, and membership in the same discourse community, such as academic, legal, athletic, literary, scientific, or theological. Given such similarities, the reader is more likely to bring to the text the prior knowledge, acquaintance with linguistic and literary conventions, and assumptions about social situations required for understanding implications or allusions and noting nuances of tone and thought.

Yet, because each individual's experience is unique, differences due to social, ethnic, educational, and personal factors exist, even with contemporaries.

The reading of works written in another period bespeaks an inevitable difference in linguistic, social, or cultural context. Here, especially, readers may agree on interpretations without necessarily assuming that their evocations from the text fit the author's intention (Rosenblatt, 1978, p. 109ff).

Differences as to the author's intention often lead to consultation of extra-textual sources. For works of the past especially, scholars call on systematic methods of philological, biographical, and historical research to discover the personal, social, and literary forces that shaped the writer's intention. The contemporary reception of the work also provides clues. Such evidence, even if it includes an author's stated intention, still yields hypothetical results and cannot dictate our interpretation. We must still read the text to decide whether it supports the hypothetical intention. The reader is constantly faced with the responsibility of deciding whether an interpretation is acceptable. The question of validity of interpretation must be faced before considering implications for teaching and research.

## Validity of Interpretation

The problem of validity of interpretation has not received much attention in reading theory or educational methodology. Despite the extraordinary extent of the reliance on testing in our schools, there seems to be little interest in clarifying the criteria that enter into evaluation of "comprehension." Actual practice in the teaching of reading and in the instruments for testing of reading ability has evidently been tacitly based on, or at least has indoctrinated, the traditional assumption that there is a single determinate "correct" meaning attributable to each text. The stance factor, the efferent–aesthetic continuum, has especially been neglected; operationally, the emphasis has been on the efferent, even when "literature" was involved.

The polysemous character of language invalidates any simplistic approach to meaning, creating the problem of the relationship between the reader's interpretation and the author's intention. The impossibility of finding a single absolute meaning for a text or of expecting any interpretation absolutely to reflect the writer's intention is becoming generally recognized by contemporary theorists. "Intention" itself is not absolutely definable or delimitable even by the writer. The word *absolute*, the notion of a single "correct" meaning inherent "in" the text, is the stumbling block. The same text takes on different meanings in transactions with different readers or even with the same reader in different contexts or times.

## Warranted Assertibility

The problem of the validity of any interpretation is part of the broader philosophical problem cited at the beginning of this piece. Perception of the world is always through the medium of individual human beings transacting with their worlds. In recent decades, some literary theorists, deriving their arguments from poststructuralist Continental writers and taking a Saussurean view of language as an autonomous system, have arrived at an extreme relativist position. They have developed a reading method that assumes all texts can be "deconstructed" to reveal inner contradictions. Moreover, the language system and literary conventions are said to completely dominate author and reader, and agreement concerning interpretation simply reflects the particular "interpretive community" in which we find ourselves (Fish, 1980; Rosenblatt, 1991).

Such extreme relativism is not, however, a necessary conclusion from the premise that absolutely determinate meaning is impossible. By agreeing on criteria of evaluation of interpretations, we can accept the possibility of alternative interpretations yet decide that some are more acceptable than others.

John Dewey, accepting the nonfoundationalist epistemological premises and foregoing the quest for absolutes, solved the scientists' problem by his idea of "warranted assertibility" as the end of controlled inquiry (1938, pp. 9, 345). Given shared criteria concerning methods of investigation and kinds of evidence there can be agreement concerning the decision as to what is a sound interpretation of the evidence, or "a warranted assertion." This is not set forth as permanent, absolute truth, but leaves open the possibility that alternative explanations for the same facts may be found, that new evidence may be discovered, or that different criteria or paradigms may be developed.

Although Dewey used primarily scientific interpretation or knowledge of the world based on scientific methods to illustrate warranted assertibility, he saw the concept as encompassing the arts and all human concerns. It can be applied to the problem of all linguistic interpretation (Rosenblatt, 1978, chap. 7; 1983, p. 151ff). Given a shared cultural milieu and shared criteria of validity of interpretation, we can, without claiming to have the single "correct" meaning of a text, agree on an interpretation. Especially in aesthetic reading, we may find that alternative interpretations meet our minimum criteria, and we can still be free to consider some interpretations superior to others.

In contrast to the notion of readers locked into a narrow "interpretive community," the emphasis on making underlying or tacit criteria explicit provides the basis not only for agreement but also for understanding tacit sources of disagreement. This creates the possibility of change in interpretation, acceptance of alternative sets of criteria, or revision of criteria. Such self-awareness on the part of readers can foster communication across social, cultural, and historical differences between author and readers, as well as among readers (Rosenblatt, 1983).

In short, the concept of warranted assertibility, or shared criteria of validity of interpretation in a particular social context, recognizes that some readings may satisfy the criteria more fully than others. Basic criteria might be (1) that the context and purpose of the reading event, or the total transaction, be considered; (2) that the interpretation not be contradicted by, or not fail to cover, the full text, the signs on the page; and (3) that the interpretation not project meanings which cannot be related to signs on the page. Beyond these items arise criteria for interpretation and evaluation growing out of the whole structure of shared cultural, social, linguistic, and rhetorical assumptions.

Thus, we can be open to alternative readings of the text of *Hamlet*, but we also can consider some readings as superior to others according to certain explicit criteria, for example, complexity of intellectual and affective elements and nature of implicit value system. Such considerations permit comparison and "negotiation" among different readers of the same text as well as clarification of differences in assumptions concerning what constitutes a valid interpretation (Rosenblatt, 1978, 1983). On the efferent side of the continuum, current discussions of alternative criteria for interpretation of the U.S. Constitution provide another complex example.

### *Criteria for the Efferent–Aesthetic Continuum*

Precisely because, as Figure 1 indicates, both public and private elements are present in all reading, the criteria of validity of interpretation differ for readings at various points on the efferent–aesthetic continuum. Because the predominantly efferent interpretation must be publicly verifiable or justifiable, the criteria of validity rest primarily on the public, referential aspects of meaning and require that any affective and associational aspects not dominate. The criteria for the predominantly aesthetic reading call for attention to the referential, cognitive aspects but only as they are interwoven and colored by the private, affective, or experiential aspects generated by the author's patterns of signs. Especially in the middle ranges of the efferent–aesthetic continuum, it becomes important for writers to provide clear indications as to stance and for readers to be sensitive to the writer's purpose and the need to apply relevant criteria.

### *"Literary" Aspects of Efferent Reading*

In recent decades, in one scientific field after another, the opposition between scientific and "literary" writing has been found to be illusory. Writers in the natural and social sciences have become aware of the extent to which they engage in semantic and syntactic practices that have usually been considered "literary" and that they, too, have been using narrative, metaphor, and other rhetorical devices. Examples are the importance of metaphor in writings about economics or the idea that the historian writes narrative and that he can never be completely objective in selecting his facts. Sensitivity to sexist and racist tropes has increased awareness of the extent to which metaphor permeates all kinds of texts and, indeed, all language. Sometimes the efferent–aesthetic distinction seems to be completely erased (for example, the historian is sometimes said to write "fiction").

It becomes necessary to recall that the stance reflecting the aesthetic or efferent purpose, not the syntactic and semantic devices alone, determines the appropriate criteria. For example, in a treatise on economics or a history of the frontier, the criteria of validity of interpretation appropriate to their disciplines, which involve primarily verifiability and logic, would still apply. When an economist remarks that "the scientists had better devise good metaphors and tell good stories" (McCloskey, 1985), the concept of a dominant stance becomes all the more essential. The criteria for "good" should be not only how vivid and appealing the stories are but also how they gibe with logic and facts and what value systems are implied.

The relevance of the efferent–aesthetic continuum (Figure 1) may be illustrated by the example of metaphor: The scientist speaks of the "wave" theory of light, and we focus on the technical concept at the extreme efferent end of the continuum. Shakespeare writes, "Like as the wave makes toward the pebbled shore/So do our minutes hasten to their end," and our aesthetic attention to the feeling of inevitability of the succeeding waves enhances the feeling of the inevitability of the passage of time in our lives. A political analysis suggested surrendering to the inevitability of fascism by calling it "the wave of the future. . . . There is no fighting it" (Lindbergh, 1940, p. 934). Despite the vividness of the metaphor, efferent attention should have remained dominant, applying the efferent criterion: Did logic and factual evidence support the persuasive appeal?

## Implications for Teaching

### Reading and Writing: Parallelisms and Differences

Parallelisms between reading and writing processes have raised questions concerning their connections, especially in the classroom. The reading and writing processes both overlap and differ. Both reader and writer engage in constituting symbolic structures of meaning in a to-and-fro, spiral transaction with the text. They follow similar patterns of thinking and call on similar linguistic habits. Both processes depend on the individual's past experiences with language in particular life situations. Both reader and writer therefore are drawing on past linkages of signs, signifiers, and organic states in order to create new symbolizations, new linkages, and new organic states. Both reader and writer develop a framework, principle, or purpose, however nebulous or explicit, that guides the selective attention and the synthesizing, organizing activities that constitute meaning. Moreover, every reading and writing act can be understood as falling somewhere on the efferent–aesthetic continuum and as being predominantly efferent or aesthetic.

The parallels should not mask the basic differences—the transaction that starts with a text produced by someone else is not the same as a transaction that starts with the individual facing a blank page. To an observer, two people perusing a typed page may seem to be doing the same thing (namely, "reading").

But if one of them is in the process of writing that text, different activities will be going on. The writer will be engaged in either expression-oriented or reception-oriented authorial reading. Moreover, because both reading and writing are rooted in mutually conditioning transactions between individuals and their particular environments, a person may have very different experiences with the two activities, may differ in attitudes toward them, and may be more proficient in one or the other. Writing and reading are sufficiently different to defeat the assumption that they are mirror images: The reader does not simply reenact the author's process. Hence, it cannot be assumed that the teaching of one activity automatically improves the student's competence in the other.

Still, the parallels in the reading and writing processes described above and the nature of the transaction between author and reader make it reasonable to expect that the teaching of one can affect the student's operations in the other. Reading, essential to anyone for intellectual and emotional enrichment, provides the writer with a sense of the potentialities of language. Writing deepens the reader's understanding of the importance of paying attention to diction, syntactic positions, emphasis, imagery, and conventions of genre. The fact that the sign–interpretant–object triad is, as Peirce said, dependent on habit indicates an even more important level of influence. Cross-fertilization will result from reinforcement of linguistic habits and thinking patterns resulting from shared transactional processes of purposive selective attention and synthesis. How fruitful the interplay between the individual student's writing and reading will be depends largely on the nature of the teaching and the educational context.

## The Total Context

Here we return to our basic concept that human beings are always in transaction and in a reciprocal relationship with an environment, a context, a total situation. The classroom environment, or the atmosphere created by the teacher and students transacting with one another and the school setting, broadens out to include the whole institutional, social, and cultural context. These aspects of the transaction are crucial in thinking about education and especially the "literacy problem." Because each individual's linguistic–experiential reservoir is the residue of past transactions with the environment, such factors condition the sense of possibilities, or the potential organizing frameworks or schema and the knowledge and assumptions about the world, society, human nature, that each brings to the transactions. Socioeconomic and ethnic factors, for example, influence patterns of behavior, ways of carrying out tasks, even understanding of such concepts as "story" (Heath, 1983). Such elements also affect the individual's attitude toward self, toward the reading or writing activity, and toward the purpose for which it is being carried on.[3]

The transactional concept of the text always in relation either to author or reader in specific situations makes it untenable to treat the text as an isolated entity or to overemphasize either author or reader. Recognizing that language is not a self-contained system or static code on the one hand avoids the traditional obsession with the product—with skills, techniques, and conventions, essential though they are—and, on the other, prevents a pendulum swing to overemphasis on process or on the personal aspects.

Treatment of either reading or writing as a dissociated set of skills (though both require skills) or as primarily the acquisition of codes and conventions (though both involve them) inhibits sensitivity to the organic linkages of verbal signs and their objects. Manipulating syntactic units without a sense of a context that connects them into a meaningful relationship may in the long run be counterproductive.

Nor can the transactional view of the reading and writing processes be turned into a set of stages to be rigidly followed. The writer's drafts and final texts—or the reader's tentative interpretations, final evocation, and reflections—should be viewed as stopping points in a journey, as the outward and visible signs of a continuing process in the passage from one point to the other. A "good" product, whether a well-written paper or a sound textual interpretation, should not be an end in itself—a terminus—but should be the result of a process that builds the strengths for further journeys or, to change the metaphor, for further growth. "Product" and "process" become interlocking concerns in nurturing growth.

Hence, the teaching of reading and writing at any developmental level should have as its first concern the creation of environments and activities in which students are motivated and encouraged to draw on their own resources to make "live" meanings. With this as the fundamental criterion, emphasis falls on strengthening the basic processes that we have seen to be shared by reading and writing. The teaching of one can then reinforce linguistic habits and semantic approaches useful in the other. Such teaching, concerned with the ability of the individual to generate meaning, will permit constructive cross-fertilization of the reading and writing (and speech) processes.

Enriching the individual's linguistic–experiential reservoir becomes an underlying educational aim broader than the particular concern with either reading or writing. Especially in the early years, the linkage between verbal sign and experiential base is essential. The danger is that many current teaching practices may counteract the very processes presumably being taught. The organization of instruction, the atmosphere in the classroom, the kinds of questions asked, the ways of phrasing assignments, and the types of tests administered should be scrutinized from this point of view.

The importance of a sense of purpose, of a guiding principle of selection and organization in both writing and reading, is being increasingly recognized. The creation of contexts that permit purposive writing and reading can enable the student to build on past experience of life and language, to adopt the appropriate stance for selective attention, and to develop inner gauges or frameworks for choice and synthesis that produce new structures of live meaning.

## Collaborative Interchange

In a favorable educational environment, speech is a vital ingredient of transactional pedagogy. Its importance in the individual's acquisition of a linguistic–experiential capital is clear. It can be an extremely important medium in the classroom. Dialogue between teacher and students and interchange among students can foster growth and cross-fertilization in both the reading and writing processes. Such discussion can help students develop insights concerning transactions with texts as well as metalinguistic understanding of skills and conventions in meaningful contexts.

Students' achievement of insight into their own reading and writing processes can be seen as the long-term justification for various curricular and teaching strategies. For example, writers at all levels can be helped to understand their transactional relationship to their readers by peer reading and discussion of texts. Their fellow students' questions, varied interpretations, and misunderstandings dramatize the necessity of the writer's providing verbal signs that will help readers gain required facts, share relevant sensations or attitudes, or make logical transitions. Such insights make possible the second, reader-oriented authorial reading.

Similarly, group interchange about readers' evocations from texts, whether of their peers or adult authors, can in general be a powerful means of stimulating growth in reading ability and critical acumen. Readers become aware of the need to pay attention to the author's words in order to avoid preconceptions and misinterpretations. When students share responses to transactions with the same text, they can learn how their evocations from the same signs differ, can return to the text to discover their own habits of selection and synthesis, and can become aware of, and critical of, their own processes as readers. Interchange about the problems of interpretation that a particular group of readers encounters and a collaborative movement toward self-critical interpretation of the text can lead to the development of critical concepts and interpretive criteria. Such metalinguistic awareness is valuable to students as both readers and writers.

The teacher in such a classroom is no longer simply a conveyor of ready-made teaching materials and recorder of results of ready-made tests or a dispenser of ready-made interpretations. Teaching becomes constructive, facilitating interchange, helping students to make their spontaneous responses the basis for raising questions and growing in the ability to handle increasingly complex reading transactions (Rosenblatt, 1983).[4]

## The Student's Efferent–Aesthetic Repertory

The efferent–aesthetic continuum, or the two basic ways of looking at the world, should be part of the student's repertory from the earliest years. Because both stances involve cognitive and affective as well as public and private elements, students need to learn to differentiate the circumstances that call for one or the other stance. Unfortunately, much current practice is counterproductive, either failing to encourage a definite stance or implicitly requiring an inappropriate one. Favorite illustrations are the third-grade workbook that prefaced its first poem with the question "What facts does this poem teach you?" and the boy who complained that he wanted information about dinosaurs, but his teacher only gave him "storybooks." Small wonder that graduates of our schools (and colleges) often read poems and novels efferently or respond to political statements and advertisements with an aesthetic stance.

Despite the overemphasis on the efferent in our schools, failure to understand the matter of the public–private "mix" has prevented successful teaching even of efferent reading and writing. Teaching practices and curriculums, from the very beginning, should include both efferent and aesthetic linguistic activity and should build a sense of the different purposes involved. Instruction should foster the habits of selective attention and synthesis that draw on relevant elements in the semantic reservoir and should nourish the ability to handle the mix of private and public aspects appropriate to a particular transaction.

Especially in the early years, this should be done largely indirectly, through, for example, choice of texts, contexts for generating writing and reading, or implications concerning stance in the questions asked. In this way, texts can serve dynamically as sources from which to assimilate a sense of the potentialities of the English sentence and an awareness of strategies for organizing meaning and expressing feeling. Emphasis on analysis of the evocations, or terminology for categorizing and describing them, has no value if they overshadow or substitute for the evoked work. Such activities acquire meaning and value when, for example, they answer a writer's own problems in expression or explain for a reader the role of the author's verbal strategies in producing a certain felt response.

The developmental sequence suggested here is especially important in aesthetic reading. Much teaching of poetry at every level, including high school and college, at present takes on a continuously repeated remedial character because of the continued confusion about stance through emphasis on efferent analysis of the "literary" work. Students need to be helped to have unimpeded aesthetic experiences. Very young children's delight in the sound and rhythms of words, their interest in stories, and their ability to move easily from verbal to other modes of expression too often fade. They need to be helped to hold on to the experiential aspect. When this can be taken for granted, efferent, analytical discussions of form or background will not be substitutes for the literary work but become a means of enhancing it. Discussion then can become the basis for assimilating criteria of sound interpretation and evaluation appropriate to the various points on the continuum and to the student's developmental status.

# Implications for Research

Research based on the transactional model has a long history (Applebee, 1974; Farrell & Squire, 1990). Until fairly recently, it has generated research mainly by those concerned with the teaching of literature in high schools and colleges, rather than by those concerned with reading per se in the elementary school (Beach & Hynds, 1990; Flood et al., 1991; Purves & Beach, 1972). It is not possible here to survey this already considerable body of research, much of it exploring aspects of response to literature; nor does space allow discussion of recent volumes dealing with applications of transactional theory in elementary school, high school, and college (Clifford, 1991; Cox & Many, 1992; Hunger-ford, Holland, & Ernst, 1993; Karolides, 1992). I shall instead suggest some general considerations concerning research topics and theoretical and method-ological pitfalls.

The transactional model of reading, writing, and teaching that has been presented constitutes, in a sense, a body of hypotheses to be investigated. The shift it represents from the Cartesian to the post-Einsteinian paradigm calls for removal of the limitations on research imposed by the dominance of positivis-tic behaviorism. Instead of mainly treating reading as a compendium of sepa-rate skills or as an isolated autonomous activity, research on any aspect should center on the human being speaking, writing, reading, and continuously trans-acting with a specific environment in its broadening circles of context. And as Bartlett (1932) reminds us, any secondary theoretical frameworks, such as schemata or strategies, are not stable entities but configurations in a dynamic, changing process. Although the focus here will be on reading research, the interrelationship among the linguistic modes, especially reading and writing, broadens the potential scope of problems mentioned.

The view of language as a dynamic system of meaning in which the affec-tive and the cognitive unite raises questions about the emphasis of past research. Researchers' preoccupation with the efferent is exemplified by their focus on Piaget's work on the child's development of mathematical and logical concepts and the continuing neglect of the affective by behaviorist, cognitive, and artificial intelligence psychologists. This is slowly being counterbalanced by growing interest in the affective and the qualitative (e.g., Deese, 1973; Eisner & Peshkin, 1990; Izard, 1977). We need to understand more fully the child's growth in capacity for selective attention to, and synthesis of, the vari-ous components of meaning.

Research in reading should draw on a number of interrelated disciplines, such as physiology, sociology, and anthropology, and should converge with the general study of human development. The transactional theory especially raises questions that involve such broad connections. Also, the diverse subcul-tures and ethnic backgrounds represented by the student population and the many strands that contribute to a democratic culture present a wide range of questions for research about reading, teaching, and curriculum.

## Developmental Processes

The adult capacity to engage in the tremendously complex process of reading depends ultimately on the individual's long developmental process, starting with "learning how to mean" (Halliday, 1975; Rosenblatt, 1985b). How does the child move from the earliest, undifferentiated state of the world to "the referential, emotive and associative part processes" (Rommetveit, 1968, p. 167)? Developmental research can throw light on the relation of cognitive and emotional aspects in the growth of the ability to evoke meaning in transactions with texts.

Research is needed to accumulate systematic understanding of the positive environmental and educational factors that do justice to the essential nature of both efferent and aesthetic linguistic behavior, and to the role of the affective or private aspects of meaning in both stances. How can children's sensorimotor explorations of their worlds be reinforced, their sensitivity to the sounds and qualitative overtones of language be maintained? In short, what can foster their capacity to apprehend in order to comprehend, or construct, the poem, story, or play? Much also remains to be understood about development of the ability to infer, or make logical connections, or, in short, to read efferently and critically.

How early in the child's development should the context of the transaction with the text create a purpose for one or the other dominant stance, or help the reader learn to adopt a stance appropriate to the situation? At different developmental stages, what should be the role or roles of reflection on the reading experience through spoken comments, writing, and the use of other media?

An overarching question is this: How can skills be assimilated in a context that fosters understanding of their relevance to the production of meaning? How can the young reader acquire the knowledge, intellectual frameworks, and sense of values that provide the connecting links for turning discrete verbal signs into meaningful constructs? The traditional methods of teaching and testing recognize the important functions of the symbolic system, the alphabetic and phonological elements (the "code"), and linguistic conventions by fragmenting processes into small quantifiable units. These are quantitatively and hence economically assessable. But do such methods set up habits and attitudes toward the written word that inhibit the process of inferring meaning, or organizing and synthesizing, that enters into even simple reading tasks? How can we prepare the way for increasingly rich and demanding transactions with texts?

## Performance

Assessment of performance level is usually required as a means of assuring the accountability of the school. Whether standardized tests accurately measure the student's ability is currently being called into question. Research on correlation of reading ability with factors such as age, gender, ethnic and socioeconomic background, and so on has confirmed the expectation that they are active factors. However, such research reports a state of affairs that is interpreted according to varying assumptions, not all conducive to the development of mature readers and writers. The transactional emphasis on the total context of the reading act reinforces the democratic concern with literacy and supports the call for vigorous political and social reform of negative environmental factors. At the same time teachers must recognize that the application of quantitatively based group labels to individual students may unfairly create erroneous expectations that become self-fulfilling prophecies.

## Teaching Methods

In the current transition away from traditional teaching methods, there is the danger that inappropriate research designs may be invoked to evaluate particular teaching methods. What criteria of successful teaching and what assumptions about the nature of linguistic processes underlie the research design and the methods of measurement? Any interpretations of results should take into account the various considerations concerning reader, text, and context set forth in the transactional model.

Results of research assessing different teaching methods raise an important question: Did the actual teaching conform to the formulaic labels attached to the methods being compared? The vagueness of a term such as *reader-response method* can illustrate the importance of more precise understanding of the actual teaching processes being tested in a particular piece of research. The same term has been applied to teachers who, after eliciting student responses to a story, fall back on habitual methods of demonstrating the "correct" interpretation and to teachers who make the responses the beginning of a process of helping students grow in their ability to arrive at sound, self-critical interpretations.

Much remains to be done to develop operational descriptions of the approaches being compared. Studies are needed of how teachers lead, or facilitate, without dominating or dictating. Ethnographic study of classroom dynamics, records of interchange among teacher and students, videotapes of classrooms, and analyses of text give substance to test results.

## Response

Students' empirical responses to a text (mainly written protocols) form the basis of much of the research on methods generally referred to as reader response or transactional. (The term *response* should be understood to cover multiple activities.) Protocols provide indirect evidence about the students' evocation, the work as experienced, and reactions to it. Such research requires a coherent system of analysis of students' written or oral reports. What evidence, for example, is there that the reading of a story has been predominantly aesthetic?

The problem of empirical assessment of the student's aesthetic reading of a text offers particular difficulties, especially because no single "correct" interpretation or evaluation is posited. This requires setting up criteria of interpretation that reflect not only the presence of personal feelings and associations, which are only one component, but also their relationship to the other cognitive and attitudinal components. In short, the assessment must be based on clearly articulated criteria as to signs of growing maturity in handling personal response, relating to the evoked text, and use of personal and intertextual experience vis-à-vis the responses of others.

In order to provide a basis for statistical correlation, content analysis of protocols has been used largely to determine the components or aspects of response. The purpose is to distinguish personal feelings and attitudes from, for example, efferent, analytic references to the sonnet form. This requires a systematic set of categories, such as *The Elements of Writing About a Literary Work* (Purves & Rippere, 1968), which has provided a common basis for a large number of studies. As the emphasis on process has increased, refinements or alternatives have been devised. The need is to provide for study of the relationship among the various aspects of response, or the processes of selecting and synthesizing activities by which readers arrive at evocations and interpretations (Rosenblatt, 1985a). Qualitative methods of research at least should supplement, or perhaps should become the foundation for, any quantitative methods of assessing transactions with the written word.

Experimental designs that seek to deal with the development of the ability to handle some aspect of literary art should avoid methodologies and experimental tasks that instead serve to test efferent metalinguistic capacities. For example, levels of ability to elucidate metaphor or to retell stories may not reflect children's actual sensing or experiencing of metaphors or stories so much as their capacity to efferently abstract or categorize (Verbrugge, 1979).

The dependence on single instances of reading in assessing an individual's abilities is currently being called into question. The previous reminder that we are dealing with points in a continuing and changing developmental process is especially relevant. Habits are acquired and change slowly; it may be found that the effects of a change, for example, from traditional to response methods of teaching literature, cannot be assessed without allowing for a period of transition from earlier approaches and the continuation of the new approaches over time.

Basal readers have in the past offered especially clear examples of questions and exercises tacitly calling for an efferent stance toward texts labeled stories and poems. There has been little to help students assimilate and make automatic the aesthetic mode of relating to a text. Here, preparations for reading, the teacher's questions both before and after reading, and the mode of assessment, which powerfully influences teaching, should be scrutinized.

Studies that seek to generalize about the development of abilities by simultaneous testing of the different age levels have the problem of taking into account the factor of schooling. To what extent do changes in children's ability to retell or comment on the grammar of a story reflect schooling in the appropriate way to talk about a story? Similarly, to what extent are reported changing literary interests in the middle years not a reflection of personality changes but of too narrow definitions of *literary*?

### Research Methodologies

The preceding discussion has centered on suggesting problems for research implied by the transactional model. Research methods or designs have been mentioned mainly in reference to their potentialities and limitations for providing kinds of information needed and to criteria for interpretation of data. Quantitatively based generalizations about groups are usually called for, but currently there is interest in clarifying the potentialities and limitations of both quantitative and qualitative research. Empirical experimental designs are being supplemented or checked by other research approaches, such as the case study (Birnbaum & Emig, 1991), the use of journals, interviews during or after the linguistic event, portfolios, and recordings in various media. Because the single episode test has various limitations, research in which researcher and teacher collaborate—or carefully planned research carried on by the teacher—provides the opportunity for extended studies. The transactional model especially indicates the value of ethnographic or naturalistic research because it deals with problems in the context of the ongoing life of individuals and groups in a particular cultural, social, and educational environment (Kantor, Kirby, & Goetz, 1981; Zaharlick & Green, 1991). The developmental emphasis also supports the call for longitudinal studies (Tierney, 1991). Interdisciplinary collaboration, desirable at any time, seems especially so for longitudinal studies. Research will need to be sufficiently complex, varied, and interlocking to do justice to the fact that reading is at once an intensely individual and an intensely social activity, an activity that from the earliest years involves the whole spectrum of ways of looking at the world.

## Acknowledgments

I want to thank June Carroll Birnbaum and Roselmina Indrisano for reading this manuscript, and Nicholas Karolides and Sandra Murphy for reading earlier versions.

## Notes

1. The 1949 volume marks Dewey's choice of transaction to designate a concept present in his work since 1896. My own use of the term after 1950 applied to an approach developed from 1938 on.

2. By 1981, transactional theory, efferent stance, and aesthetic stance were sufficiently current to be listed and were attributed to me in *A Dictionary of Reading and Related Terms* (Harris & Hodges, 1981). But the often confused usage of the terms led me to write "Viewpoints: Transaction Versus Interaction—A Terminological Rescue Operation" (1985).

3. The transactional model of reading presented here covers the whole range of similarities and differences among readers and between author and reader. Always in the transaction between reader and text, activation of the reader's linguistic–experiential reservoir must be the basis for the construction of new meanings and new experiences; hence, the applicability to bilingual instruction and the reading of texts produced in other cultures.

4. *Literature as Exploration* emphasizes the instructional process that can be built on the basis of personal evocation and response. Illustrations of classroom discussions and chapters such as "Broadening the Framework," "Some Basic Social Concepts," and "Emotion and Reason" indicate how the teacher can democratically moderate discussion and help students toward growth not only in ability to handle increasingly complex texts but also in personal, social, and cultural understanding.

# References

Ames, A. (1955). *The Nature of Our Perceptions, Prehensions, and Behavior*. Princeton, NJ: Princeton University Press.

Appenzeller, T. (1990, November/December). "Undivided Attention." *The Sciences*.

Applebee, A.N. (1974). *Tradition and Reform in the Teaching of English*. Urbana, IL: National Council of Teachers of English.

Bartlett, F.C. (1932). *Remembering: A Study in Experimental and Social Psychology*. London: Cambridge University Press.

Bates, E. (1979). *The Emergence of Symbols*. New York: Academic.

Beach, R., & Hynds, S. (1990). "Research on Response to Literature." In E. Farrell & J.R. Squire (Eds.), *Transactions with Literature* (pp. 131–205). Urbana, IL: National Council of Teachers of English.

Birnbaum, J., & Emig, J. (1991). "Case Study." In J. Flood, J.M. Jensen, D. Lapp, & J.R. Squire (Eds.), *Handbook of Research on Teaching the English Language Arts* (pp. 195–204). New York: Macmillan.

Blumenthal, A.L. (1977). *The Process of Cognition*. Englewood Cliffs, NJ: Prentice Hall.

Bohr, N. (1959). "Discussion with Einstein." In P.A. Schilpp (Ed.), *Albert Einstein, Philosopher-Scientist* (p. 210). New York: HarperCollins.

Cantril, H., & Livingston, W.K. (1963). "The Concept of Transaction in Psychology and Neurology." *Journal of Individual Psychology*, 19, 3–16.

Chomsky, N. (1968). *Language and Mind*. New York: Harcourt Brace.

Clifford, J. (Ed.). (1991). *The Experience of Reading: Louise Rosenblatt and Reader Response Theory*. Portsmouth, NH: Boynton/Cook.

Cox, C., & Many, J.E. (Eds.). (1992). *Reader's Stance and Literary Understanding.* Norwood, NJ: Ablex.

Culler, J. (1982). *On Deconstruction.* Ithaca, NY: Cornell University Press.

Damasio, A.R. (1989). "The Brain Binds Entities by Multilingual Activities for Convergence Zones." *Neural Computation,* 1.

Deese, J. (1973). "Cognitive Structure and Affect in Language." In P. Pliner & T. Alloway (Eds.), *Communication and Affect.* New York: Academic.

Dewey, J. (1938). *Logic: The Theory of Inquiry.* New York: Henry Holt.

Dewey, J., & Bentley, A.F. (1949). *Knowing and the Known.* Boston: Beacon.

Eisner, E.W., & Peshkin, A. (1990). *Qualitative Inquiry in Education: The Continuing Debate.* New York: Teachers College Press.

Emig, J. (1983). *The Web of Meaning.* Portsmouth, NH: Boynton/Cook.

Farrell, E., & Squire, J.R. (Eds.). (1990). *Transactions with Literature.* Urbana, IL: National Council of Teachers of English.

Fish, S. (1980). *Is There a Text in This Class?* Cambridge, MA: Harvard University Press.

Flaubert, G. (1926). *Correspondance* (Vol. 2). Paris: Louis Conard.

Flood, J., Jensen, J.M., Lapp, D., & Squire, J.R. (Eds.). (1991). *Handbook of Research on Teaching the English Language Arts.* New York: Macmillan.

Halliday, M.A.K. (1975). *Learning How to Mean.* New York: Elsevier.

Harris, T.L., & Hodges, R.E. (Eds.). (1981). *A Dictionary of Reading and Related Terms.* Newark, DE: International Reading Association.

Heath, S.B. (1983). *Ways with Words: Language, Life, and Work in Communities and Classrooms.* Cambridge, UK: Cambridge University Press.

Hungerford, R., Holland, K., & Ernst, S. (Eds.). (1993). *Journeying: Children Responding to Literature.* Portsmouth, NH: Heinemann.

Izard, C.E. (1977). *Human Emotions.* New York: Plenum.

James, W. (1890). *The Principles of Psychology* (2 vols.). New York: Henry Holt.

Kantor, K.J., Kirby, D.R., & Goetz, J.P. (1981). "Research in Context: Ethnographic Studies in English Education." *Research in the Teaching of English,* 15(4), 293–309.

Karolides, N.J. (Ed.). (1992). *Reader Response in the Classroom: Evoking and Interpreting Meaning in Literature.* White Plains, NY: Longman.

Kuhn, T. (1970). *The Structure of Scientific Revolutions* (2nd ed.). Chicago: University of Chicago Press.

Lindbergh, A.M. (1940). *The Wave of the Future.* New York: Harcourt Brace.

McCloskey, D. (1985). *The Rhetoric of Economics.* Madison: University of Wisconsin Press.

Miller, G.A., & Johnson-Laird, P.N. (1976). *Language and Perception.* Cambridge, MA: Harvard University Press.

Myers, G. (1986). *William James: His Life and Thought.* New Haven, CT: Yale University Press.

Peirce, C.S. (1933, 1935). *Collected Papers* (Vol. 3, Vol. 6) (P. Weiss & C. Hartshorne, Eds.). Cambridge, MA: Harvard University Press.

Purves, A.C., & Beach, R. (1972). *Literature and the Reader: Research in Response to Literature.* Urbana, IL: National Council of Teachers of English.

Purves, A.C., & Rippere, V. (1968). *Elements of Writing About a Literary Work: A Study of Response to Literature.* Urbana, IL: National Council of Teachers of English.

Rommetveit, R. (1968). *Words, Meanings, and Messages.* New York: Academic.

Rosenblatt, L.M. (1978). *The Reader, the Text, the Poem: The Transactional Theory of the Literary Work.* Carbondale: Southern Illinois University Press.

Rosenblatt, L.M. (1983). *Literature as Exploration* (4th ed.). New York: Modern Language Association. (Original work published 1938)

Rosenblatt, L.M. (1985a). "The Transactional Theory of the Literary Work: Implications for Research." In C. Cooper (Ed.), *Researching Response to Literature and the Teaching of Literature.* Norwood, NJ: Ablex.

Rosenblatt, L.M. (1985b). "Viewpoints: Transaction Versus Interaction—A Terminological Rescue Operation." *Research in the Teaching of English,* 19, 96–107.

Rosenblatt, L.M. (1991). "Literary Theory." In J. Flood, J.M. Jensen, D. Lapp, & J.R. Squire (Eds.), *Handbook of Research on Teaching the English Language Arts* (pp. 57–62). New York: Macmillan.

Rosenblatt, L.M. (1993). "The Transactional Theory: Against Dualisms." *College English,* 55(4), 377–386.

Saussure, F. (1972). *Cours de linguistique générale.* Paris: Payot.

Tierney, R.J. (1991). "Studies of Reading and Writing Growth: Longitudinal Research on Literacy Development." In J. Flood, J.M. Jensen, D. Lapp, & J.R. Squire (Eds.), *Handbook of Research on Teaching the English Language Arts* (pp. 176–194). New York: Macmillan.

Verbrugge, R.R. (1979). "The Primacy of Metaphor in Development." In E. Winner & H. Gardner (Eds.), *Fact, Fiction, and Fantasy in Childhood.* San Francisco: Jossey-Bass.

Vygotsky, L.S. (1962). *Thought and Language* (F. Hanmann & G. Vakar, Eds. & Trans.). Cambridge, MA: MIT Press.

Werner, H., & Kaplan, B. (1962). *Symbol Formation.* New York: Wiley.

Zaharlick, A., & Green, J. (1991). "Ethnographic Research." In J. Flood, J.M. Jensen, D. Lapp, & J.R. Squire (Eds.), *Handbook of Research on Teaching the English Language Arts* (pp. 205–223). New York: Macmillan.

# Chapter Two

# Viewpoints: Transaction Versus Interaction—A Terminological Rescue Operation

Abstract. *This article differentiates the usages of* transaction *and* interaction *as reflections of differing paradigms. The transactional theory of reading is dissociated from information-processing and interactive processing. The implications for research of various concepts basic to the total transactional theory of reading are discussed.*

This paper might perhaps have been subtitled "The Pleasures and Dangers of Being Cited." Ultimately, it has been prompted by the realization that the term, *transaction*, which I apply to the reading-act or reading-event, and the term, *transactional*, by which I designate my theory of reading, are being increasingly encountered in publications on reading, writing, and literary theory. (A further indication: A professor at a midwestern university reported that several people had remarked on the number of times the term *transaction* had been invoked at the May, 1984, meetings of the International Reading Association.) I would be very churlish, indeed, if I did not feel some satisfaction at this development. It was also pleasant, for example, to find confirmation in an "ERIC/RCS Report: An Examination of the Construct of 'Reader-Text Relationship'" in the May, 1984, issue of *English Education* (Koenke, 1984). This stated that the *Dictionary of Reading and Related Terms* (Harris & Hodges, 1981), although it does not contain an entry for the concept of reader-text relationship, does include an entry for *transactional theory*, with a quote from my 1978 book, and, as I discovered, entries for my concepts of "efferent reading" and "aesthetic reading."

However, I must admit that I began to feel somewhat uneasy when *information-processing* and *literary criticism* were presented as cognate theoretical sources. And the impulse to write the present paper was triggered when I found my transactional theory being said to share "common ground" with information-processing, and "top-down" and "bottom-up" processing being shown as squatters on that common ground under the rubic of "interactive processing." This model, it is explained, presents comprehension as "an interaction between the processing of the text and the use of the reader's experiences and expectancies." "Interaction" and "transaction" seem to be accepted as interchangeable. For example:

> It is at this point that the information-processing theory and the literary criticism theory of at least one recognized authority, Louise Rosenblatt, seem to find common ground. Rosenblatt (1978) describes the relationship between reader and text as one in which the elements of a total situation are conditioning others and being conditioned by others. This takes place within the framework of a transaction and she conceptualizes various types of reading-text relationships. (Koenke, 116)

Now, this article seems a valiant effort to bring order out of current reading research, and, instead of attributing responsibility for the confusions that I wish to point out, I am grateful that the report brings them so clearly into the open. The looseness in usage of theoretical concepts is not untypical of some recent doctoral theses and even of writings or classifications by some of their mentors, established writers in the field. Hence the following effort is to clarify the reasons why I cannot accept a blurring of the distinctions between, on the one hand, *transaction, transactional*, and *transactional theory* and, on the other, *information-processing, interactive processing*, and *interaction*. The distinction between *interaction* and *transaction* is basic.

At stake here is not a matter simply of definitions of single, discrete terms, but of what C. S. Peirce called "the ethics of terminology" (1932). After decades when simply to insist on the importance of the reader was considered, if not subversive, scientifically unorthodox and irrelevant, it is gratifying that the reader's contribution is now being recognized. All the more reason, therefore, for clarifying the nature of the reader's role as symbolized by the term *transactional* applied to my reading theory. At stake, basically, is recognition and assimilation of what has come to be rather fashionably termed a new scientific "paradigm" (Kuhn, 1962, 1970), a shift in the whole way of thinking about human beings in the natural world and their knowledge of it. Usually this shift is illustrated by changes in the philosophy of science reflecting developments in physics. The *paradigm* underlying Newtonian physics, based on Descarte's dualistic view of man as separate from nature, held sway for 300 years, but Einsteinian and subatomic developments revealed its limitations. Since the 1970s especially, there has been much discussion of this change in the scientific atmosphere. Thus when John Dewey and Arthur F. Bentley published *Knowing and the Known* in 1949, they could point to at least half a century of such developments in physics, biology, and other sciences. They were concerned that the changes in scientific approach and method had not been matched by changes in terminology, and they sought to counteract the resulting confusions and ambiguities.

"The stress in physical inquiry," Dewey and Bentley state (p. 105), "lay upon locating units or elements of action, and determining their interactions." Physics was "a system of interactions involving particles, boundaries and laws" (p. 68). "Interaction," then, was seen as the impact of separate, already-defined entities acting on one another. (Recall the entities, stimuli, responses, factors, elements, of traditional language and of mechanical analysis.) The scientist was an objective "onlooker." The metaphor appropriate to this system was, of course, the machine. Without denying the effectiveness of the mechanical, interactional paradigm for certain problems, Dewey and Bentley noted the emergence of a new paradigm. Humankind was seen, not as separate from nature, but as within nature, and, to use Niels Bohr's (1959) phrasing "the observer," e.g., the scientist, was viewed as "part of his observation." In subatomic physics, for example, the acts of observation were seen to alter the states of the particles observed.

## Transaction

In order to differentiate this new paradigm from the old, Dewey and Bentley suggested in *Knowing and the Known* (1949) that the term *transaction* be used. Instead of breaking the subject matter into fragments in advance of inquiry, the observer, the observing, and the observed were to be seen as aspects of a total situation. The metaphor for "interaction," we have seen, was the machine, with separable elements or entities acting on one another. Another analogy would be an event such as two billiard balls colliding and then going their separate unchanged ways. In the new paradigm, the metaphor for "transaction" was organic, the living organism. The human being is not seen as a separate entity, acting upon an environment, nor the environment as acting on the organism, but both as parts or aspects of a total event. Recent developments in ecology have made this way of thinking clearer to many people. *Transaction*, then, designates an ongoing process in which the elements or parts are seen as aspects or phases of a total situation.

There is, of course, nothing inherent in the words *interaction* or *transaction* that requires this effort to disengage them. The problem lies in the history of the word, *interaction*, its association with the mechanistic Newtonian model of research and the behaviorist research model patterned on it. *Transaction* also offers the slight problem of the popular association of the term with business. But note that there is nothing inherently commercial about a transaction; the business aura derives only from the fact that it describes the relationship between a buyer and a seller—you can't buy unless there is someone selling and vice versa. It is unfortunate that James Britton (1984), with whose approach I have much in common, should have wasted the word on designating a practical kind of writing, in contrast to *poetic*. The transaction, after all, is something that happens between the buyer and the seller, and it is meaning that happens between reader and text. Actually, to offset the commercial usage, we find that the OED lists a 1460 usage: "*Roman and Civil law*: The adjustment of a dispute between parties by mutual concession; compromise." From the very beginning, evidently, transaction carried overtones of mutuality, a blending of components.

The transactional view also refutes the notions of language as a self-contained, ungrounded system, such as the deconstructionists derive from the dyadic formulation of the great French linguist, de Saussure (1972) stressing the relation between the signifier and the signified, the word and its object. In contrast, Peirce's semiotic theory offers a triadic formulation—sign, object, interpretant. "A sign," Peirce wrote, "is in a conjoint relation to the thing denoted and to the mind. . . . The sign is related to its object only in consequence of a mental association, and depends upon a habit" (1933). This model, providing for the human element in the symbolizing process, is consonant with the transactional paradigm and is supported by contemporary studies of language acquisition (Bates, 1979; Werner & Kaplan, 1963). Language, socially generated and individually internalized, has for each of us public and personal aspects. The "sense" of a word is "the sum of all the psychological events aroused in our consciousness by the word" (Vygotsky, 1962; James, 1890). This is the experiential and linguistic reservoir, the cognitive and affective residue of our past experience with life and language, on which each must draw in any linguistic transaction, whether speaking or listening, writing or reading (Rosenblatt, 1983).

## Stimulus-Response and Transaction

I have emphasized Dewey and Bentley's 1949 generalizations about the changing paradigm (which is still in process of formulation, as the recent spate of books on the subject testifies) because I adopted their terminology when I read the book, as Bentley reported to Dewey in a letter of April 20, 1950 (Dewey & Bentley, 1964, p. 630). However, this book was a late development in Dewey's break with the dualistic Cartesian mechanistic view. That break can be traced back at least to his articles written in 1896 and 1930 (Dewey, 1931) in which he rejected the accepted notion of stimulus and response as involving a set of elements subject to prior definition. Instead of the notion of a fixed already-defined stimulus acting on a passive organism, Dewey pointed out that the prior state of that organism affected the character of the stimulus. A clap of thunder, for example, would be a different stimulus to a scholar so absorbed in his studies that he heard only a vague sound than to a timorous person waiting anxiously for the next thunderclap. Over the next half-century, Dewey went on to attempt to stress this rejection of the behaviorist stimulus-response paradigm by using various terms, such as *situation* or *experience*, to emphasize the dynamic, fluid process involved in the interrelationships being studied. "Interaction," with its mechanical associations, tended to blur the new approach Dewey was developing.

Thus when in 1949 Dewey called for *transaction* in place of *interaction*, he was drawing on a theoretical position he had long espoused. And, if I may be forgiven the inescapably personal character of these remarks, in adopting Dewey's terminology for the relationship between reader and text, I was finding a new designation for a theory of reading that I had been developing since 1938. In *Literature as Exploration*, published in that year, I wrote: "The reading of any work of literature is, of necessity, an individual and unique occurrence, involving the mind and emotions of some particular reader" (p. 32). Throughout, I was concerned to reject such dualisms as form and content, social and esthetic, and to see them, though distinguishable analytically, as inseparable in their "living context," which required also recognition of a personal, social, and cultural matrix.

In the following decades, I presented this view of the dynamic relationship of reader and text (e.g., 1964, 1968, 1969, 1977). In the second and later editions of *Literature as Exploration* (1968, 1976, 1984), I indicated that I preferred *transaction* to my use of *interaction*, and in the Winter, 1969, issue of *Journal of Reading Behavior*, published "Towards a Transactional Theory of Reading."

## Information-Processing

The reason for my distress at the effort to merge "information processing" and my view of reading becomes apparent. Information processing theory rests on a mechanical or electronic analogy or metaphor. The "interactive processing model," which is said (not only in the ERIC article mentioned above, but in other quarters) to share "common ground" with my transactional theory basically retains the old mechanistic view of separate personal "top" and textual "bottom" elements acting on one another. No matter how much one might build elements labeled top-down or bottom-up into a machine, the result would still be a machine, and not an organism. The same is true of the introduction of "the feedback loop" in an effort to impart transactionality. This, too, is a mechanical concept that cannot effect the transformation.

Instead of trying to plaster over the distinction between the dualistic, mechanistic, linear, interactional view, in which the text, on the one hand, and the personality of the reader, on the other, can be separately analyzed, with the impact of one on the other studied in a vacuum, we need to see the reading act as an event involving a particular individual and a particular text, happening at a particular time, under particular circumstances, in a particular social and cultural setting, and as part of the ongoing life of the individual and the group. We still can distinguish the elements, but we have to think of them, not as separate entities, but as aspects or phases of a dynamic process, in which all elements take on their character as part of the organically-interrelated situation. Instead of thinking of reading as a linear process, we have to think rather of a complex network or circuit of interrelationships, with reciprocal interplay.

Both the "bottom-up" and "top-down" approaches to the reading process need a thorough critical rethinking in the light of the transactional theory of reading, which sees both reader and text as active, but in an organic, rather than a linear mechanical, way. "Inferring" is not something that is simply to be added on to "decoding," for example. "Expectations" and "experiences" which the reader brings are not entities for interaction, but stances or states of the organism, as are linguistic activities.

## Efferent and Aesthetic Reading

I have already mentioned my disquiet at the tendency, especially among those concerned with "reading" per se, to place "reading research" or "information processing" over against "literary criticism" or "literary theory" as though the latter were somehow not also concerned with reading. The truth of the matter is that in general this separation does reflect the lacks in the theoretical under-pinnings of both of these groups. The reading experts ignore what is usually called "literature," and the "literary" folk, starting with an agreed-upon canon of "literary works," usually ignore the problems of the reading of "ordinary" prose and how it differs from "literary" reading. Each group therefore tends to fall back on seeing "literariness" as inherent in the text, seeking this in content and in syntactic and semantic conventions.

In searching for a theoretical basis for the teaching of literature, I found that I had arrived at a general theory of the reading process. And I concluded that the source of "literariness" could not be relegated to the text. No one of the subjects, literary conventions, technical devices, types of discourse cited as determinate was essential to all literary works of art, however much these devices might enhance the literary or aesthetic quality of the reading transaction. The differ-ence, it became apparent, resided in what the reader does in these two kinds of reading—what is brought into the center of attention, what is pushed into the periphery or ignored. Any reading act, I point out (1978, Ch. 3) falls somewhere on a continuum between predominantly efferent (from the Latin, *efferre*, to carry away), and the predominantly aesthetic (or "literary") reading.

Both cognitive and affective aspects of consciousness are activated in the transaction with verbal signs. The difference between the two kinds of reading lies in the reader's "selective attention" to what is being stirred up in the expe-riential reservoir. The predominantly efferent reader focuses attention on public meaning, abstracting what is to be retained after the reading—to be recalled, paraphrased, acted on, analyzed. In aesthetic reading, the reader's selective attention is focused primarily on what is being personally lived through, cogni-tively and affectively, *during* the reading event. The range of ideas, feelings, associations activated in the reservoir of symbolizations is drawn upon. (The reader may retain much afterwards, but that is not the differentiating aspect.)

Any text (e.g., a sonnet or a story) can be read either way. Obviously, much reading falls near the middle of the continuum, with some degree of attention to the subordinate mode, but any reading event can be characterized as primarily efferent or aesthetic.

The concepts of "stance" and "selective attention" rest, of course, on the view of language indicated above, and are an integral part of the total transactional model of the reading process set forth in the 1938 and 1978 books and many articles. The reader transacts with the particular aspect of the environment which is the text, the pattern of signs on the page. It is not possible to summarize here the dynamics, the interplay, the fusions, of the to-and-fro process as it proceeds in time, the constant activity of choice and revision, the structuring and testing that constitute the total transaction.

In the October, 1984, issue of *Research in the Teaching of English*, Britton suggests that his "participant" and "spectator" categories are interchangeable respectively with my "efferent" and "aesthetic" categories. My esteem for the work of Britton and his colleagues makes it difficult to disentangle our agreements and differences. We share a recognition of the importance of the reader's attitude, as against the general preoccupation simply with the text. However, our two sets of categories are not congruent. Emphasis on the "spectator" aspect does not do justice to the total transactional (in my sense) relationship with the text. The "object" on which the aesthetic reader concentrates is not "verbal," but experiential; the "object" is the cognitive and affective structure which the reader calls forth and lives through. Thus the reader is in a sense both spectator and participant. Perhaps it is his "verbal" phrasing that leads Britton into the self-contradiction of accepting at times formulations of textual traits as the essential determinants of the aesthetic (pp. 321, 325).

Actually, my categories cut across both of Britton's concepts, since my concern at this point is with the linguistic process, the reader's stance toward the process of symbolization. Is not the "pure" scientist concentrating on observing some segment of the world as much a "spectator" cut off from practical concerns as the poet, but bringing an efferent stance to bear? And just as in reading a poem we can shift from the aesthetic stance to efferently notice some technical device, so the scientist can shift to an aesthetic stance, savoring the private and personal aspects of what is being perceived, whether the elegance of a mathematical equation or the rings of Saturn. Since much of our linguistic activity hovers near the middle of the efferent-aesthetic continuum, it becomes essential that in any particular speaking/listening/writing/reading event we adopt the predominant stance appropriate to our purpose.

## Evocation and Response

*Literature as Exploration* is often credited with being the first formulation of "reader-response" criticism or theory (Tompkins, 1980; Suleiman & Crosman, 1980). It is true that, to counter the traditionalists' and the New Critics' neglect of the reader, I insisted on the reader's role. This emphasis was shared by those who later, in the 1970s and 1980s, came to react against the New Critical formalism. Many, nevertheless, continued to treat the literary work as an object, a static set of meanings, with the reader responding or reacting to a literary work "out there," apart from the reader. Even some of those who have belatedly espoused what sounds like a transactional view of the relationship between reader and text still often tend to emphasize one to the practical neglect of the other. In contrast, the transactional concept has always kept both reader and text in focus. Some, especially those applying the psychoanalytic doctrines, so emphasize the reader's personality that the text becomes practically passive (cf. Holland, 1975; Bleich, 1975). Others (e.g., lser, 1978) whose theoretical phrasings at times seem transactional nevertheless concentrate primarily on analyses of the text and see the reader's contribution only as filling in "the gaps" rather than transactionally creating meaning through the aesthetic stance and the triadic relationship with all the verbal signs.

Also, much so-called "reader-response" theory does not make clear *what* the reader is "responding" to. It seems as though the "response" is directed at the text (which in some unexplained way embodies the work). In the transactional theory, "text" refers to a set of verbal signs. The poem, the novel, the play, the story, i.e., the literary work of art, comes into being, happens, during the aesthetic transaction. This lived-through current of ideas sensations, images, tensions, becomes shaped into what the reader sees as the literary work or the evocation corresponding to the text. This is what the reader starts reacting or responding to *during* the reading event. Later, there will be recall of the experience, remembering of, and reflection on, the evocation and the reactions.

The evocation together with the concurrent responses are the subject matter of interpretation, which is the effort to report on the nature of the structure of thought and feeling called forth during the transaction with the text. Criticism should make the aesthetic transaction the starting point of a further transactional relationship between reader/critic and text—or between reader/historian and text, or reader/semiotician and text. Thus the transactional theory deals not only with the initial reading process, but also with such problems as criteria of validity of interpretation, questions relating to texts from different periods or cultures, and criteria of evaluation. If I spell out these aspects of the theory, it is simply in order to make clear why I deplore the tendency to be satisfied simply with the term *transaction* as a synonym for *interaction*, or the tendency to accept the basic concept of "transaction" without acknowledging its developed corollaries in the full transactional theory.

"Context" takes on scope and importance from the transactional view of the reading event as a unique coming-together of a particular personality and a particular text at a particular time and place under particular circumstances. The reader's evocation, like the author's text, is seen as "the organic expression, not only of a particular individual, but also of a particular cultural setting"

(Rosenblatt, 1938, p. 139). The importance of what has recently been termed "the interpretive community" (Fish, 1980) was thus recognized, related to its social sources, and placed in this broader cultural setting (Rosenblatt, 1938, and 1978, pp. 121–23, 128–30). *Literature as Exploration* underlines the importance of seeing any reading event in its personal, social, cultural matrix. Not only what the reader brings to the transaction from past experience with life and language, but also the socially molded circumstances and purpose of the reading, provide the setting for the act of symbolization. The reading event should be seen in its total matrix.

## Implications for Research

The transactional model of reading provides the basis for important shifts in emphasis and methods in the teaching of reading, both efferent and aesthetic. And the contrast between the linear, mechanistic, behaviorist research model based on the concept of "interaction" as against the organic model based on "transaction," has important implications for research, not only in terms of the formulation of hypotheses but also, of course, in the methods used to test them. In an essay on the implications of the transactional theory for research on response and the teaching of reading (Rosenblatt, 1984), I have sketched some of these considerations: transactional conceptualizations, for example, affect the nature of basic problems to be studied in the area of language development, especially in the acquisition of habits of selective attention and synthesis. The situations and teaching methods that foster the retention and strengthening of aesthic capabilities are only now beginning to receive notice from researchers; it is particularly important that psychologists should catch up with the new paradigm in literary theory.

Research on "response" especially needs to be liberated from the restriction to problems amenable to the older research designs, with their emphasis on translation into quantitative terms. Questions about the process of evocation and response especially need to be faced. Problems of differentiating purposes and situations appropriate to the efferent and aesthetic stances, respectively, arise both in literary and educational research. The transactional emphasis on the personal literary transaction as the starting-point for growth in reading abilities has important repercussions on teaching methods and hence on ways of studying and evaluating them.

In research on the processes of efferent and aesthetic reading, and on the teaching of efferent and aesthetic reading, such problems and hypotheses call for the fullest methodological range. In pointing to the necessity for the new paradigm, Dewey and Bentley, like the physicists, recognize the relevance of the older paradigm to certain types of problems, while insisting on its limitations and the need for the new paradigm for other problems. The failure of reading research thus far to contribute much to solving the literacy problem may be due to lack of recognition of the limitations of the old experimental design, with its neat definition of variables and "treatment." A too-ready extrapolation from the laboratory or research situation to the school may have paralleled the confusion between *interaction* and *transaction*.

Dewey and Bentley point out that even in biological investigations, there may be "interactional" studies of, say, the effect of a drug on a particular organ. But the important thing is to recognize that this must be reinterpreted in the transactional framework of the total human organism. Similarly, in research on the reading process and the teaching of reading, the earlier more limited interactional studies should be scrutinized and evaluated thoroughly in a transactional framework, with a healthy skepticism toward the tendency to hypostatize as entities what should be viewed as aspects of a transaction. (To what extent, for example, are "schema" and "schemata" being hypostatized as fixed entities, static explanations for what is actually a fluid, nonlinear process or situation?)

It is being more generally recognized that any investigation of human activities should honor above all the scientist's admission that the observer is part of the observation. The investigation, as has been indicated, needs to be placed in its broadest matrix. The assumptions the investigator brings, the relationship between investigator and subject, the past experiences of the subjects and their understanding of the situation, the extent to which their present activities reflect past indoctrinations, the practical institutional, professional, and political influences present in the situation—such concerns apply no matter what the particular research methodology: experimental, case study, interview, or ethnographic.

## Ethnographic Research

The ethnographic approach, which utilizes the techniques of the anthropologist and the sociologist, is especially appropriate to research based on the transactional theory. As indicated earlier, the social or cultural setting of the investigation should be acknowledged. The appropriateness of ethnographic methods for problems of language and literature (and its relevance to my theory) has already received lively presentation in this journal (see especially, Kantor, Kirby, & Goetz, 1981). The flexibility and variety of methods possible through the ethnographic approach can counteract the artificiality and static character of ideas derived from the older research designs. New hypotheses and more realistic problems may emerge from such study of transactional processes, and may stimulate the development of new strategies for testing the hypotheses.

At the same time, the ethnographic method must be developed as a systematic disciplined approach, and the pitfalls of such methods must be avoided. The questions raised, the research designs, and the interpretations of the findings will benefit from a cultural perspective: problems need to be fitted into the broader framework of the development of the capacities of individual human beings, and of the role of language and literature in our society and other cultures. The transactional theory, with its sense of the individual reader and the individual text as bearers of culture creating new cultural events in unique transactions provides a critical framework.

Again, this assumes that, not simply the difference between the terms *interaction*, and *transaction* will be honored, but also that the transactional theory of reading as a whole will be given a chance to make its contribution toward further scientific research in reading.

# References

Bates, E. (1979). *The Emergence of Symbols*. New York: Academic Press.

Bleich, D. (1975). "The Subjective Character of Critical Interpretation." *College English, 37* (7), 739–55.

Bohr, N. (1959). "Discussion with Einstein." In P.A. Schilpp (Ed.), *Albert Einstein, Philosopher-Scientist*. New York: Harper.

Britton, J. (1970). *Language and Learning*. Coral Gables, FL: University of Miami Press.

Britton, J. (1984). "Viewpoints: The Distinction Between Participant and Spectator Role Language in Research and Practice." *Research in the Teaching of English, 18* (3), 320–31.

Dewey, J. (1896). "The Reflex Are Concept in Psychology." *Psychological Review, 3* (4), 357–70.

Dewey, J. (1925). *Experience and Nature*. New York: W. W. Norton.

Dewey, J. (1931). *Philosophy and Civilization*. New York: Minton Balch.

Dewey, J. (1934). *Art as Experience*. New York: Minton Balch.

Dewey, J., & Bentley, A.F. (1949). *Knowing and the Known*. Boston: Beacon Press.

Fish, S. *Is There a Text in This Class?* Cambridge, MA: Harvard University Press.

Harris, T.L., & Hodges, R.E. (1981). *A Dictionary of Reading and Related Terms*. Newark, DE: International Reading Association.

Holland, N. (1975). *5 Readers Reading*. New Haven, CT: Yale University Press.

Iser, W. (1978): *The Act of Reading*. Baltimore: Johns Hopkins University Press.

James, W. (1890). *The Principles of Psychology*. New York: Henry Holt.

Kantor, K.J., Kirby, D.R., & Goetz, J.P. (1981). "Research in Context: Ethnographic Studies in English Education." *Research in the Teaching of English, 15* (4), 293–309.

Koenke, K. (1984). "ERIC/RCS Report: An Examination of the Construct of "Reader-Text Relationship." *English Education, 16* (2), 115–20.

Kuhn, T. (1970). *The Structure of Scientific Revolutions* (2nd ed.). Chicago: University of Chicago Press.

Peirce, C.S. (1932, 1933). *Collected Papers* (Vols: 2 & 3). P. Weiss and C. Hartshorne (Eds.). Cambridge, MA: Harvard University Press.

Rosenblatt, L.M. (1938). *Literature as Exploration*. New York: Appleton-Century. Revised ed., New York: Noble & Noble, 1968; London: Heinemann, 1970; 3rd ed., New York: Noble & Noble, 1976; New York: Modern Language Association, 1983.

Rosenblatt, L.M. (1964). "The Poem as Event." *College English, 26* (2), 123–28.

Rosenblatt, L.M. (1968). "A Way of Happening." *Educational Record, 49* (3), 339–46.

Rosenblatt, L.M. (1969, Winter). "Towards a Transactional Theory of Reading." *Journal of Reading Behavior, 1* (1), 31–49.

Rosenblatt, L.M. (1978). *The Reader, the Text, the Poem: The Transactional Theory of the Literary Work.* Carbondale: Southern Illinois University Press.

Rosenblatt L.M. (1982). "The Literary Transaction: Evocation and Response." *Theory into Practice, 21* (4), 268–77.

Rosenblatt, L.M. (1983). *Writing and Reading.* A paper presented at the 1983 Convention of the Modern Language Association.

Rosenblatt, L.M. (1984). "The Transactional Theory of the Literary Work: Implications for Research." In C. Cooper (Ed.), *Researching Response and the Teaching of Literature.* Norwood, NJ: Ablex Press.

Saussure, F. de (1972). *Cours de linguistique générale.* Paris: Payot.

Suleiman, S.R. & Crosman, I. (Eds.). (1980). *The Reader in the Text.* Princeton: Princeton University Press.

Tompkins, J.P. (Ed.) (1980). *Reader-Response Criticism.* Baltimore: Johns Hopkins University Press.

Vygotsky, L. (1962). *Thought and Language* (F. Hanfmann & G. Vakar, Eds. and trans.). Cambridge: MIT Press.

Werner, H., & Kaplan, B. (1963). *Symbol Formation.* New York: Wiley.

## Chapter Three

# Toward a Cultural Approach to Literature

President Roosevelt's warning that "if civilization is to survive we must cultivate the science of human relationships—the ability of all peoples, of all kinds, to live together and work together in the same world, at peace"—has gained even more drastic urgency since it was written on the day before his death. International understanding and the moral and intellectual solidarity of all peoples must be achieved—under penalty of extinction if we fail. Educators have been especially alert to this need, and there has been a renewed concern to clarify the ways in which each field of study can better serve those ends. In the field of literature the need to acquaint American youth with the literary achievements of foreign peoples has been urged as an important means of eliminating provincialism and fostering sound international understanding. And, since international sympathies must be reinforced by moral solidarity at home, the study of foreign literatures has been urged, too, as a means of eliminating prejudice against people of various foreign ancestries within our own country.

An enveloping philosophy for the study of foreign literatures and a clear sense of the basic attitudes and insights that we seek to foster are essential. The crux of the problem lies in the development of attitudes toward cultural differences. It is not necessary to document here the existence, even among American college graduates, of attitudes of rejection or superiority toward those, abroad or at home, who diverge from accepted American norms. To be fruitful, the study of foreign literature should be permeated by consistent ways of thinking about cultural differences. In particular circumstances, with particular instructors and students, one or another type of course or series of texts may be desirable; but their effectiveness for fostering humane attitudes will depend on the concepts about people and cultures which make up the climate of thought within which the reading and study are carried on. The following remarks are an attempt to initiate discussion by sketching some of the ideas which should be implicit in any treatment of foreign literatures which seeks to serve our ultimate humanistic goals.

# I

The anthropologists, through their study of primitive and modern societies, or, to use the anthropological term, cultures, have provided us with the ideological framework for our problem. They have reinforced our awareness of the amazing diversity of social patterns that men have created—strikingly different modes of behavior, types of personal relationships, ideas of good and evil, religious beliefs, social organizations, economic and political mechanisms, and forms of art. But the anthropologists find these differences evidence only of the extreme plasticity of the human creature. They have made us understand that men have fashioned these divergent patterns of living out of the raw materials of their common humanity, out of the common drives which all human beings share.

The scientific evidence is that race or any inherited physical traits cannot be recognized as causal factors in the diverse patterning of cultures. Each culture utilizes, at any time, only a limited number out of the vast range of potentialities possessed by the human creature. Everything from physical traits to the ability to dream dreams and see visions may receive different valuations in different societies, and a people may at different times in its history pour its personal and group life into widely contrasting molds. There will be many differences from individual to individual within a society, of course; but all will be shaped by reaction to the dominant pressures, the accepted habits, and the system of values of that culture. There would be a great difference in the resulting personality, for example, according to whether the same human organism were born into a society which rewards gentleness, moderation, and co-operativeness or one that prizes aggressiveness, violence, and individualism. For each society develops some of the individual's latent possibilities and represses or rejects others.

Thus we come to see our American society as playing out one among the many modes of living that mankind has developed and as one among the many diverse cultural patterns man has evolved from his common drives and capacities. If we tend to feel that our ways have an inherent rightness and divine sanction, that, too, is an illusion that we share with individuals shaped by other cultures, which seem equally self-justified to them.

When the individual sees himself and all that he takes for granted in our American society as a product of the same process of cultural conditioning that has produced other personalities in very different types of society, he can acquire the objectivity necessary for meeting the impact of those differences. They will be recognized as variations on the common human theme and need not be met with blind and self-justified suspicion or fear or repugnance. The emotional rejection of differences can give way to intelligent reflection on them.[1]

1. This statement of key ideas is necessarily sketchy. See Ruth Benedict, *Patterns of Culture* (Houghton Mifflin, 1934), and *Race: Science and Politics* (Viking Press, 1943), and the general works by Franz Boas, Ralph Linton, Bronislaw Malinowski, Margaret Mead, Robert H. Lowie, *et al.*

Infused with this cultural approach, the study of foreign literature should indeed have a liberating effect. (I am assuming, of course, that any study of foreign literature will, above all, help the student to have direct, personal enjoyment of literary works as works of art.) Literature gives us concrete evidence of how differently men have phrased their lives in different societies. But literature, by its very nature, helps also to bridge those differences. For literature, which permits us to enter emotionally into other lives, can be viewed always as the expression of human beings who, in no matter how different the ways, are, like us, seeking the basic human satisfactions, experiencing the beauties and rigors of the natural world, meeting or resisting the demands of the society about them, and striving to live by their vision of what is important and desirable in life. Imaginative sharing of human experience through literature can thus be an emotionally cogent means of insight into human differences as part of a basic human unity.

The ultimate human meaning of a work of literature, and especially a foreign work, is not that of a photographic document but emerges as we penetrate beneath the exotic social forms and themes to discover the structure of emotional relationships and moral emphases it embodies. Our delight in the picturesque or dramatic externals of foreign life, our interest in strange folkways, need not obscure our sense of the literary work as a crystallization of human emotions and aspirations, as a patterning of attitudes toward the world of man and nature. Sometimes these are explicit in the work, sometimes implicit, clothed in story and symbol. But always it is possible to reach through the literary work to the broader human patterns it reflects. Through the study of foreign literature, then, we are seeking to help our students to broaden their vision of the varied images of life, of the different patterns of values, of the contrasting habits of emotional response, that other peoples have created out of our common human potentialities. And these differences are to be seen as alternatives, beside which our way of life and our own system of values are to be placed.

Nor will the images of human behavior and personality encountered in literature fall into a neat hierarchy, with American society perched at the summit. It will not always be easy to decide in what direction the balance should fall, if these patterns are weighed in terms of their meaning for the fulfilment of human capacities. In some societies, as in the Greek or the feudal, men will be seen, for example, to have elaborated ideals of a different range of personal loyalties, a more exacting code of honor, than in our own, or to have envisaged stronger claims of friendship (cf. Pater's *Two Early French Stories*). Again, some societies tend to give greater prestige than we do to the artist and the intellectual. Or it may be necessary to make clear at what social cost certain types of elegance in art and manners, as in seventeenth-century France, were achieved. Moreover, in the same society—and in the same great work of art— high sensitivity on some points may coexist with great callousness on others. An acceptance of cruelty or violence, a view of the child as a little savage to be tamed, a suppression of women, and a glorification of brute power may be associated with much that we admire ethically and aesthetically. Perhaps such insights may lead to the question whether America, too, may not have cultural blind spots, juxtaposed to humane sensitivity at other points.

A concern with attitudes toward cultural differences gives special point to the literary scholar's interest in clarifying the relationship between the literary work and the society which produced it—and especially the relationship between the author and his audience. Of course, we know that literature is not a mere mirror of life. Literature is itself an integral part of a culture and has its own complex relationship to the rest of the cultural setting. A literary work often reflects only some one segment of the society, to which it may be addressed. If sometimes it offers a realistic description, at other times it may represent an escape from, or compensation for, actual conditions. And always it implies the temperament of the author—more or less at one with the dominant modes of thought and feeling in the society about him. It would be self-defeating, if in our zeal to find "characteristic" or "representative" foreign works we minimized these considerations and unwittingly reinforced the tendency to make hasty generalizations about foreign peoples.[2] Moreover, we are less insulated from the full human impact of the great masterpieces if we see how they often reflect only one part of the arc of a society.

Perhaps all of this sums up merely to insistence that we approach the literature of other peoples with the same concern for its intrinsic human meaning with which we approach our own literature today. The value of such intercourse with, and such an open mind toward, the cultural alternatives encountered through foreign literature of the past and present lies in the objectivity which it can foster. Such a comparative approach opens the path to escape from unquestioning acceptance of the familiar and from consequent crude prejudice against all other ways. If we are indeed seeking to foster international understanding, it must be based on such objectivity toward our own and other ways of life.

The same approach to differences can help to dissolve attitudes of rejection toward the minorities within our American society, who possess differentiating traits due to their national ancestry, their religious training, their segregation because of color, their belonging to one or another economic group. And the view of differences as alternatives due to environmental variations may lead even to the recognition that minority groups may possess some qualities, may follow some standards of behavior, such as habits of group aid, or may value some kinds of temperaments that, instead of being spurned as divergent from American norms, should be incorporated as an accepted part of the American pattern.

---

2. How disillusioning it was for many Frenchmen in 1870 to discover that the image of the romantic, sentimental, dreamy, contemplative Germans—based largely on the reading of German romantic literature—did not at all correspond to the full reality! See Fernand Baldensperger, *La Littérature: création, succès, durée* (Paris: Flammarion, 1927), p. 201.

# II

Awareness of the cross-fertilization of cultures is another insight militating against provincialism that can be fostered through the study of literature. Interchange from society to society has been one of the important factors in cultural growth and enrichment. Even among primitive cultures, the anthropologists point to those marginal peoples who have remained culturally impoverished and static because they were cut off from contact with other societies. The history of our Western civilization embodies a long series of such fructifying contacts. Within our own field of literature our problem is an embarrassment of riches in seeking to do justice to the intermingled cultural streams that have fed us. We must include at least the Hebrew, Greek, and Roman among the ancient literatures; the Middle Ages and the Renaissance must be presented as European developments with various influences from the East; and, in more recent times of national literatures, what a vast network of crosscurrents, of give-and-take across national frontiers!

Students of comparative literature remind us that, when such borrowings, such "influences," occur, it is because native conditions have created a favorable soil on which the foreign seed can be implanted. Each literature possesses, and continues to maintain, its own special characteristics, and the foreign influence may undergo a sea-change as it is incorporated into the new literary setting. Yet beneath the surface similar emotional needs and intellectual tendencies have made possible the transfusion of ideas, themes, or artistic forms.

This view of the intricate interpenetration of cultures both prevents a smug cultural egotism and permits a hopeful sense of possibilities for the future. No society is justified in the belief that it has produced the supermen toward which all history has been tending. We are not the supremely superior heirs who incorporate all that was good in the past. We see that peoples, at one time looked upon as barbarians and inherently inferior by the more advanced societies about them, have later, in the course of cultural interchange and growth, developed new and undreamed-of outlets for human capacities and have produced writers speaking across the barriers of language and time to their fellow-humans.

A reason frequently stated for studying the foreign works which have contributed to our own cultural heritage is that we shall thus inculcate a respect and sympathy for the peoples who produced these great writings: the Bible will demonstrate oneness in ethical and religious ideals with the Jews; Dante will lead to a sense of fraternity with the Italians; Homer, the Greeks; and so on. Such an increased appreciation and sympathy for specific peoples should surely be fostered.

But should there not be an equal emphasis on the fact of our common indebtedness to a multi-national, or multi-cultural, ancestry? The Bible, Homer, Shakespeare, Molière, Goethe, Ibsen, and the others are not only bonds between us and the people whose national pride they are. Such works are bonds also between us and all the other peoples they have enriched. The inter-marriages of minds in the course of history have given us and other modern peoples many of the same cultural ancestors. Are not the Greek and Latin classics cultural links between us and the French, for example? And are not Shakespeare, Goethe, Ibsen, or the Bible, mediators among many cultures?

Indeed, when we look at the histories of literature as they now exist, we may well wonder if the nationalist obsession of recent centuries has not too strongly dominated our thinking and obscured the realities. Such revolutions have come about in the course of any national literature that an Englishman of the eighteenth century, for instance, might feel more at home with a French contemporary than with his own English descendant of the romantic period. Our national cultures are so complex, and include such a wide range of temperaments and philosophies, that an American poet today may find himself more akin to, say, a contemporary French poet than to another American poet. Fortunately, we do not always put nationalist categories first in treating literature. Courses in medieval literature and the Renaissance perforce cut across national and linguistic boundaries. Even in dealing with more recent times of intense nationalism, we are breaking away from distorting national compartmentalizations to concentrate on great common movements of ideas and feeling, as in courses on the romantic movement, realism in fiction, the symbolist and post-symbolist trends. The study of different genres, drama, the short story, the novel, poetry, also leads us to move back and forth across national frontiers. More of this emphasis on parallel developments should permeate courses focused on American or English literature if we wish to present modern civilization as a co-operative enterprise transcending national frontiers. The evidence of the rich harvest of cultural interchanges in the past can be made the source of a receptive attitude toward such interchange with an everwidening circle of peoples in the future.

The approach to cultural differences that has been sketched thus far is equally pertinent to the problem of affecting attitudes toward differences within our own society. Not only do we Americans share the general multiple indebtedness of our Western civilization, but we are living embodiments of a very special illustration of cultural intermingling. American history is coming to be understood more and more in terms of the interplay of peoples and patterns drawn from many lands. The period of zealous "Americanization," with its image of differences merged in the American melting pot, has given way to a growing realization of the fact that unity need not mean uniformity. The newer and more constructive image is that of an *orchestration*[3] of individual and group differences into a harmonious national unity. Differences can be welcomed as a national asset, a condition making for cultural fertility.

3. Horace M. Kallen, *Culture and Democracy in the United States* (Boni & Liveright, 1924), p. 124.

Teachers of English, both in the colleges and in the schools, may have to admit more than a small share of the responsibility for having perpetuated too narrow a conception of what is American. The tendency to overstress the so-called "Anglo-Saxon" elements in our culture is understandable. But without scanting this major aspect of our American literary tradition, we can do greater justice to the values in our life and literature that have resulted from the incorporation into our American society of people with varied traditions of behavior, feeling, and expression. The emphasis should not be on differences in themselves but rather on the fact that, out of this wealth of diverse temperaments and ways, we have laid the foundations for, and are together continuing to create, an integrated American culture. The special mark of this culture can be its flexibility, its fostering of a broad and fertile range of individual differences—some of which may be due to diversity of ancestry—within the framework of a creatively democratic society.

Given the complexity of the cultural picture, let us be especially careful that the study of foreign literature not lead to the mistaken notion that the label—English or French or Chinese or Polish—can be equated with any individual. The very laudable effort in the schools, at present, to stress the contributions of the various groups to our cultural heritage seems sometimes to fall into this error. Such labels denote broad cultural patterns, within which there can be great individual variations. The boy of Italian ancestry, for instance, may weary of having it assumed that he will take special pride in Dante and Leonardo da Vinci or that his schoolmates will value him more because of these great Italians. The boy may himself respond more to Homer or Walt Whitman—and they are as much his heritage as is Dante. Above all, we must remember that his Italian ancestry is only one of the factors in the complex process of cultural conditioning to which his life in America has exposed him. The concept of the interplay of cultural elements may thus help us to liberate ourselves from too rigid national or cultural categorizations and may permit us to look at individuals within our own and other cultures *as* individuals.

# III

The comparative approach to cultures, the placing of our own beside the others, represents only the first step in the process of developing international and human understanding. Students, it may be objected, becoming acquainted with cultures extremely different from, yet in their own terms as valid as, our own, may lose their provincialism but retain only a sterile relativism, arguing that what is "good" in one culture may be "evil" in another. A similar confusion may result from the turning with equal enthusiasm from one great work to another in, let us say, a course in world literature. Nor do we wish to exchange the feeling of superiority of the smugly complacent American for the feeling of inferiority endured by another kind of American. A recurrent phenomenon in our country has been the intellectual or the artist who has reached out for the aesthetic riches of foreign lands and has become alienated from the American life about him.

The answer to these objections has been implicit throughout this discussion: the comparative approach, the awareness of cultural differences as cultural alternatives, to serve as a basis for a sound educative process, must be buttressed by an active sense of values. Only by turning a *critically* appreciative eye upon our own and other cultures, our own and other literatures, shall we avoid either excessive smugness or excessive humility. The fundamental criteria for such a critical attitude are provided by our democratic ideals. The belief in the value and dignity of the human being that has been the leaven throughout our history can be the foundation for such a system of values. Though we have in many ways fallen far short of our democratic ideals, the common awareness of those ideals has been our conscience and our goad. The fact that within our own society there are tendencies that sometimes frustrate and obstruct our democratic aspirations can be a reminder that in all cultures there are varied and often conflicting elements. There must be developed the kind of international understanding that respects the validity of other cultures and does not seek stupidly to impose our own but yet, at the same time, discriminates between those patterns that threaten and those that serve the democratic ideal and the mutually helpful relations among peoples. The problem becomes one of discriminating, in our own and other literatures, between those elements that nourish the sense of man's dignity and worth and those that, no matter how satisfying aesthetically, reinforce attitudes inimical to this view or reflect an authoritarian spirit. Thus the student is liberated imaginatively to look objectively upon his own and other societies and to envisage the possibility of even greater approximation toward our democratic goals.

If we claim that the study of literature has value for life today, if we believe that through such study we can contribute toward creation of the ways of thinking and feeling so sorely needed in our domestic and international life, we must make much more important than ever before this critical process based on a vital awareness of democratic values. These should not, of course, be made the subject of constant preachments. Nor need courses in literature include lectures on cultural anthropology. Such insights can usually be fostered in terms of specific literary works, for in their personal and human import lies a potent means for affecting attitudes. This will be accomplished through constantly recurring emphases, through the approach to literary works in terms of their underlying structure of emotional relationships and social values, and through a consistent attitude toward cultural differences. The ends we are so eager to serve can, I believe, be achieved when the study of foreign literature embodies such a critically comparative approach, based on the democratic system of values.

# Chapter Four

# Foreword

*The teaching of language and literature can be a potent means of nourishing the democratic appreciation of each human being as an individual, unobscured by any group label—racial, religious, national, social, or economic—which may be applied to him.* To this thesis the present issue of the *English Journal* is devoted. The fulfilment of these potentialities of the English classroom is a responsibility more crucial than ever before. The atomic bomb has shocked us into awareness of the life-and-death urgency of many long-present and basic moral problems of our age. Peace abroad must be reinforced by moral solidarity at home. The existence of widespread habits of prejudiced feeling and behavior toward many groups in America is recognized as one of the vital threats to the health of our democracy. The ultimate cure will depend on the reshaping of many factors—social, political, and economic—in our society; but to all spheres of American education falls a major task—that of helping American youth to free themselves from prejudice and to become capable of creating together in mutual respect a society of free men.

The term "intercultural education" has come to be associated with this effort to establish wholesome attitudes toward the many groups in our society. The term is unfortunate, for it may suggest the existence of utterly distinct cultures in America rather than a single but pluralistic American culture, including a broad range of individual and group differences within its framework. The currency of a new term should not, at any rate, mislead us into thinking that we are promulgating a new concept of the teaching of English or adding a new subject to the province of English. We are merely, under stress of urgent necessity, seeking to do better what we have endeavored to do all along. We have sought to help our students acquire the power of using language as an instrument for understanding themselves and others, as a medium for co-operating effectively with their fellow-men. We have striven to transmit a living sense of literature, to develop in our students the capacity to respond to all that the work of art can give in heightened sensitivity to the quality and value of temperaments and ways of life different from their own. Only as these aims permeate our daily teaching of English, only in the context of the pervasive inculcation of democratic attitudes and a humane sense of values, does the special theme of this issue take on meaning. If we concentrate here on the subject of the relations among individuals of diverse group origins, it is only to explore the application of our generally accepted aims to this problem.

Recognition of the important role of the English teacher in this crisis is reflected in the generous response of our distinguished authors to the invitation to participate in this symposium. Thomas Mann heartens us for the task before us and speaks to us out of his profound knowledge of the powers of language and literature for good and for evil. The underlying theme of this issue is developed by Horace Kallen, who more than thirty years ago challenged the gray conformism of the melting-pot image and offered the pioneering symbol of an orchestration of differences. He evokes for us the diversity within unity which is the American pattern. We perceive that the very diversity which is the creative principle in American life is made possible by a unifying faith in the dignity and value of the individual, a unifying aspiration toward equality of opportunity and freedom for all. Helen Papashvily, through the medium of her art, brings home to us the intimate values of the American's participation in the riches of many "worlds." From the high-school student Noble Oyanagi we receive heart-warming testimony of the readiness of American youth to live in the American spirit.

Ruth Benedict, whose anthropological works have widely extended understanding of the facts and fallacies about race, and Ernst Kris, eminent psychiatrist, provide the scientific approach to racism and the psychology of prejudice, without which our efforts might become futilely expended good will.

James T. Farrell not only invigorates our sense of literature as an emotionally charged revelation of the human meaning of the "social problems" about which we so glibly speak; he also places the question of the human cost of group prejudice squarely within the broader question of the economic and social values in our society which impede rounded personal fulfilment for all individuals, of all classes and groups. Similarly, Alain Locke stresses the need for treating the literature of any minority group in its relation to, and as part of, the main stream of American literature. Edna Ferber reminds us that, through knowledge of one another, our sense of differences may become, not a barrier, but a bond of understanding.

The articles which follow bring us even more directly into the English classroom. Lou La Brant illuminates the ways in which language affects attitudes toward people. Margaret Heaton shows how literature—not as texts on which to moralize, but through the imaginative insights it offers—can foster the development of a sense of individuals as complex human personalities. Charles K. Cummings, Jr., illustrates by specific cases the kind of understanding needed for the tactful guidance of students toward sound human relations. Mrs. Smiley's survey of teachers' reports of work in intercultural education in various parts of the country demonstrates that our responsibilities can be fulfilled in the normal course of the English program. This account should be read in the light of the guiding ideas provided by the preceding articles and by Marion Edman's concluding analysis of pitfalls and possibilities.

Our aim, as Hawthorne phrased it, is to keep unbroken "the magnetic chain of humanity"—to efface the barriers between man and man. To combat group prejudice, we must transcend the habit of thinking mainly in terms of groups. Otherwise, in our eagerness to defend the group, we may, as effectively as those who are prejudiced, imprison the individual within his group. For it is the opportunity to live in many worlds at once that ensures the ultimate freedom of the individual American to be an individual.

On behalf of the Committee on Inter-cultural Relations, I wish to thank the Editor for opening the pages of the *English Journal* to us and for his hearty cooperation. We are indebted also to the National Conference of Christians and Jews for its generous and unrestricting sponsorship of this issue.

# Chapter Five

# The Acid Test
# for Literature Teaching

This is a critical hour for the teaching of literature in the schools of America. Many of our high school and college graduates, it is being demonstrated, have not developed the habit of reading literary works. This, quite rightly, raises questions concerning the efficacy of what in the past has been happening in English classrooms. Meanwhile the pressure of increasing numbers in the schools creates a trend toward larger classes and therefore toward the kind of teaching that can be done for large groups sitting in rows, passively receiving information. In this shifting situation, a mass production approach to education, converging with a revived academicism, may lead to the abandonment of the very elements of literature teaching that are essential.

Of course, many factors other than teaching methods are involved in the present crisis in culture. Often the teachers of English are closer to the young people of America, and closer to the essence of literature, than the scholarly gentlemen who view with alarm and yearn for the genteelly literate élite of the past. Yet the danger does exist that the whole cause of literature training as a part of general culture may suffer defeat. If there has been only limited success in the past, a reason has been the confusion about the essential nature of the subject-matter of literature teaching. Unless this confusion ceases, English teachers will not know what to defend and what to sacrifice under pressure of increasing numbers and academic attacks. My aim in the following discussion is to present what seems to me to be at the very heart of any literature teaching.

## Transactions Between Readers and Books

Our business seems usually to be considered the bringing of books to people. But books do not simply happen to people. People also happen to books. A story or poem or play is merely inkspots on paper until a reader transforms them into a set of meaningful symbols. When these symbols lead us to live through some moment of feeling, to enter into some human personality, or to participate imaginatively in some situation or event, we have evoked a work of literary art. Literature provides a *living through*, not simply knowledge *about*: not information that lovers have died young and fair, but a living-through of *Romeo and Juliet*; not just facts about Rome, but a living-through of the tensions of *Julius Caesar* or the paradoxes of *Caesar and Cleopatra*.

For the reader, the literary work is a particular and personal event: the electric current of his mind and personality lighting up the pattern of symbols on the printed page. Or perhaps we should say that the symbols take meaning from the intellectual and emotional context the reader provides. The current of his thoughts and feelings has for the time of his reading been channeled by the printed symbols. The result has been a more or less organized imaginative experience, and the word, "story," or the word, "poem," points towards this segment of the reader's experience.

When we teach literature, we are therefore concerned with the particular and personal way in which students learn to infuse meaning into the pattern of the printed symbols. We are not dealing with books as separate and fixed and neatly outlined and summed-up entities. We are dealing with each student's awareness, no matter how dim or confused, of a certain part of the ongoing sequence of his life, as he seeks to marshall his resources and organize them under the stimulus of the printed page.

Our subject-matter as teachers of literature, then, is the transactions between readers and books. If we are to "teach literature," certain kinds of experiences known as literary must first be brought about—that is our primary responsibility. This means helping specific students to have such experiences.

Once an organic relationship has been set up between young readers and books, many kinds of growth are possible, and the teacher can proceed to fulfill his function. Above all, students need to be helped to have personally satisfying and personally meaningful transactions with literature. Then they will develop the habit of turning to literature for the pleasures and insights it offers. Moreover, the sense of the intimate meaningfulness of literature is basic to wholesome growth in the kinds of abilities traditionally thought of as literary and critical.

This view is becoming more widely accepted today, and few teachers of English would deny that the individual's ability to read and enjoy literature is the primary aim of literary study. In practice, however, this concern tends to be overshadowed by the emphasis on whatever can be easily systematized and measured. Or the English program becomes whatever can be more easily justified to colleagues and administrators, whose own past English training has often produced only skepticism about our whole literary activity. Various attitudes and practices within our own professional training also tend to obstruct, and some of these will be pointed out later in this discussion.

To place any particular problem in teaching in proper focus, we must keep in mind that our concern is with developing lifelong personal relationships between books and people.[1] Thus we may develop criteria for judging the short-term motivations we provide our students, the works we ask them to read, and the teaching methods we employ.

Before we can logically consider such matters as the selection of works to be read, or the value of different approaches to literature, an underlying requirement must be faced. The atmosphere in the classroom, the relationship between teacher and pupil, and among the pupils, must *permit* a personal response to what is read. The variety and unpredictability of life need not be alien to the classroom. Teachers and pupils need to be relaxed enough to face what indeed happened as they interpreted the printed page. Frank expression of boredom, or even vigorous rejection, are more valid starting points for learning than are docile attempts to feel "what the teacher wants." The young reader, in learning to inquire about why he has responded inadequately to a given work, is learning both to seek the personally meaningful and to read more adequately.

Often, the teacher is eager to create such an atmosphere of untrammeled, frank responsiveness to books but is unsuccessful. This seems frequently to be the result of a failure to see how certain conventional notions about literature, certain approaches and emphases, can come between the student and the book. The following discussion will seek to point out some of these.

## Creating a Live Circuit

Perhaps all of us, at no matter what school or college level we teach, should have the opportunity to observe that second miracle of language (the first, of course, being acquisition of the spoken word), the child's entrance into the world of the printed page. What a delicate process it is, and with what pitfalls it is beset! We know the importance of "readiness": physical and neurological readiness to perform the highly complex operation which is the act of reading; emotional readiness to meet the challenge. Also essential is a sufficiently rich experience to make the words into meaningful signs, pointing to things and ideas. The queer black shapes must not only come to have sounds attached to them; these sounds must also be related to the appropriate object or idea. A set of black shapes on a page—*CAT*—becomes linked to a certain crisp sound in the ear. This becomes a word *read* only when that sound is linked to a certain class of furry, four-footed creatures. The beginning reader, then, should bring to the printed symbols a certain fund of experience with life and language. And the reading materials offered to the youngster should bring him verbal symbols that can be linked with that experience.

With the beginning reader, we can easily follow the process as he draws on past experience to achieve meaning from printed symbols. We can see, too, how

1. A conference devoted to surveying some of the general implications of this emphasis is reported in Grambs, Jean D., *The Development of Lifetime Reading Habits* (New York, published for the National Book Committee by R. R. Bowker Co., 1954).

he uses the printed words to organize and interpret that past experience. Moreover, we can glimpse the moment when, through words, he reorganizes past knowings and attains new insights. There is a continual shuttling back and forth between words and past experience and newly crystallized understanding.

But how easily this web of relationships can be broken, and the habit of mere verbalization fasten itself on the child! How easily he can come to feel that reading is simply associating the right noises with print, and have little or no comprehension of what it symbolizes.

In working with older pupils, whether in elementary or high school, or even college, we do not always recognize that we are faced with a problem parallel to that of the beginning reader. The six-year-old is perhaps readier to admit, and indeed to sense, the break between symbol and referent. The older child has too often already acquired the habit of being satisfied with only a general notion of the meaning of a passage. Fortunately, few become as extremely indifferent to words as the college sophomore who wrote, "the lemon meringue pie, its chocolate filling dotted with mounds of cocoanut." He defended this by saying that as he did not know just what a meringue pie was, any collection of good flavors would do! Many read story or poem or play with a similar willingness to let the printed symbols evoke only a pallid, generalized notion about the work, rather than as full a living-into it as possible.

The beginner, sounding out correctly the words found on the printed page without comprehension of their meaning, has failed to link words to experience. Parallel to this is the high school student who reads a story or poem or play as an academically and socially required exercise in words. It is something to verbalize about, to summarize, to analyze, but not something to be related to the ongoing stream of his own life.

Surely, like the beginner, the adolescent reader needs to encounter literature for which he possesses emotional and experiential "readiness." He, too, must possess the raw materials out of which to evoke in a meaningful way the world symbolized on the printed page. To avoid the mere translation from one set of words to another, that world must be fitted into the context of his own understanding and interests. If the language, the setting, the theme, the central stituation, all are too alien, even a "great work" will fail. All doors to it are shut. The printed words will at best conjure up only a ghost of a literary experience. The literary work must hold out some link with the young reader's own past and present preoccupations, emotions, anxieties, ambitions.

Hence a standard literary diet, prescribed for all in standard sequence, negates the reality of our school situation. In our heterogeneous society, variations from group to group, and within groups from individual to individual, make it necessary for us to plan our reading program in terms of the specific group and the individual differences within it. We need to be guided by an understanding of such matters as the pupils' general background, level of maturity, major interests, social difficulties and aspirations.

Sometimes, if the group is sufficiently homogeneous, they will be able to share much of their reading. With other groups, differences may require that there be a greatly diversified pattern of individual reading. Indeed, for any young reader both kinds of opportunity are needed—the chance to share and compare literary reactions and the chance to follow his own personal bent.

Some educators fear that this emphasis will degenerate into limiting young people to books dealing directly with their immediate environment and present problems. This would indeed be a frustration of the power of literature to carry us into new and broader realms. A steady diet of books about the students' own age group, their own minority or majority group, their own social or psychological problems, would probably result in the reading of the works simply as sociological or psychological documents. But even more misguided are those who, out of a fear of such misinterpretation, seek to use only an abstract ideal of literary culture as their guide of what should be presented to the student. A false dilemma has been set up, for it is not necessary to choose between these two extreme alternatives. To some students today, *Jane Eyre* can be more personally and immediately compelling than, for instance, *A Tree Grows in Brooklyn*, not simply, however, because *Jane Eyre* is a better book and a classic, but because the personality and situation of its heroine offer so many linkages with the emotional preoccupations of these contemporary adolescents.

There are some young readers of literature who will kindle at once to a magical phrase, who will respond to the subtle chemistry by which word acts upon word, image upon image, to create a unique effect. For most, however, the path leads from personal preoccupations to literary awakening. Sometimes the linkage between reader and book may be rather accidental. The attempted assassination of the President in 1950 shocked a young man into a sense of the immediacy of *Julius Caesar*. The play gave him, he realized, much understanding even of the present that could not be derived from the current newspaper. But contemporary relevance is not summed up in the morning paper, and the immediacy of the literary work can derive from much more fundamental sources. For example, the adolescent's need to see physical or social handicaps overcome has for many surmounted the remoteness of style or time or place or age level in *Cyrano de Bergerac, Of Human Bondage,* or *The Old Man and the Sea.* Youth seeks to understand itself and its world, to feel from within what it means to be different kinds of personalities, to discover the possibilities in human relationships, to develop a usable image of adult aims and roles. Such are the deep-seated interests that can be brought into play to nourish a vital interest in literature.

Especially in the high school years, we should help young people to discover the power of literature to enable us to experiment imaginatively with life, to get the feel and emotional cost of different adult roles, to organize and reflect on a confused and unruly reality, and to give us pleasure through the very language that accomplishes these things. Both our classroom atmosphere and the selection of reading materials should therefore be guided by the primary concern for creating a live circuit between readers and books.

## Initiating a Process of Growth

Yet how often is actual practice still guided by vestiges of the scholarly patterns of a quarter-century ago. How often is it a matter of exposing the youngsters to the traditional materials and of being resigned when the exposure does not "take"! Of course, our young people should be acquainted with American writers of the past, but will "Snow-Bound" be equally vital to all eighth graders? For a certain group, *Macbeth* may best serve the aim of developing a lasting interest in good reading, but for some pupils this play might better give way for a while to such works as *Mutiny on the Bounty*. Some recent first novel in which the author broods over his own adolescence may be more powerful than *David Copperfield*. Again, *David Copperfield* may offer more points of contact with a contemporary reader than *Silas Marner, Vanity Fair,* or *A Portrait of the Artist as a Young Man.*

From the world of teen-age stories, of *Seventeenth Summer*, the path can lead to *Romeo and Juliet*. From Zane Grey to Guthrie to Rölvaag to Cather has been another progression. Stories about parent-child relations, and minority group characters, and historical figures, and farmers, and scientists—whatever may strike the spark of personal relevance can create the conditions for leading the young reader into ever richer and more challenging literary experiences.

A process of growth is involved. To *initiate* that process, each young reader needs works that his own past experiences and present preoccupations enable him to evoke with personal meaningfulness. Without this, literature remains something inert, to be studied in school and henceforth avoided. But when books arouse an intimate personal response, the developmental process can be fostered. No particular type of reading is being urged here as the panacea. There is no formula: not contemporary literature as against literature of the past, nor minor as against major works, nor even syntactically simpler as against more demanding works. Rather, we need to be flexible, we need to understand where our pupils are in relation to books, and we need a sufficient command of books to see their potentialities in this developmental process. Our main responsibility is to help the student to find the right book for growth.[2]

## Avoiding Substitutes for Literature

Having created the situation for a live response to books, we must scrutinize carefully the way in which teaching methods and approaches will either foster or hinder a lasting sense of personal meaningfulness. In high school, just as with the beginning reader, teaching techniques can be successful in the short run and set up bad habits for the long run. The adolescent can be easily led into

2. Some of the bibliographical aids available for the teacher are: the reviews of new books in this journal; the book lists of the National Council of Teachers of English; Lenrow, Elbert, *Reader's Guide to Prose Fiction* (New York, Appleton-Century Co., 1940); *Reading Ladders for Human Relations* (Washington, D.C., American Council on Education, 1955).

an artificial relationship with literature. Year after year, as freshmen come into college, one finds that even the most verbally proficient of them, often those most intensely drawn to literature, have already acquired a hard veneer, a pseudo-professional approach. They are anxious to have the correct labels— the right period, the biographical background, the correct evaluation. They read literary histories and biographies, critical essays, introductions to editions, and then, if they have time, they read the works. The quest is for the sophisticated interpretation and the accepted judgment. At worst, their interest in the author's life seems to be on a par with the Hollywood gossip column. At best, it tends to make the literary work a document in the author's biography.

Shock and confusion often result when they are asked about the impact of the work on themselves as unique personalities. They tend not to linger on that, or even to pay much attention to it. They have learned hastily to substitute someone else's experience with the work. Already they seem shut off from the full personal nourishment that literature can give.

It is much easier in the classroom to deal with ideas and information *about* literature than it is with literature itself, as it resides in the myriad transactions between individuals and books. To help a young reader to reflect critically on his own response is indeed challenging to him and to the teacher. Naturally, the tendency is to concentrate on the easily checked "facts" of the story or play, or to present information about literary history, or to discuss the often entertaining items about the life of the author. Hence it is that in many classrooms pupils learn to ignore or even distrust their own responses to literature. They may therefore reject literature altogether as irrelevant to themselves. Or they may divert their original interest in literature to studies around and about literature. The student comes to substitute these for the kind of reflection on his response that would enable him to approach the next work in a sounder way.

Knowledge of literary history, information about the lives of authors— surely, we wish our high school graduates to possess as much of these as possible. There is, of course, no inherent contradiction between such concerns and the development of a living sense of literature. The contradiction often results, however. Knowledge about literature becomes an end in itself, and the literary work becomes largely an object to be described, manipulated, catalogued, categorized.

Sometimes, however, the young reader's attempt to understand his response to the work raises pressing questions about the difference between his own times and the context in which the work was written. Then the knowledge about the intellectual and social setting of the work helps the reader directly to assimilate the work and to understand both himself and his own age better. When the high school girl feels only pity for Katherina at a performance of *The Taming of the Shrew*, we are inevitably involved in the problem of why that response is out of key with the total work, and that in turn involves us in historical matters—literary and social.

We shall solve our dilemma by placing such concerns in perspective and by staunchly refusing to sacrifice the more important for the less important. We shall resist the temptation to treat the literary work primarily as a document in the author's biography, or as a document explaining the age when it was written, or as a document illustrating shifts in literary technique. These are indeed temptations, it must be admitted, because such knowledge is more conventionally a sign of literary "culture," and is more easily taught and tested, particularly with large classes.

The criterion for high school teaching should remain: relevance to the nourishment of a personal sense of literature as a mode of experience. If that job is considered central, we can move happily on to historical and social approaches in their properly secondary place. For they will no longer lead away from the work of art, but feed back into the reader's heightened awareness of how it fits into the context he himself provides.

## Analysis of the Literary "Transaction"

Another danger to the development of a relationship of personal integrity with literature stems insidiously from the apparent concern with the literary work itself. An extreme illustration of this was the exclamation of a core curriculum teacher, "We would like to include novels in our assignments. Why can't you English teachers give us a simple method for analyzing a novel? Something that pupils could be quickly taught to apply to any novel." Unfortunately, "a method" for analyzing a novel is not useful in the way that "a method" for division of fractions is—something to be applied routinely. This routine approach, of course, is the danger: a systematic dissection of plot, setting, characters, theme, style, or, if the emphasis is more sociological, the routine items may be author's life and times, setting of the novel, main problem, and so on. Similarly, when the influence of the "New Criticism" has permeated secondary teaching, the potentially valuable emphasis on "close reading" often has been nullified also by the creation of routine formulae for analysis. Literary works then seem to exist only to illustrate the use of symbolism or the method of irony.

All such approaches may seem to be forcing the pupil to focus on "the novel itself." But the existence of such a pattern that the pupil knows he must follow tends to stultify his experience of the work. He is reading in order to say something about these items. His attention is turned away from where the novel fits into his experience of life and literature, and any item—plot or theme or style—is as remote from himself as any other item.

Sensitivity to the different aspects of the literary work is highly desirable, of course, but when the eye of the reader is focused on the work as personally perceived, he will not march impartially through a set of items or apply again and again a single type of analysis. He will be aglow with a particular response. He will need first to register this response, to get the particular quality of it.

And he will need to reflect on it. For it will be the result of the way the work fits into his own past experience of books and life.

This approach to reading is a safeguard against still another danger—sentimentalizing about the characters in a literary work and opinionated discussion of topics tangentially suggested by it. Because we are concerned with the total development of our students, we value the power of literature to enhance their understanding of themselves and of human problems. When the focus of our teaching is the transaction between reader and book, such concerns do not lead away from the work into sheer emotionality and theorizing. The student scrutinizes the two-way circuit set up between himself and the literary work. He tests whether his particular personal response is justified, whether it has incorporated as adequately as possible what the printed page offers. He is often helped in this self-criticism by comparison of his interpretation with that of others.

Should not this process of reflection deal with such questions as: What happened, not simply in the story, but rather within me as I read the story? What things struck me forcibly? What were the "clues" in the story that "added up" to a meaning for me? What puzzled me? What meanings did others see in it—my classmates, my teacher, perhaps critics in published comments? Do they defend their interpretations by pointing to things in the story that I overlooked? Does this help me to see my blind spots? Or did they overlook some things that make my interpretation at least equally possible? How can I make this reflection the means of arriving at a more complete response to this and other works?

Raising such questions will inevitably lead to analysis of the work, but the basic question will be: What in this book, *and in me*, caused this response? Such a query will not produce the flabby clichés—the "Keats-has-a-fine-command-of-words" sort of thing—nor will there be a facile listing of recurrent images or a glib repetition of standard comments. The primary concern, after all, should not be the counting of different kinds of images in Keats' poem, but the savoring of a particular way of thinking and feeling evoked by it. From that might follow, for example, a clumsy but purposeful probing into the specific themes, phrases, images, patterns, that lead to "a mixed-up feeling of sadness and happiness." Instead of, "The plot holds your interest," the question may arise, "Why did I care so much about what happened to a feeble, ignorant old man?" Or it may be "Why did I jump to such wrong conclusions, and ignore so many clues, about the character of the husband in that story?" Such concerns will help the young reader to discover, let us say, the way the author has enlisted his sympathy and built up the tension of the story. But they will also at the same time help the young reader to handle the ideas and assumptions, the sensitivities and blind spots, that he brings to his reading.

The student can thus learn to avoid projecting his own attitudes on the work. He can discover that a strong emotional response to a book does not necessarily prove its literary merit. He can learn not to accept shoddy writing and stereotyped characters simply because he agrees with the moral or political theme. He may become able to admire the masterly technique of an author yet question his view of man and the world. To reflect on what one thought and felt while reading, in order to sort out the ideas and emotions relevant to the work, and in order to relate them to other experiences in life and literature: this is an essential part of growth in ability to read.

The various frameworks for analysis of the literary work should perhaps most often be something for the teacher to keep in mind in guiding the young reader. Whatever the specific framework may be, one requirement seems fundamental: the problems should be phrased in terms of the transaction between the reader and the book. The analysis of the "how" of the book will be a logical otucome of the "what," the actual quality of the experience with it. Such understanding of technique and background will not become an end in itself, but will serve to illuminate or organize the pupil's sense of the work as a total experience.

Some years ago, a latter-day Monsieur Jourdain applied to me for a private course in literature. As he talked, it dawned on me that he wanted me to teach him who Goethe was, when Shakespeare lived, whether *Hamlet* was a comedy or tragedy, but that he had no intention of reading any of the literary works! It would be comparatively easy to drill the vast numbers coming into our high schools in that kind of get-rich-quick knowledge about literature and to leave them impervious to literature as a personal mode of experience, as an art.

We need to resist the pressures from without and from within ourselves that lead to such empty results. As we review our current high school programs in literature, we need to hold on to the essentials, or take the opportunity as readjustments come about, to create the practices that will meet the acid test: Does this practice or approach hinder or foster a sense that literature exists as a form of personally meaningful experience? Is the pupil's interaction with the literary work itself the center from which all else radiates? Is the student being helped to grow into a relationship of integrity to language and literature? Is he building a lifetime habit of significant reading?

# Chapter Six

# The Literary Transaction:
# Evocation and Response

The term *response* seems firmly established in the vocabulary of the theory, criticism, and teaching of literature. Perhaps I should feel some satisfaction at the present state of affairs since I am sometimes referred to as the earliest exponent of what is termed *reader-response* criticism or theory.[1] Yet the more the term is invoked, the more concerned I become over the diffuseness of its usage. In the days when simply to talk about the reader's response was considered practically subversive, it would undoubtedly have been premature to demand greater precision in the use of the term. Now that the importance of the reader's role is becoming more and more widely acknowledged, it seems essential to differentiate some of the aspects of the reading event that are frequently covered by the broad heading of "response."

Response implies an object. "Response to what?" is the question. There must be a story or a poem or a play to which to respond. Few theories of reading today view the literary work as ready-made in the text, waiting to imprint itself on the blank tape of the reader's mind. Yet, much talk about response seems to imply something like that, at least so far as assuming the text to be all-important in determining whether the result will be, say, an abstract factual statement or a poem. Unfortunately, important though the text is, a story or a poem does not come into being simply because the text contains a narrative or the lines indicate rhythm and rhyme. Nor is it a matter simply of the reader's ability to give lexical meaning to the words. In order to deal with my assigned topic, it becomes necessary, therefore, to sketch some elements of my view of the reading process,[2] to suggest some aspects of what happens when reader meets text. (Note that although I refer mainly to reading, I shall be defining processes that apply generally to encounters with either spoken or written symbols.) This will require consideration of the nature of language, especially as manifested in early childhood. Only then shall I venture to develop some implications concerning children, literature, and response.

## The Reading Process and the Reader's Stance

Reading is a transaction, a two-way process, involving a reader and a text at a particular time under particular circumstances. I use John Dewey's term, transaction, to emphasize the contribution of both reader and text. The words in their particular pattern stir up elements of memory, activate areas of consciousness. The reader, bringing past experience of language and of the world to the task, sets up tentative notions of a subject, of some framework into which to fit the ideas as the words unfurl. If the subsequent words do not fit into the framework, it may have to be revised, thus opening up new and further possibilities for the text that follows. This implies a constant series of selections from the multiple possibilities offered by the text and their synthesis into an organized meaning.

But the most important choice of all must be made early in the reading event—the overarching choice of what I term the reader's stance, his "mental set," so to speak. The reader may be seeking information, as in a textbook; he may want directions for action, as in a driver's manual; he may be seeking some logical conclusion, as in a political article. In all such reading he will narrow his attention to building up the meanings, the ideas, the directions to be retained; attention focuses on accumulating what is to be carried away at the end of the reading. Hence I term this stance *efferent*, from the Latin word meaning "to carry away."

If, on the other hand, the reader seeks a story, a poem, a play, his attention will shift inward, will center on what is being created *during* the actual reading. A much broader range of elements will be allowed to rise into consciousness, not simply the abstract concepts that the words point to, but also what those objects or referents strip up of personal feelings, ideas, and attitudes. The very sound and rhythm of the words will be attended to. Out of these ideas and feelings, a new experience, the story or poem, is shaped and lived through. I call this kind of reading *aesthetic*, from the Greek word meaning "to sense" or "to perceive." Whether the product of the reading will be a poem, a literary work of art, depends, then, not simply on the text but also on the stance of the reader.

I am reminded of the first grader whose teacher told the class to learn the following verses:

In fourteen hundred and ninety-two
Columbus crossed the ocean blue.

When called on the next day, the youngster recited:

In fourteen hundred and ninety-three
Columbus crossed the bright blue sea.

Questioned as to why she had changed it, she simply said she liked it better that way.

I submit that this represents a problem in stance. The teacher had wanted her to read efferently, in order to retain the date "1492." The pupil had read aesthetically, paying attention to the qualitative effect, to her own responses, not only to the image of the ship crossing the sea, but also to the sound of the words in her ear, and in this instance the discomfort evidently occasioned by the reversal of the normal adjective-noun order.

Freeing ourselves from the notion that the text dictates the stance seems especially difficult, precisely because the experienced reader carries out many of the processes automatically or subconsciously. We may select a text because it suits our already chosen, efferent or aesthetic, purposes. Or we note clues or cues in the text—the author announces the intention to explain or convince, for example, and we adopt the appropriate efferent stance. Or we note broad margins and uneven lines, and automatically fall into the stance that will enable us to create and experience a poem.

Any text, however, can be read either way. We may approach novels as sociological documents, efferently seeking to accumulate evidence concerning, say, the treatment of children in the 19th century. The "pop" poet may select a "job wanted" advertisement, arrange its phrases in separate lines, and thus signal us to read it aesthetically, to experience its human meaning, as a poem. Sometimes, of course, readers adopt an inappropriate attitude—for example, reading a political article aesthetically when they should be efferently paying attention to facts. And many people, alas, read the texts of stories and poems efferently.

Recognizing that the reader's stance inevitably affects what emerges from the reading does not deny the importance of the text in the transaction. Some texts offer greater rewards than do others. A Shakespeare text, say, offers more potentialities for an aesthetic reading than one by Longfellow. We teachers know, however, that one cannot predict which text will give rise to the better evocation—the better lived-through poem—without knowing the other part of the transaction, the reader.

Sometimes the text gives us confusing clues. I'm reminded of a letter a colleague received. "Dear Professor Baldwin," it began, "You will forgive my long silence when you learn about the tragedy that has befallen me. In June, my spouse departed from the conjugal domicile with a gentleman of the vicinity." The first sentence announces that we should adopt an aesthetic stance. The second would be appropriate in a legal brief, since the vocabulary seems adapted to an impersonal, efferent stance.

Any reading event falls somewhere on the continuum between the aesthetic and the efferent poles; between, for example, a lyric poem and a chemical formula. I speak of a *predominantly* efferent stance, because according to the text and the reader's purpose, some attention to qualitative elements of consciousness may enter. Similarly, aesthetic reading involves or includes referential or cognitive elements. Hence, the importance of the reader's *selective* attention in the reading process.

We respond, then to what we are calling forth in the transaction with the text. In extreme cases it may be that the transaction is all-of-a-piece, so to speak. The efferent reader of the directions for first aid in an accident may be so completely absorbed in the abstract concepts of the actions advised that nothing else will enter consciousness. Or an aesthetic reader may be so completely absorbed in living through a lyric poem or may so completely identify with a character in a story that nothing else enters consciousness. But in most reading there is not only the stream of choices and syntheses that construct meaning: there is also a stream of accompanying reactions to the very meaning being constructed. For example, in reading a newspaper or a legal document, the "meaning" will be constructed, and there will be an accompanying feeling of acceptance or doubt about the evidence cited or the logical argument.

In aesthetic reading, we respond to the very story or poem that we are evoking during the transaction with the text. In order to shape the work, we draw on our reservoir of past experience with people and the world, our past inner linkage of words and things, our past encounters with spoken or written texts. We listen to the sound of the words in the inner ear; we lend our sensations, our emotions, our sense of being alive, to the new experience which, we feel, corresponds to the text. We participate in the story, we identify with the characters, we share their conflicts and their feelings.

At the same time there is a stream of responses being generated. There may be a sense of pleasure in our own creative activity, an awareness of pleasant or awkward sound and movement in the words, a feeling of approval or disapproval of the characters and their behavior. We may be aware of a contrast between the assumptions or expectations about life that we brought to the reading and the attitudes, moral codes, social situations we are living through in the world created in transaction with the text.

Any later reflection on our reading will therefore encompass all of these elements. Our response will have its beginnings in the reactions that were concurrent with the evocation, with the lived-through experience. Thus an organized report on, or articulation of, our response to a work involves mainly efferent activity as we look back on the reading event—an abstracting and categorizing of elements of the aesthetic experience, and an ordering and development of our concurrent reactions.

I have tried briefly to suggest some major aspects of my view of the reading process—reading as basically a transaction between the reader and the text; the importance of the reader's selective attention to what is aroused in consciousness through intercourse with the words of the text; the need to adopt a predominant stance to guide the process of selection and synthesis; the construction of efferent meaning or the participation in aesthetic evocation; the current of reactions to the very ideas and experiences being evoked. To develop the capacity for such activities is the aim of "the teaching of reading and literature." We shall find support and clarification in going on to consider children's early entrance into language and into literature. It will then perhaps be possible to arrive at some implications for desirable emphasis in the child's early transactions with texts.

## Entrance into Language

The transactional view of the human being in a two-way, reciprocal relationship with the environment is increasingly reflected in current psychology, as it frees itself from the constrictions of behaviorism.[3] Language, too, is less and less being considered as "context-free."[4] Children's sensorimotor exploration of the physical environment and their interplay with the human and social environment are increasingly seen as sources and conditions of language behavior. During the prelinguistic period, the child is "learning to mean,"[5] learning the functions of language through developing a personal sound-system for communicating with others before assimilating the linguistic code of the social environment.

Recent research on children's early language supports William James's dynamic picture of the connection among language, the objects and relations to which it refers, and the internal states associated with them—sensations, images, percepts and concepts, feelings of quality, feelings of tendency. James says, "The stream of consciousness matches [the words] by an inward coloring of its own. . . . We ought to say a feeling of *and*, a feeling of *if*, a feeling of *but*, and a feeling of *by*, quite as readily as we say a feeling of *blue* or a feeling of *cold*."[6]

Werner and Kaplan, in their study of symbol formation, show us the child at first internalizing such "a primordial matrix" of sensations and postural and imaginal elements. The child's early vocables "are evoked by total happenings and are expressive not only of reference to an event external to the child," but also of "the child's attitudes, states, reactions, etc."[7] Evidence of this early sense of words as part of total happenings is the fact that some children at five years of age may still believe that the name is an inherent part of the referent. *Cat* at first is as much an attribute of the creature as its furry pointed ears. Thus, in language as in experience in general, the child is faced with the need for a process of differentiation of perception.[8] The child's movement toward conventional linguistic forms entails a sorting out of these various elements.

Werner and Kaplan describe the sorting-out process as an "inner-dynamic or form-building" or "schematizing" activity. Acquisition of language is a "twin process," they show us, because the child must learn to link the same internal, organismic state both to the sense of an external referent or object, on the one hand, and to a symbolic or linguistic vehicle, on the other. What links a word, cat, to its referent, the animal, is their connection with the same internal state.

Bates similarly sees the emergence of symbols as "the selection process, the choice of one aspect of a complex array to serve as the top of the iceberg, a light-weight mental token" that can stand for the whole "mental file drawer" of associations and can be used for higher-order cognitive operations.[9] In other words, the child learns to abstract from the total context in order to arrive at a generalized concept of "cat."

This process of decontextualization is, of course, essential to the development of the ability to think, to apply the symbol to new contexts and situations. The "mental token" is the public meaning of the word. Understandably, parents and schools welcome and foster this phase. But much less attention has been paid to the broad base of "the iceberg" of meaning.[10] "The sense of a word," Vygotsky reminds us, "Is the sum of all the psychological events aroused in our consciousness by the word. It is a dynamic, fluid, complex whole. . . . The dictionary meaning of a word is no more than a stone in the edifice of sense. . . ."[11] Along with the cognitive abstraction from past experiences, which is the public meaning of the word, there are the private kinesthetic and affective elements that comprise the complex, fluid matrix in which language is anchored.

## The Literary Transaction

The connection can now be made with the view of the reading process that I have sketched. The role of selective attention in the two kinds of reading becomes apparent. In predominantly efferent reading, the child must learn to focus on extracting the public meaning of the text. Attention must be given mainly to the "token" top-of-the-inner-iceberg, to organizing the abstract concepts the verbal symbols point to. These can yield the information, the directions, the logical conclusions that will be the residue of the reading act.

In aesthetic reading, the child must learn to draw on more of the experiential matrix. Instead of looking outward mainly to the public referents, the reader must include the personal, the qualitative, kinesthetic, sensuous inner resonances of the words. Hence attention is turned toward what is immediately lived-through in transaction with the text, toward what is being shaped as the story or the poem.

Both efferent reading and aesthetic reading should be taught. If I concentrate on aesthetic reading, it is not only because our interest here today is in children and literature, but also because it is the kind of reading most neglected in our schools.

Contrary to the general tendency to think of the efferent, the "literal," as primary, the child's earliest language behavior seems closest to a primarily aesthetic approach to experience. The poet, Dylan Thomas, told a friend, "When I experience anything, I experience it as a thing and as a word at the same time, both amazing."[12] Such a bond between language and the inner experiential matrix continues to be stressed in recent studies of children's early language. Words are primarily aspects of sensed, felt, lived-through experiences:

> Beginning about the last quarter of the first year and continuing through the second, increased differentiations of self and other, the

sharpening of self-awareness and the self-concept, and the ability to
form and store memories enable the infant to begin the development
of affective-cognitive structures, the linking or bonding of particular
affects or patterns of affects with images and symbols, including
words and ideas. . . .

Since there is essentially an infinite variety of emotion-symbol
interactions, affective-cognitive structures are far and away the predominant motivational features in consciousness soon after the acquisition of language.[13]

Dorothy White, in her classic diary of her child's introduction to books
before age five, documents the transactional character of language. She notes
how, at age two, experience feeds into language, and how language helps the
child to handle further experience.

The experience makes the book richer and the book enriches the personal experience even at this level. I am astonished at the early age this
backward and forward flow between books and life takes place. With
adults or older children one cannot observe it so easily, but here at this
age when all a child's experiences are known and the books read are
shared, when the voluble gabble which is her speech reveals all the
associations, the interaction is seen very clearly. Now and again Carol
mystifies me with a reference to life next door, or with some trans-
posed pronunciation which defeats me, but on the whole I know her
frame of reference.[14]

White also illustrates the private facet of the child's acquisition of the public language. Having observed the actual experiences that fed into the child's
words, the mother realizes that she understands the child's particular meanings
and emphasis on words that even the father cannot grasp. Of course, it is such
private overtones that we all draw on in our aesthetic reading.

Parents and teachers have generally recognized signs of the young child's
affinity for the aesthetic stance. Joseph Conrad tells us that the aim of the novelist is "to make you hear, to make you feel—it is, before all, to make you see."[15]
Children enthralled by hearing or reading a story or a poem often give various
nonverbal signs of such immediacy of experience. They delightedly sway to
the sound and rhythm of words; their facial expressions reveal sensitivity to
tone; their postural responses and gestures imitate the actions being described.
That they are often limited by lack of knowledge, by immature cognitive
strategies, in no way contradicts the fact that they are living through aesthetic
experiences, their attention focused on what, in their transaction with the
words, they can see and hear and feel.

A most eloquent verbal sign that the story or poem is being aesthetically
experienced is the child's "Read it again." White's account of her daughter's
"voluble gabble" as stories are read testifies that a relaxed, receptive atmosphere,

with no questions or requirements, is conducive to children's verbal expressions of that second stream of reactions to the work that is the source of "responses." White's book shows a child, even before age five, offering various kinds of verbal signs of aesthetic listening—questions, comments, comparisons with life experiences and with other stories, rejection because the story puzzles or frightens, or because it offers no links with the child's past experiences.

When an adolescent girl calls the story of a wallflower at her first dance "the greatest tragedy I have ever read" we must recognize that this is a sign of the intensity of the lived-through transaction with the text, and not a judgment on the relative potentialities of this book and, say, *King Lear.* This transactional process is especially demonstrated in early reading and listening to stories. White tells of reading to her three-year-old the story of a small boy who wakes one morning to find himself the sole inhabitant of his town. White remarks:

> All this to an older child might well represent a delirium of joy and liberty, but to Carol, whose pleasure is the presence of people, not their absence, it was stark tragedy. "He's all by himself," she said, overcome and deeply mournful. Paul's isolation obviously wounded and shocked her, but I had the feeling that in creating this dismay, the book provided her with the most tremendous emotional experience she has known in all her reading. However, here's the rub, this emotional experience was of a kind totally different from anything the author had planned to provide, for planned he had.[16]

The author, she points out, may plan a particular book, but "one cannot plan what children will take from it."

Understanding the transactional nature of reading would correct the tendency of adults to look only at the text and the author's presumed intention, and to ignore as irrelevant what the child actually does make of it. As in the instance just cited, it may be that the particular experience or preoccupations the child brings to the spoken or printed text permit some one part to come most intensely alive. Let us not brush this aside in our eagerness to do justice to the total text or to put that part into its proper perspective in the story. It is more important that we reinforce the child's discovery that texts can make possible such intense personal experience. Other stories, continued reading, the maturation of cognitive powers, will contribute to the habit of attending to the entire text or organizing the sequence of episodes into a whole. We have the responsibility first of all to develop the habit and the capacity for aesthetic reading. Responsibility to the total text and the question of "the author's intention" comes later—with all the indeterminacy of meaning that implies.[17]

The notion that first the child must "understand" the text cognitively, efferently, before it can be responded to aesthetically is a rationalization that must be rejected. Aesthetic reading, we have seen, is not efferent reading with a layer of affective associations added on later. (I call this the "jam on bread" theory of literature.) Rather, we have seen that the aesthetic stance, in shaping what is understood, produces a meaning in which cognitive and affective, referential and emotive, denotational and connotational, are intermingled. The child may listen to the sound, hear the tone of the narrative "voice," evoke characters and actions, feel the quality of the event, without being able to analyze or name it. Hence the importance of finding ways to ensure that an aesthetic experience has happened, that a story or a poem has been lived through, before we hurry the young listener or reader into something called "response." This is often largely an efferent undertaking to paraphrase, summarize, or categorize. Evocation should precede response.

## Maintaining Aesthetic Capacity

Why, if the capacities for aesthetic experience are so amply provided at the outset of the child's linguistic development, do we encounter in our schools and in our adult society such a limited recourse to the pleasures of literature? We cannot take the easy route of blaming television for this, since it was a problem already lamented at least 50 years ago.

One tendency is to assume a natural developmental loss of aesthetic capacity, or at the least, interest, as the child grows older. We often still share Wordsworth's romantic view that "Shades of the prison-house begin to close/Upon the growing boy."[18] Some believe that in the early school years children become mainly concerned with the "real" and reject "the worlds of the imaginative and the fantastic." This idea, and confusion of the aesthetic stance with the fictive, with the imaginative or fantasy, may have contributed to the neglect of literature in the middle years.

The child's problem of delimiting the objects and the nature of the real world may at a certain stage foster a preoccupation with clarifying the boundary between reality and fantasy. But distrust of fantasy should not be equated with rejection of aesthetic expereience. Literary works representing "real" events and "real" people can be read with all the sensuous kinesthetic, imaginative richness that are applied to fantasy. Imagination is needed also in cognitive processes, in the process of remembering, in thinking of the past, in thinking of alternative solutions to a problem. Again, we need to see that the reader's stance transcends the distinction between the real and the fictive.

The obvious question, in all such developmental generalization, is—to what extent the changes observed (are due to innate factors and to what extent they are the result of environmental influences). Fortunately, an ethnographic emphasis is beginning to be valued in contemporary research on the teaching of English,[19] and I should wish only to broaden its purview. Hence the question: to what extent does the emphasis in our culture on the primarily practical, technical, empirical, and quantitative contribute to the reported loss of aesthetic receptivity as the child grows older? Why do we find teachers at every level, from the early years through high school and college, seeming always to be having to start from scratch in teaching poetry?

The fact of the great diversity of the cultures evolved by human beings is in itself testimony to the power of the environment into which the child is born. Anthropologists are making us aware of how subtle signals from adults and older children are assimilated by the infant. "In depth" studies of child-rearing and particular customs or rituals document the complexity of the individual's assimilation to his culture.[20] All who are concerned about education and children have a responsibility to our society to interpret this process, and to be actively critical of the negative aspects of our culture. Just as the medical profession is helping us relate our physical health to general environmental and cultural conditions, so we as professionals need to emphasize the importance of the child's general social, economic, and intellectual environment both outside and in the school.

A nurturing environment that values the whole range of human achievements, the opportunity for stimulating experiences, cultivation of habits of observation, opportunities for satisfying natural curiosity about the world, a sense of creative freedom—all of these lay the foundation for linguistic development. Reading, we know, is not an encapsulated skill that can be added on like a splint to an arm. If I have dwelt so long on the organismic basis of all language, it is because reading draws on the whole person's past transactions with the environment. Reading, especially aesthetic reading, extends the scope of that environment and feeds the growth of the individual, who can then bring a richer self to further transactions with life and literature. We must at least indicate awareness of broader underlying societal or cultural needs before we go on to talk about the teaching of reading, and especially the teaching of literature, the kind of reading our economy-minded school boards often consider elitist and dispensable.

In my sketch of the child's acquisition of the environing language system, I presented as a natural and desirable development the selective process by which the child detaches a sense of the public meaning of a verbal symbol from its personal organismic matrix. But in our society the emphasis, at home and at school, is almost entirely on that decontextualizing, abstracting process. Parents quite rightly welcome the child's abstracting-out of words so that they can be applied to other instances of the same category and be used in new situations. Of course, the child needs to participate in the public, referential linguistic system. Of course, the child needs to distinguish between what the society considers "real" and what fantasy. Of course, the rational, empirical, scientific, logical components of our culture should be transmitted.

Nevertheless, are these aptitudes not being fostered—or at least favored— at the expense of other potentialities of the human being and of our culture? The quality of education in general is being diluted by neglect of, sacrifice of, the rich organismic, personal, experiential source of both efferent and aesthetic thinking. Is there not evidence of the importance of the affective, the imaginative, the fantasizing activities even for the development of cognitive abilities and creativity in all modes of human endeavor?

Throughout the entire educational process, the child in our society seems to be receiving the same signal: adopt the efferent stance. What can be quantified—the most public of efferent modes—becomes often the guide to what is taught, tested, or researched. In the teaching of reading, and even of literature, failure to recognize the importance of the two stances seems to me to be at the root of much of the plight of literature today.

One of the most troubling instances of the confusion of stances is the use of stories to teach efferent reading skills. Is it not a deception to induce the child's interest through a narrative and then, in the effort to make sure it has been (literally, efferently) "understood," to raise questions that imply that only an efferent reading was necessary? Even more disconcerting is the neglect of the aesthetic stance when the declared aim is "the teaching of literature," when stories and poems are presented, not as exercises for reading skills, but presumably for their value as literature, for their capacity to present images of life, to entertain, to deal with human situations and problems, to open up vistas of different personalities and different milieus. Here, too, the concern in most classes still seems to be first of all with the kinds of response that can be met by efferent reading. Questions often ask for highly specific factual details—What did the boy do, where did he go, what did he see, what does this word mean? At the other extreme is the tendency to nudge the young reader toward a labeling, a generalization, a paraphrase, a summary that again requires an abstracting analytic approach to what has been read. Repeated questions of that sort soon teach the young reader to approach the next texts with an efferent stance. Studies of students' responses to literature have revealed the extent to which in a seemingly open situation the young reader will respond in ways already learned from the school environment.[21] Results of the 1979–80 National Assessment of Reading and Literature demonstrate that the traditional teacher-dominated teaching of literature, with its emphasis on approved or conventional interpretations, does not produce many readers capable of handling their initial responses or relating them to the text. Questions calling for traditional analyses of character or theme, for example, reveal such shallowness of response.

Educators and psychologists investigating children's aesthetic activities and development reflect a similar tendency to focus on the efferent—a legacy, perhaps, from the hegemony of traditional behaviorist experimental research methodology. Investigations of children's use of metaphor seem often actually to be testing children's cognitive metalinguistic abilities. Studies of the "grammar" of story tend also to eliminate the personal aesthetic event and to center on the cognitive ability to abstract out its narrative structure. Stories of poems can thus become as much a tool for studying the child's advance through the Piagetian stages of cognitive or analytic thinking as would a series of history texts or science texts.

## Implications for Teaching

What, then, are the implications for teaching? The view of language and the reading process I have sketched demonstrates the importance of the early years for the development of adult readers able to share in the pleasures and benefits of literature. The theoretical positions I have sketched apply, I believe, throughout the entire educational span, from the beginning reader to the adult critic. At every stage, of course, knowledge of students and books is essential to the sound application of any theoretical guidelines. At best, I can only suggest criteria for differentiating between potentially counterproductive or fruitful practices. I shall undoubtedly only be offering theoretical support for what many sensitive teachers are already doing.

A reading stance is basically an expression of purpose. Children will read efferently in order to arrive at some desired result, some answer to a question, some explanation of a puzzling situation, some directions as to procedures to be followed in an interesting activity.

Aesthetic reading, by its very nature, has an intrinsic purpose, the desire to have a pleasurable, interesting experience for its own sake. (The older the students, the more likely we are to forget this.) We should be careful not to confuse the student by suggesting other, extrinsic purposes, no matter how admirable. That will turn attention away from participating in what is being evoked.

Paradoxically, when the transactions are lived through for their own sake, they will probably have as by-products the educational, informative, social, and moral values for which literature is often praised. Even enhancement of skills may result. By the same token, literary works often fail to emerge at all if the texts are offered as the means for the demonstration of reading skills.

Exercises and readings that do not satisfy such meaningful purposes for the child, but are considered defensible means of developing skills, should be offered separately, honestly, as exercises. If needed, they should be recognized as ancillary and supplementary to the real business of reading for meaning, whether efferent or aesthetic.[22]

I speak of both the teaching of efferent reading and the teaching of aesthetic reading because the distinctions in purpose and process should be made clear from the outset. (Of course, I do not mean to imply theoretical explanation of them to the child.) If reading is presented as a meaningful, purposive activity, and if texts are presented in meaningful situations, the two kinds of stance should naturally emerge. Texts should be presented that clearly satisfy one or another purpose. Given the linguistic development of the child, probably there should be greater emphasis in the earlier stages on aesthetic listening and reading.

This view of the two stances opens up the necessity for a new and more rounded concept of comprehension in both efferent and aesthetic reading. I shall venture here only the suggestion that this will involve attention to the transactional, two-way, process and to affective as well as cognitive components of meaning. Recent interest of some psychologists in the role of context in comprehension indicates movement in this direction.[23]

In the teaching of literature, then, our primary responsibility is to encourage, not get in the way of, the aesthetic stance. As the child carries on the process of decontextualization that serves the logical, analytic, cognitive abilities whose development Piaget traced so influentially, we need also to keep alive the habit of paying selective attention to the inner states, the kinesthetic tensions, the feelings, the colorings of the stream of consciousness, that accompany all cognition, and that particularly make possible the evocation of literary works of art from texts.

Much of what we need to do can fortunately be viewed as a reinforcement of the child's own earliest linguistic processes, richly embedded in a cognitive-affective matrix. Transactions with texts that offer some linkage with the child's own experiences and concerns can give rise aesthetically to new experiences. These in turn open new linguistic windows into the world. Recall that when I refer to a reading event, it can be either hearing the text read or having the printed text. Both types of literary experience should continue into the elementary years.

A receptive, nonpressured atmosphere will free the child to adopt the aesthetic stance with pleasant anticipation, without worry about future demands. There will be freedom, too, for various kinds of spontaneous nonverbal and verbal expression during the reading. These can be considered intermingled signs of participation in, and reactions to, the evoked story or poem.

After the reading, our initial function is to deepen the experience. (We know one cannot predict developments in a teaching situation, but we can think in terms of priority of emphasis.) We should help the young reader to return to, relive, savor, the experience. For continuing the focus on what has been seen, heard, felt teachers have successfully provided the opportunity for various forms of nonverbal expression or response: drawing, painting, play-acting, dance. These may sometimes become ends in themselves, perhaps valuable for a child's development, but only very generally relevant to the reading purposes. Such activities can, however, offer an aesthetic means of giving form to a sense of what has been lived through in the literary transaction. This can give evidence of what has caught the young reader's attention, what has stirred pleasant or unpleasant reactions. This can lead back to the text.

Requests for verbal responses create the greatest hazards. Adults may, often unconsciously, reveal a testing motive. Perhaps there will be a suggestion of what the approved or "correct" response should be. Sometimes there is a tacit steering toward an efferent or analytic stance, toward the kinds of subjects the adult thinks interesting or important. The reader is often hurried away from the aesthetic experience and turned to efferent analysis by questions such as those appended to stories in various basal readers and anthologies and by teachers' questions or tests "checking whether the student has read the text." Questions that call for the traditional analyses of character, setting, and plot are often premature or routine, contributing to shallow, efferent readings.

Some object that the formalists and post-structuralists are right in identifying literature with its system of conventions, its technical traits. My reply is that, by focusing on these components of the text, they fail to do justice to the total aesthetic experience. Metaphor, narrative structure, linguistic conventions, verbal techniques are, of course, important elements of "literary" texts, and they contribute much to the quality of the aesthetic transaction. But they are vacuous concepts without recognition of the importance of stance. Poetic metaphors or narrative suspense, for example, become operative, come into existence, only if the reader pays attention to the inner states that these verbal patterns arouse. After this repeatedly happens, we can communicate to our students the appropriate terminology—when they need it! "Form" is something felt on the pulses, first of all.

How, then, can we deal with the young reader's responses without inhibiting the aesthetic experience? Two answers to this quite real dilemma suggest themselves. First, a truly receptive attitude on the part of teacher and peers—and this requires strong efforts at creating such trust—can be sufficient inducement to children to give spontaneous verbal expression to what has been lived through. Once nonverbal or verbal comments have given some glimpse into the nature of what the young readers have made of the text, the teacher can provide positive reinforcement by leading to further reflection on what in the experienced story or poem had triggered the reactions. Comments by other children and the teacher, of course, also contribute to this imaginative recall of the experience.

Second, if for some reason the teacher finds it appropriate to initiate discussion, remarks (or questions, if necessary!) can guide the reader's attention back toward the reading event. Questions can be sufficiently open to enable the young readers to select concrete details or parts of the text that had struck them most forcibly. The point is to foster expressions of response that keep the experiential, qualitative elements in mind. Did anything especially interest? annoy? puzzle? frighten? please? seem familiar? seem weird? The particular text and the teacher's knowledge of the readers involved will suggest such open-ended questions. The habit of the aesthetic stance, of attention to concrete detail, will be strengthened for further reading. Cognitive abilities, to organize, to interpret, or to explain, will be rooted in the ability to handle responses. (And enhanced "reading skills" will probably be a by-product!)

The young reader will be stimulated to make the connections among initial responses, the evoked work, and the text. He may then be motivated to return to the actual words of the text, to deepen the experience. As students grow older, sharing of responses becomes the basis for valuable interchange. Discovering that others have had different responses, have noticed what was overlooked, have made alternative interpretations, leads to self-awareness and self-criticism.[24]

At the opening of these remarks, I mentioned the need to clarify my own version of reader-response theory, but felt no urge to survey the gamut of competing theories. It seems important, however, to recall that the transactional theory avoids concentration solely on the reader's contribution or on feeling for its own sake,[25] but centers on the reciprocal interplay of reader and text. For years I have extolled the potentialities of literature for aiding us to understand ourselves and others, for widening our horizons to include temperaments and cultures different from our own, for helping us to clarify our conflicts in values, for illuminating our world. I have believed, and have become increasingly convinced, that these benefits spring only from emotional and intellectual participation in evoking the work or art, through reflection on our own aesthetic experience. Precisely because every aesthetic reading of a text is a unique creation, woven out of the inner life and thought of the reader, the literary work of art can be a rich source of insight and truth. But it has become apparent that even when literature is presented to young readers, the efferent emphasis of our society and schools tends to negate the potential interest and benefits of the reading. Literature is "an endangered species." By establishing the habit of aesthetic evocation and personal response during the elementary years, teachers of children's literature can make a prime contribution to the health of our culture.

# Notes

1. Tompkins, Jane P. (Ed.) *Reader-Response Criticism.* Baltimore: Johns Hopkins University Press, 1980, p. xxvi; Suleiman, Susan R. and Crosman, Inge (Eds.) *The Reader in the Text.* Princeton: Princeton University Press, 1980, p. 45.

2. Rosenblatt, Louise M. *The Reader, the Text, the Poem.* Carbondale, Ill.: Southern Illinois University Press, 1978 presents the fullest statement of the transactional theory. The present article cannot deal with such matters as "correctness" of interpretation, the author's intention, the openness and constraints of the text, or the role of the critic.

3. This is conveniently documented by articles by 11 leading psychologists (Jerome Bruner, Richard Lazarus, Ulric Neisser, David McClelland, et al.) on "the state of the science" in *Psychology Today*, May 1982, pp. 41–59. See especially the article by Ulric Neisser.

4. Keller-Cohen, Deborah. "Context in Child Language," *Annual Review of Anthropology*, 1978, 7, pp. 433–482.

5. Halliday, M.A.K. *Learning to Mean.* New York: Elsevier, 1975.

6. James, William. *The Principles of Psychology.* New York: Dover Publications, pp. 245–246.

7. Werner, Heinz, and Kaplan, Bernard. *Symbol Formation.* New York: Wiley, 1963, p. 18.

8. Gibson, E.J. *How perception really develops.* In David Laberge and S. Jay Samuels (Eds.), *Basic Processes in Reading.* Hillsdale, N.J.: Lawrence Erlbaum, 1975, p. 171; Rommetveit, Ragnar. *Words, Meanings, and Messages.* New York: Academic Press, 1968, pp. 147, 167; Werner and Kaplan, *Symbol Formation*, pp. 23–24 and *passim*.

9. Bates, Elizabeth. *The Emergence of Symbols.* New York: Academic Press, 1979, pp. 65–66.

10. See Dewey, John. *How We Think.* Lexington, Mass.: D.C. Heath, 1933, Ch. X; Dewey, John. "Qualitative Thought," *Philosophy and Civilization.* New York: Minton, Balch, 1931, pp. 93–116.

11. Vygotsky, L.S. *Thought and Language,* (Eugenia Hanfmann and Gertrude Vakar, Eds. and trans.) Cambridge, Mass.: MIT Press, 1962, p. 8.

12. Tedlock, Ernest (Ed.), *Dylan Thomas.* New York: Mercury, 1963, p. 54.

13. Izard, Carroll E. "On the ontogenesis of emotions and emotion-cognition relationships in infancy." In Michael Lewis and Leonard Rosenblum (Eds.), *The Development of Affect.* New York: Plenum Press, 1978, p. 404.

14. White, Dorothy. *Books before Five.* New York: Oxford University Press, 1954, p. 13.

15. Conrad, Joseph, Preface. *The Nigger of the Narcissus.* New York: Doubleday, Page, 1922, p. x.

16. White, p. 79.

17. The problems of validity in interpretation and of the author's intention are treated in Rosenblatt, *The Reader, the Text, the Poem,* Chapters 5 and 6.

18. Wordsworth, William, "Ode, Intimations of Immortality." *Poetics/Works.* London: Oxford University Press, 1959, p. 46.

19. See *Research in the Teaching of English, 15* (4), December 1981, pp. 293–309, 343–354, and *passim.*

20. Bateson, Gregory, and Mead, Margaret. *Balinese Character.* New York: New York Academy of Sciences, 1942; Geertz, Clifford. *The Interpretation of Cultures.* New York: Basic Books, 1973.

21. Purves, Alan. *Literature Education in Ten Countries.* Stockholm: Almqvist and Wiksell, 1973.

22. Cf. Huey, Edmund Burke. *The Psychology and Pedagogy of Reading.* Cambridge, Mass.: MIT Press, 1968 (original edition, 1908), pp. 345, 380.

23. See Harste, Jerome C., and Carey, Robert F. "Comprehension as Setting." In *New Perspectives on Comprehension,* Monograph in Language and Reading Studies, Indiana University, No. 3, October 1979.
     In a volume and an article that reflect the psychologists' usual preoccupation with efferent reading, I find this concession: "It may be in the rapid interplay of feelings . . . that the source of the creation of ideas, later to receive their analytic flesh and bones, may be found. If so, how sad it would be if it were discovered that the real problem of many readers is that their instruction so automatizes them that they do not develop a feeling for what they read or use the feelings available to them in the development of new understandings from reading." Spiro, Rand J. "Constructive Processes in Prose Comprehension and Recall." In Rand J. Spiro, Bertram Bruce, and William Brewer (Eds.), *Theoretical Issues in Reading Comprehension.* Hillside, N.J.: L Eribaum, 1980, p. 274.

24. Rosenblatt, L. *Literature as Exploration,* 1976 (distributed by the National Council of Teachers of English) develops further the implications for teaching.

25. The recent publication of *On Learning to Read*, by Bruno Bettelheim and Karen Zelan, with its subtitle, *The Child's Fascination with Meaning*, and its emphasis on response, leads me to disclaim any actual resemblance to my views. These authors reiterate what many of us, from Dewey on, have been saying about the importance of meaning and the child's own feelings, and about the narrow, dull approach of much teaching of beginning reading. But the book's concentration on a doctrinal psychoanalytic interpretation of response, disregard of the process of making meaning out of printed symbols, and treatment of the text as a repository of ready-made meanings or didactic human stereotypes, add up to an inadequate view of the relationship between reader and text.

# Chapter Seven

# Literature—S.O.S.!

"Literature-based language arts"; "the use of literature for literacy instruction"; "the contribution of the aesthetic in the teaching of mathematics"; "aesthetic response in content area studies." Such phrases are increasingly encountered in our journals. In the past, literature and the aesthetic have been neglected in our schools; now, finally, their importance is being recognized. Surely, this is a matter for rejoicing. Alas, the contrary is true: There are signs that the very efforts to rescue literature, though often excellent, may become self-defeating.

No one seems to think it necessary to explain what is meant by *literature*, or *the aesthetic*.

If one analyzes the use of these terms in their contexts, a variety of tacit assumptions seems to operate. Sometimes, all that is required is that a text already has been designated as "literature." Sometimes, the presence of story, of a narrative, is the clue. Sometimes, the presence of rhymed words, or of verse rhythms, or of metaphoric language seems sufficient to justify the claim that "literature," or at least "the aesthetic," has been operating. Sometimes, the aesthetic is attributed to the presence of emotion, as when students become excited about scientific information.

All of these elements can indeed be found in texts read as literature. Yet none of these, either singly or all together, can ensure the presence of "literature." The fact is that any text, even if it contains such elements, can be the occasion for *either* a "literary" *or* a "nonliterary" reading.

After all, narrative (story) is found not only in novels but also in scientific accounts of geological change or historical accounts of political events or social life. When we speak of the "arm" of a chair, we are using a metaphor. The physicist who uses "wave" in his theory of light is using a metaphor. As for the term *literature*—I recently received a phone call offering me "literature" about a retirement home!

The term *literature*, when it is used in contrast, say, to scientific exposition, refers to a particular mode of experience. It requires a particular kind of relation between reader and text. It requires a particular kind of reading process.

## Two Ways of Reading

Take, for example, the couplet:

> In fourteen hundred and ninety-two
> Columbus crossed the ocean blue.

Why are we reluctant to accept:

> In fourteen hundred and ninety-three
> Columbus crossed the dark blue sea.

The point, of course, is that we want to use the verse and rhyme as a mnemonic device for the date of Columbus' arrival in America. In other words, we read the couplet in the way we read an expository essay. We pay some attention to the sound and rhythm, but our predominant interest is in acquiring information that we wish to retain after the reading has ended. I use the term *efferent* (from the Latin for "carry away") to refer to this nonliterary kind of reading.

Still, we can, if we wish, shift gears and pay attention mainly to what we are thinking and feeling as we read or speak the couplet. We can disregard the inaccuracy of the date in the second couplet and decide that it is, from an aesthetic point of view, preferable (e.g., we feel more comfortable with the order of words in "the dark blue sea"). We should then be adopting an *aesthetic* stance toward the text—reading it with attention, of course, to what the words refer to, but *mainly* to what we are experiencing, thinking, and feeling *during* the reading.

Obviously, these verses about Columbus do not provide much reward for the aesthetic stance. Yet they share with even the most valued poetry—say, Shakespeare's *Macbeth*—the potential for being read either aesthetically or efferently.

I was once asked to classify the metaphors in Shakespeare's plays. (This was supposed to reveal biographical information.) That would have meant approaching each play efferently, with my attention focused on how each metaphor should be classified—e.g., as nature, law, animal, etc. It would simply have been irrelevant to pay attention to what states of mind the metaphors were arousing in me. *That* kind of attention to what the metaphors were stirring up—associations, ideas, attitudes, sensations, or feelings—would have had to be reserved for the kind of reading that I call *aesthetic* reading.

Consider the following metaphor:

> I am the captain of my soul.

If my purpose is to select the class of metaphors to which this might belong, an efferent reading of this line would be required. My mind would be carrying on an analytic, reasoning activity, in which "captain of a ship" would be seen as implied in the metaphor. Of course, I would have to reason, for someone else "captain" might produce an association with the army. I might have to classify it as naval *or* military.

In an aesthetic reading, on the other hand, I would be registering the effect on me, the states of mind produced by the idea or image of a ship's captain. If interrupted and questioned, I might report a feeling of strength, of independence, of mastery over "my soul." I would probably not explicitly analyze this feeling as resulting from the comparison implied in the metaphoric use of "captain." If asked, I could shift my attention away from the metaphoric effect and recognize this.

## Adopting a Predominant Stance

It's the either-or habit of thinking that has caused the trouble. True, there are two primary ways of looking at the world. We may experience it, feel it, sense it, hear it, and have emotions about it in all its immediacy. On we may abstract generalizations about it, analyze it, manipulate it, and theorize about it. These are not contradictory activities, however. We cannot, for example, identify the efferent with cognition and the aesthetic, or literary, with emotion.

Instead of thinking of the *text* as either literary or informational, efferent or aesthetic, we should think of it as written for a particular *predominant* attitude or stance, efferent or aesthetic, on the part of the reader. We have ignored the fact that our reading is not all-of-one-piece. We read for information, but we are also conscious of emotions about it and feel pleasure when the words we call up arouse vivid images and are rhythmic to the inner ear. Or we experience a poem but are conscious of acquiring some information about, say, Greek warfare. To confuse matters even further, we can switch stances while reading. And we can read aesthetically something written mainly to inform or read efferently something written mainly to communicate experience. Our present purpose and past experiences, as well as the text, are factors in our choice of stance.

Teachers need constantly to remind themselves that reading is always a particular event involving a particular reader at a particular time under particular circumstances. Hence, we may make different meanings when transacting with the same text at different times. And different readers may make different defensible interpretations of the same text. We need think only of the text of the Constitution or the text of *Hamlet* to document this (Rosenblatt, 1978).

The reader brings to the text a reservoir of past experiences with language and the world. If the signs on the page are linked to elements in that reservoir, these linkages rise into consciousness. The reader recognizes them as words in a language; the child is often slowly making such connections. All readers must draw on past experiences to make the new meanings produced in the transaction with the text. This experience then flows into the reservoir brought to the next reading event.

Psychologists (e.g., Bates, 1979) have pointed out that these connections between verbal signs and what they signify involve both what the words are understood to refer to (their public, dictionary meaning) and the feelings, ideas, and attitudes (their private associations) that have become linked with them through past reading or life experiences. A mixture of such public and private elements is present in all linguistic events. The differences among them result from the individual's focus of attention.

A reading event during which attention is given *primarily* to the public aspect, I call, as indicated above, *efferent* reading. If the reader focuses attention *primarily* on the private element, I term it *aesthetic*. But each case involves both public and private aspects of meaning.

Actually, we have been talking about a continuum, not an opposition. In a sequence from 1 to 10, for example, these two numbers are not opposites or contraries but simply the end points of a continuum. In the continuum from efferent to aesthetic, these terms are end points in a changing proportion, or "mix," of elements. In any reading, at any point in the continuum, there are both cognitive and affective, publicly referential and privately associational,

**Figure 1.** The Efferent/Aesthetic Continuum

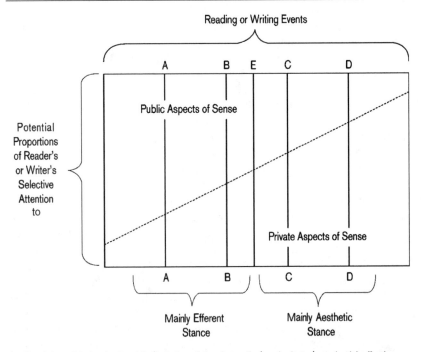

Any linguistic activity has both public (lexical, analytic, abstracting) and private (experiential, affective, associational) components. Stance is determined by the proportion of each component admitted into the scope of selective attention. The efferent stance draws mainly on the public aspect of sense; the aesthetic stance includes proportionally more of the experiential, private aspect.

Reading or writing events A and B fall into the efferent part of the continuum, with B admitting more private elements. Reading or writing events C and D both represent the aesthetic stance, with C according a higher proportion of attention to the public aspects of sense. Because the reader gives the efferent and aesthetic aspects about equal attention in E, he may adopt a stance not appropriate to his purpose, e.g., an aesthetic attitude toward a discussion of economics.

and abstract and concrete elements (see Figure 1). The place where any reading event falls on the continuum reflects the proportion of what, for brevity, we can call the public and private elements. In the predominantly efferent half of the continuum, the area of attention to the public elements will be greater than the area of the private. Some readings may lean more heavily on the private aspects than others and will be closer to the middle of the continuum. A book about a foreign country read for information, for example, could entail mainly concentration on abstract generalizations (Figure 1, A) or involve much attention to experiential aspects of descriptions (Figure 1, B).

Similarly, aesthetic readings will result when the reader's attention is focused mainly on the private, experiential aspects. But some aesthetic readings pay more attention to the public, referential, and cognitive aspects than do others. An aesthetic reading of *Encyclopedia Brown and the Case of the Mysterious Handprints* (Sobol, 1986), which invites the reader to solve a problem, will probably fall closer to the efferent side of the continuum (Figure 1, C) than will an aesthetic reading of a story such as *Charlotte's Web* (White, 1952) (Figure 1, D).

Precisely because all readings tend to have such a "mix," it becomes important for readers (and writers) to keep their main purposes clear. Beautiful and moving as the words urging us to vote for a candidate may be, it's important that we keep clear that our purpose is to get accurate information. And if we want to experience a text as a poem or a story, we need to learn to evoke experiential meaning from the text and to focus attention on that, rather than simply "the message" or "the facts." Readings that fall near the middle of the continuum especially need to keep the primary purpose, the primary focus of attention, clear.

## Clarifying a Sense of Purpose

Confusion about the purpose of reading has in the past contributed to failure to teach effectively both efferent reading and aesthetic reading. Why not help youngsters early to understand that there are two ways of reading? We do not want to give them theoretical explanations, nor do we need to. We communicate such understandings by what we do, by the atmosphere and the activities we associate with the two kinds of reading, and by the kinds of questions we ask and the kinds of tests we give. Children who know that the teacher usually quizzes them on factual aspects of a reading, even if it is called "a poem" or "a story," will adopt the efferent stance and will read to register the facts that will be required after the reading. They know that they will be successful and rewarded if they recall the color of the horse or where the bunny hid, rather than if they linger over the experiences and feelings encountered. (Actually, that kind of fragmented questioning doesn't much improve efferent reading, either!)

With younger children, perhaps the best evidence of aesthetic experience is their demand to hear the story or poem again. Or they may wish to draw a picture or retell the story. Some may be moved to comment on it. I think of the 3-year-old who exclaimed. "She's a mean lady!" when hearing the nursery rhyme about a certain old lady who spanked her many children "all round" and put them to bed. Certainly, evidence of "comprehension" can be gained in such indirect ways from readers of all ages.

Aesthetic reading happens if students have repeatedly found that, in approaching a text called a "poem" or a "story," they can assume that they are free to pay attention to what the words call to consciousness. They can savor the images, the sounds, the smells, the actions, the associations, and the feelings that the words point to. Textbooks' and teachers' questions too often hurry the students away from the lived-through experience. After the reading, the experience should be recaptured, reflected on. It can be the subject of further aesthetic activities—drawing, dancing, miming, talking, writing, role-playing, or oral interpretation. It can be discussed and analyzed efferently. Or it can yield information. But first, if it is indeed to be "literature" for these students, it must be experienced (Rosenblatt, 1983).

It is teachers who need to be clear theoretically about efferent and aesthetic reading. As they commendably seek to present more "literature" in their language arts curricula, they need to be careful not to "use" the appeal of such texts simply or mainly for the efferent purposes of teaching grammar or "skills." Also, as teachers plan to include aesthetic elements in the work in social or natural science or to utilize the interest of story in the teaching of mathematics, they need to realize that they have a responsibility not to create confusion about primary stances appropriate to different purposes.

The different purposes lead to different modes of reading and to different criteria of evaluation of the "meanings" evoked. If the emphasis is on verifiable information or practical application, not only does the mode of reading need to be efferent, but also the interpretation of the text needs to involve some public criteria of evaluation. If the purpose is literary, the important thing is that readers relate to the text, and to one another, the different experiences produced during their transactions with it.

I am decidedly in sympathy with those who, under the rubric of "whole language," speak of the importance of meaning. But I hope that they will not confuse students by using "literary works" in such a way that students read them efferently, for the primary purpose, let us say, of learning historical data. If American history is being studied, a novel about colonial life will be valuable, but only as primarily an aesthetic experience, a sharing of what it would have been like to live in those days. If the story has been read with a primarily aesthetic emphasis, one can later, of course, ask students to recall incidental information about, for example, methods of transportation. But it would often be helpful to suggest that the author of the poem or novel had acquired that information through verified historical sources.

The distinctions in purpose and stance can be incorporated into actual classroom practice without dwelling on theoretical distinctions. Even nursery school youngsters can sense the difference between looking at a picture book in order to learn the names of birds and looking at it because there is comfort in hearing a story about finding a home—e.g., in sharing a duck family's experience of finding a place to nest. Hickman (1981) tells about the boy who complained that his teacher had brought him only "story books about dinosaurs," whereas he really wanted to *know* about them.

Obviously, what is at stake is each child's total school experience—in speech, reading, and writing—with what is termed "literature," or "the aesthetic." No one episode, whether in kindergarten or in high school, will be decisive. But it will either reinforce or weaken the student's sense of the diverse possibilities of texts—and of the world. We need to look at the whole sweep of our language arts curricula, at our use of texts across the curriculum, and especially at our methods of evaluation. We need to make sure that students are cumulatively developing, in their transactions with texts, the ability to adopt the stance on the continuum appropriate to their particular personal purposes and to the situation—in short, the ability to read both efferently and aesthetically.

# References

Bates, E. (1979). *The Emergence of Symbols*. New York: Academic Press.

Hickman, J. (1981). "A New Perspective on Response to Literature." *Research in the Teaching of English, 15*, 293–309.

Rosenblatt, L.M. (1978). *The Reader, the Text, the Poem: The Transactional Theory of the Literary Work*. Carbondale, IL: Southern Illinois University Press.

Rosenblatt, L.M. (1980). "What Facts Does this Poem Teach You?" *Language Arts, 57*, 386–394.

Rosenblatt, L.M. (1983). *Literature as Exploration*. (4th ed.). New York: Modern Language Association.

Rosenblatt, L.M. (1989). "Writing and Reading: The Transactional Theory." In J.M. Mason (Ed.), *Reading and Writing Connections* (pp. 153–176). Boston: Allyn and Bacon.

Sobol, D. (1986). *Encyclopedia Brown and the Case of the Mysterious Handprints*. New York: Bantam/Skylark.

White, E.B. (1952). *Charlotte's Web*. New York: Harper.

# Chapter Eight

# What Facts Does This Poem Teach You?

You may recall Rachel Field's much-anthologized "Roads," which begins:

> A road might lead to anywhere—
>   To harbor towns and quays,
> Or to a witch's pointed house,
>   Hidden by bristly trees.

and ends:

> Oh, a road might lead to anywhere,
>   To Mexico or Maine;
> But then it might just fool you, and—
>   Lead you back home again!

As I once finished reading this poem to a five-year-old, he snuggled under the covers and remarked, "I like that poem. You come back again." That comment could spark many kinds of reflections; for me it illustrated the very nature of poetry. That child had not been passively listening to words. He had been travelling that road, had glimpsed places familiar and distant, and had been pleased to find himself home again. One could say that he had "imagined" the journey, but for most that would emphasize the make-believe, the fictional, the not-reality aspect of poem and story. Instead, I was impressed by the fact that the poetic experience had had for him a certain kind of reality. He had lived through that journey.

A poem is not a ready-made object to which a reader is passively exposed. A poem is a happening, an event, in which the listener or reader draws on images and feelings and ideas stirred up by the words of the text; out of these is shaped the lived-through experience.

In the coming pages, I shall relate this view of poetry to my transactional theory of reading (Rosenblatt 1978). I shall then briefly indicate how recent findings about children's acquisition of language support this model of the reading process. I shall suggest some of the implications for the teaching of reading, with emphasis on the treatment of literature in the early years. (For the sake of brevity, "poem" and "poetry" will often stand for all types of literary works of art, whether in verse or prose, whether lyric or narrative.)

## Aesthetic and Efferent Reading

We tend to talk as though the poem or story or play exists in the words alone. On the contrary, the set of sounds in the ear or the squiggles on the page are simply "the text." We all know how complex is the process by which the child learns to match those marks on the page to the sound of the words they stand for. And we know, too, that the sounds in the inner ear really become words, part of the language, only when they call up the ideas or images that have become linked with these sounds in the child's past. The reader not only interprets the visual signs, but also infuses meaning into them. Hence my emphasis on the poem or story or play as a happening during the two-way relationship, the transaction, between reader and text.

But, you are probably thinking, this is true of all reading. The reader has to actively make meaning out of a history text or a newspaper as well as the text of a poem. I agree, and therefore we must proceed beyond recognizing that any reader is active; we must ask how the reader's activities in making a poem differ from the activities involved in making a set of directions for, say, putting a toy together. Robert Graves, in his "Poem: A Reminder," tells us that we must "read carefully." But, after all, we need to read a match problem or a history text "carefully," too. Hence Graves goes on to specify how the careful reading that results in a poem differs from other kinds of careful reading: "Each word we choose/Has rhythm and sound and sense." We must pay attention not only to the sense of the words—what they refer to, the ideas we organize with their help—but also to such things as the sound and rhythm of the words. All of these are important, we know, if we are to experience a poem.

This matter of the reader's focus of attention during the reading transaction is of paramount importance. Whether a poem will result depends, first of all, on where the reader centers attention as the links with the visual or oral symbols come into consciousness as words. Graves cites the "convention" that alerts the reader that a poem is intended: "Capital letters prompting every line,/Lines printed down the center of each page,/Clear spaces between groups of these." These are signals or cues to the reader to choose the aesthetic focus of attention. When we adults see the broad margins, the uneven lines, we usually have learned to do this automatically. We must attend to the sound of the words and pulsations of the phrases as we call them up in the inner ear; we must attend to the sensations and feelings and associations triggered by the ideas, images, people, and places that we conjure up under the guidance of the text. Like the youngster listening to "Roads," we are absorbed in what we are thinking and feeling and seeing, what we are living through, *during* the reading event.

How, then, does this differ from what we do in other kinds of reading? I call such nonaesthetic reading "efferent" (from the Latin, *efferre*, "to carry away"), because the reader's attention is focused primarily on what is to be carried away, retained *after* the reading event. The medical student reading about the symptoms of heart disease must focus attention on the ideas to be accumulated for future use. Any personal physical or emotional reactions or associations must be shut out, pushed into the fringes of awareness. The person reading directions on a medicine label, the lawyer analyzing a brief, also need to adopt an efferent stance.

Note that Graves did not neglect "sense" in his explanation of the poetic, in contrast to those who equate poetry with emotion, and prose with the "cognitive." Cognition, it is now increasingly recognized, is always accompanied by affect or feeling. Hence my insistence on the importance of what William James (1950) called "selective attention." The referent of a verbal symbol has an aura of affect or feeling, even perhaps a physical component. Efferent reading will select out the desired referents and ignore or subordinate affect. Aesthetic reading, in contrast, will fuse the cognitive and affective elements of consciousness—sensations, images, feelings, ideas—into a personally lived-through poem or story.[1]

Another point to be noted: we should not think of efferent reading as basic, with poetry being a kind of second thought, or added layer of meaning, like jam spread on bread. In aesthetic reading, sound and rhythm and associations *and* sense are perceived together, blended into an experienced meaning. In the transactional model, efferent and aesthetic reading are parallel or coordinate modes. As the reader enters into a transaction with a text, there ensues the adoption, either consciously or unconsciously, of a predominant attitude or stance.

## The Making of Meaning

Thus, the process of making meaning out of verbal signs requires a continuing stream of choices on the reader's part. The choices involved in the translation from graphemes to phonemes, the recognition of words, the attribution of syntactic categories, are, of course, essential. But, as readers of this journal are aware, in the teaching of reading these activities are too often treated as separate skills, ends in themselves, instead of paths to meaning. Fortunately, there is an increasing emphasis on the importance of meaning rather than fragmented skills (e.g., Goodman 1973). I find it necessary to add a stress on

1. Even within the aesthetic reading process, there will be varying degrees of attention to the different elements. Grave's "Poem" paradoxically has a strong efferent character, since a certain didactic note is struck at the beginning, and the words stir up little more than their abstract meaning. Still, attention to sound and rhythm and rhyme offers some rewards. "Roads," however, though not the best of texts, rewards the reader for full attention to sensations, images, feelings, memories and ideas that come to mind. The lived-through journey is the important thing.

recognition of the two kinds of meaning, the two stances of the reader in relation to the text.

In approaching a text, the reader needs to fit the sequence of verbal signs into some kind of framework. The feeling of what it's about, of what to anticipate, will undoubtedly often be extremely vague, changing, fleeting. The linguists have pointed out how this happens on the syntactic level: *The* is a signal or cue to what kind of word to expect next: a noun. The noun in turn sets up expectations of a verb. It is important to see also that the noun— *house*, or *mother*, say—will activate whatever the reader's past experience of these has been, and will be a cue to the coming semantic possibilities of the text. These anticipations will help the reader to build a tentative framework of meaning into which to fit the following words. If the expectations are inappropriate to what the text actually offers next, the reader finds it necessary to revise that tentative organizing principle; sometimes a complete rereading is necessary.

Overarching this whole "choosing activity," we have seen, is the early choice of stance, the decision whether to pay attention to the whole range of overtones aroused by the words, to synthesize them into the total meaning, or whether to subordinate these associations and focus mainly on the abstract meanings to be retained for later use.

Since the reader chooses the stance, any text—"Roads" or a newspaper item—can be read either efferently or aesthetically. "Roads" can be read efferently, if one is, for example, analyzing the meter or seeing whether there are more familiar than exotic items. When the "pop" poet takes a newspaper item and breaks it up into short lines, we are being cued to adopt the aesthetic stance and to make a poetic experience out of what we should otherwise have read efferently. Just as the young boy or girl absorbs other conventions of reading, so must they absorb the habit of selecting either a predominantly efferent or a predominantly aesthetic stance.

The efferent stance, it is my observation, has generally been emphasized throughout the child's experience in the home and in the school, to the neglect of the aesthetic. In part, this has been due to the misconception that the text alone does the aesthetic job, instead of recognition of the reader's contribution. Both the learning environment and teaching approaches have tended to inculcate a predominantly efferent stance toward all texts, even those presumably "literary"—poems, stories, or plays.

Surveys of reading models (Williams 1971) confirm the fact that psychologists and reading experts view reading mainly as a complex skill, aimed at gaining information. Models of the reading process usually deal with efferent reading; little attempt has been made to incorporate affective aspects. When affect or emotional attitudes are studied, they usually turn out to be the motivations, the favorable or unfavorable, secure or insecure, attitudes that the reader brings to *efferent* reading. All of these are important subjects, of course, but they represent only one kind of reading.

## The Child's Early Language

Recent work in child development, and especially studies of the child's acquisition of language, reinforce my view of the aesthetic and efferent modes. This field, too, has until fairly recently concentrated on the referential, information-processing activities. Jean Piaget recognizes that the cognitive and the affective are always associated, and that both are important in the child's growth. Nevertheless, his influence has been mainly through his masterly series of studies of the development of children's logical and mathematical concepts (Piaget 1952, 1962). This has strengthened the general tendency to concentrate on the efferent. The child always encounters a word or concept in a particular situation, but emphasis was placed on the growth of the ability to "decontextualize," to abstract out the referent of the word, its general import, apart from the associations and feelings and particularities associated with the experienced context.

L. S. Vygotsky, whose work is becoming increasingly influential, criticized the traditional separation of intellect and affect. He argued that the "sense" of a word to the individual was broader than its referential meaning.

> The sense of a word . . . is the sum of all the psychological events aroused in our consciousness by the word. It is a dynamic, fluid, complex whole, which has several zones of unequal stability. . . . The dictionary meaning of a word is no more than a stone in the edifice of sense. (1962, p. 146)

More recent students of the child's acquisition of language have developed this view further (Werner and Kaplan 1963). The familiar instance of the child's first utterance of a recognizable word—"Ball!", let us say—has often been interpreted in terms of adult syntax, as a one-word sentence, equivalent to, perhaps, "the ball fell down." Actually, these writers point out, the child's utterance is neither a word nor a sentence. Agreeing with them, Rommetveit (1968) calls it a "word form, a peculiar fusion of processes which later will branch off into referential, emotive, and associative part processes." Thus what the word *ball* points to for the child will involve its "associative network." All of these elements are intermingled, until the child learns to sort them out.

Others have confirmed this concept of the movement from the global awareness of a situation to the separating-out of elements (Bates *et al.* 1978). The child at first, sometimes to the age of five, even sees the word as an inherent part of its referent: *cow* is just as much a feature of cows as color, size, shape, horns, and so on. Images such as the child's selecting out from "the mental file drawer" associated with a word suggest the process of differentiation among these elements. Unfortunately, most of the studies of early language acquisition have emphasized the process of abstracting a word's meaning as a class or a category. Not enough research has been concerned with the problem of how the child uses language to handle the more personal, subjective, affective—aesthetic—aspects of experience. It is perhaps natural that this should be the case, since language is a socially engendered system or code that makes communication possible. The paradox, however, is that this system of public meanings must be individually, privately, internalized. There is no question that the efferent approach is essential. My complaint is only that in our culture this aspect of language receives a greatly predominant reinforcement in homes and schools and universities. Equally essential is the parallel reinforcement of language in its relation to the personal and the experiential.

## Implications for Teaching

Doing justice to the aesthetic mode of language behavior does not require discovery of a new array of teaching techniques. Rather, our transactional theory provides the criteria for evaluating our present practices, for reinforcing some strategies and eliminating or redirecting others.

Concern for the child's first words, mentioned above, is highly relevant. The infant, in its transaction with its environment, selects the stimuli to which it responds; the sense of self is created as the sense of the surrounding world emerges. Language is an important element in this task of discovery, hence the importance of a rich and stimulating environment. Hence, too, the need to encourage the curiosity, the looking and touching and shaping and listening, the interplay with peers and adults, that feed the inner reservoir from which meanings, both efferent and aesthetic, must ultimately be drawn. Many parents and teachers of the very young child already are adept at fostering such exploring sensibilities. But as the child moves more and more into the acquisition of language, the emphasis, as I have said earlier, seems to focus more and more on rewarding the efferent, abstracting, and classifying function of language. The parent's and the teacher's concern about helping the youngster to acquire the referential language code may contribute to a stifling or at least weakening of the child's initial awareness of the sensuous, affective, and associational aspects of the experiences toward which words point.

The dictated experience chart helps the child to recognize the connection among the squiggles on the page or board, the sound of the words in the ear, and the actual personal, private experience; the word is now understood to "stand for" that personal experience. And certainly this technique is helpful in leading the child toward the generally understood referents for the words. The experience chart can also serve to keep alive the child's personal feeling for language, that rich experiential aura surrounding both the word and its referent. Delightfully suggestive of the child's personal, sensuous, emotional response to words is Aliki Barnstone's poem, excerpted below, about the names attached to "Numbers."

> The letter O
> and the number zero sound like
> poems about O snowflake. Zero
> makes me hungry. It is the emptiest
> number in the universe.

(William James spoke of our having feelings or physical states corresponding even to words such as *of* or *from*. Werner and Kaplan, whom I mentioned above, call this inner sense of words "physiognomization." Bates calls it "iconicity.")

We all have observed, too, children's delight in the rhythms, the intonations, the blending or clash of vowel and consonant—often even before the "meaning" of the words is caught. The child's response to nursery rhymes is surely largely in terms of awareness of sound, rhythm, images; the young listener often "gets" the tone or mood or emotional impact even when there are many referential blanks. I remind you of these familiar observations because these potentialities of language seem to be less and less honored the further the child is led into language activities, and especially into reading.

That the young reader needs to be helped to become aware of the two different stances was brought home to me years ago. In a reading workbook for the third grade, a page with broad margins and uneven lines of print made me think, "At last this class will read a poem!" But when I looked more closely, I found these words preceding the text: "What facts does this poem teach you?" The children were being alerted to adopt an efferent stance, to read with their attention focused on the facts to be reported later! This instance has come to symbolize for me the ways in which in our educational process the aesthetic stance is, often unwittingly, nullified or subverted. Many teachers, especially in the earlier years, avoid this pitfall and preserve the children's spontaneous sensibilities; but the pressures of the basal reader, the reading tests, the calls for "basics," more often, it seems to me, have led to an increasing neglect.

Although in recent years there has been an increased emphasis on children's literature in the early and middle years, we cannot be certain that the ability to read aesthetically actually is being developed. This is true also in the secondary school years, when the teaching of reading is replaced ostensibly by the teaching of "literature." Unfortunately, until about 1970, the critical theories dominating the college and university teaching of literature—which set the models for the high schools—simply intensified the tendency to hurry the student away from any personal aesthetic experience, in order to satisfy the efferent purposes of categorizing the genre, paraphrasing the "objective" meaning or analyzing the techniques represented by the text. When the reaction came, there developed in some quarters an equally unfortunate pendulum-swing to an excessively subjective approach which neglected the responsibility toward the text—hence the still more recent pendulum-swing back to an even more excessive demand for "basic" efferent reading. The solution, as I see it, requires a fuller understanding of the reading process in both kinds of transactions with texts.

Certain negatives become clear:

1. Do not generate an efferent stance when presenting texts as poems or stories or plays.
2. Do not use the texts being read aesthetically for the explicit teaching of reading skills.

3. Do not preface aesthetic reading with requests for information or analysis that require predominantly efferent reading.

4. Do not hurry the young reader away from the lived-through aesthetic experience by too quickly demanding summaries, paraphrases, character analyses, explanations of broad themes.

5. Do not hurry the young reader into substituting literary terminology or definitions for the lived-through work. (Not so long ago, we were reading articles about "literary criticism" of that sort in the second and third grades! Fortunately, I don't think the notion "took" in those grades.)

What, then, are the positive implications?

The underlying philosophy honors the development of the social and aesthetic sensibilities of children as of equal importance with their logical or cognitive development. These facets of the personality should be seen as mutually supportive. The school and classroom environment should provide for activities and pursuits that foster the acquisition of language by enabling the child to bring meaning to the printed page. One element in that program should be systematic provision for the growth of habits of aesthetic listening and aesthetic reading.

Ideally, the classroom should include a pleasant and inviting place for aesthetic reading. Of course, at the very least, there should be available a wide variety of texts. There is no dearth of materials to enable each child to find texts appropriate to his or her interests and abilities. Readers of this journal are well aware of the proliferation of excellent "children's literature"—picture books, poetry, stories, novels, biographies, historical and science fiction and nonfiction. Such categories do not always reveal which texts are actually mainly informative, hence to be read efferently, and which offer the potentialities for aesthetic reading—a problem not so much for the child as for the teacher who enters into the picture and who will influence the child's reading stances.

As for "reading level": since aesthetic reading should be carried on for its own sake, for its immediate rewards, common sense suggests that the texts should engage as much as possible the child's already-acquired "skills." However, we know what happens when children's interest is intense: texts seemingly beyond their "level" may become accessible. Moreover, although the explicit teaching of skills destroys the aesthetic stance, aesthetic reading may yield much incidental learning or reinforcement of skills. As for literary "conventions," such as the cues for poetry cited by Graves, or the sense of narrative "structure," or figurative language, these will be absorbed in the actual reading, if the young reader's attention is on what is being evoked from the text. Repeated experiences should precede the theoretical analysis of such conventions. Similarly, we should keep in mind that for literary terminology—e.g., *satire, sonnet*—as for any other, learning names before we experience their referents is futile (Rosenblatt 1968).

If the negative warning is against inculcating an efferent stance when it is not appropriate, the positive corollary is that the atmosphere and circumstances of aesthetic reading should make the young reader feel free to pay attention to what is being lived through under guidance of the text. There should also be the opportunity, if desired, to talk freely about the experience with peers and with the teacher. Some teachers have made the literary experience the center not only of discussions, but also of other activities, utilizing music, paintings, creative dramatics, and writing. The current interest in developing children's ability to compose their own poems and stories offers an important means of strengthening the child's sense of the aesthetic potentialities of language. (This question of the relation between writing and reading deserves fuller treatment than space permits. As indicated at the opening of our discussion, speaking and listening, writing and reading are intertwined.)

There is a danger that literary texts may be used mainly as a medium for generating other activities. Hence the need to make sure that follow-up activities are such as to maintain connection with the lived-through evocation which is the poem or story. Children's spontaneous comments should be welcomed, encouraged, and, as often as possible, made the starting-point for further discussion. If the teacher finds it necessary to spark discussion, opening questions or comments should be especially monitored for their possible effect. It is evidently very easy to impart the notion that there is a "right" answer, or that the main purpose of the reading has been to acquire information. Instead, questions or comments should lead the reader back, to savor what was seen, heard, felt, thought, during the calling-forth of the poem or story from the text. What caught the interest most? What pleased, frightened, surprised? What troubled? What seemed wrong? What things in the child's own life paralleled those in the poem or story? As differing responses are heard, there can be a continuing return to the text, to see what in the text led to those varied interpretations or judgments.

I recall a teacher of the second grade who had fulfilled many of the conditions indicated above, and whose class, in the course of lively discussion about one passage in a story, had actually started to grasp something of how language works metaphorically. But perhaps the memory of a college course in criticism aroused the feeling that she had not "done justice" to the story, for she called the class together again to admonish them that they should always "look for the main idea." A vivid recall of some one part or aspect of a reading experience, and its assimilation, may be more productive than a dutiful rehashing of the whole poem or story. The aim, let us recall, is to develop the habit of aesthetic evocation from a text. If the young readers are allowed in the early years to retain and deepen that ability, we can cheerfully leave for later years the more formal methods of literary analysis and criticism. For, after all, the experienced work is what should be being analyzed or criticized. The great problem, as I see it, in many school and college literature classrooms today is that the picture—the aesthetic experience, the work—is missing, yet students are being called upon to build an analytic or critical frame for it. No wonder they so often fall back on published "study aids," which give them all the (efferent) answers required.

Some (and not only those Gradgrinds who consider literature a dispensable "frill") fear that primary focus on aesthetic experience means a wallowing in feelings alone. Literature, we can reply, deals with all that is basic in human life, from the most humble to the most ideal. Elsewhere I have developed at length the thesis that, once there has indeed been a lived-through evocation from the text, students can be led toward increasingly self-critical and sound interpretation, and enhanced capacity to relate the experience to literary, historical, or social contexts (Rosenblatt 1976). Nurturing both efferent and aesthetic linguistic abilities, from the beginning and throughout the entire curriculum, will ensure success in the teaching of both kinds of reading.

# References

Barnstone, Aliki. "Numbers." In *Zero Makes Me Hungry*, edited by E. Lueders and P. St. John. Chicago: Scott, Foresman and Co., 1976.

Field, Rachel. "Roads." In *Poems*. New York: Macmillan, 1957.

Graves, Robert. "Poem: A Reminder." In *New Collected Poems*. New York: Doubleday, 1977.

Goodman, Kenneth. "Psycholinguistic Universals in the Reading Process." In *Psycholinguistics and Reading*, edited by Frank Smith. New York: Holt, Rinehart and Winston, 1973.

James, William. *The Principles of Psychology*. New York: Dover Publications, 1950. (Vol. 1, pp. 225–284).

Piaget, Jean. *The Origins of Intelligence in Children*. New York: International Universities Press, 1952.

———. *Plays, Dreams, and Imitation in Childhood*. New York: W.W. Norton, 1962.

Rommetveit, Ragnar. *Words, Meanings, and Messages*. New York: Academic Press, 1968. (p. 167)

Rosenblatt, Louise M. "A Way of Happening." *Educational Record* (Summer 1968): 339–346.

———. *Literature as Exploration*. New York: Noble and Noble, 1976. (Distributed by NCTE)

———. *The Reader, the Text, the Poem*. Carbondale: Southern Illinois University Press, 1978.

Vygotsky, L.S. *Thought and Language*. Translated and edited by Eugenia Hanfman and Gertrude Vakar. Cambridge, MA: MIT Press, 1962.

Werner, H., and Kaplan, B. *Symbol Formation*. New York: John Wiley and Sons, 1963. (pp. 18, 134).

Williams, Joanna P. "Learning to Read: A Review of Theories and Models." In *The Literature of Research in Reading*, edited by Frederick B. Davis. New Brunswick, NJ: Rutgers Graduate School of Education, 1971.

# Chapter Nine

# Moderns Among Masterpieces

## I

"The adventures of [a] soul among masterpieces"—Anatole France's view of the materials of criticism, you recall—suggests at least one essential consideration for a discussion of the place of masterpieces, or the "classics," in education. Without accepting France's general impressionistic theory, we can still value that phrase for its emphasis on an interaction, an interplay. Always there is some specific human being, at some particular time and place, at some special point in his life span, plunging into the adventure of sharing, through the medium of the work of art, the experiences and the insights of another human being, the author. A classic, like any literary work is, after all, merely a bundle of paper inscribed with strange hieroglyphics, until some human being responds to it in terms of sense and emotion and thought.

Our task as English teachers, then, consists essentially in furthering a fruitful interrelationship between individual books or poems or plays and individual students, living and growing up in our present portentous age. Hence my accent on the adventures of *moderns* among masterpieces.

Starting with an emphasis on the personal nature of all literary experience—on the interaction between readers and books—may at least prevent from the outset any implication that the "classics" are a body of works classified and evaluated in absolute, fixed terms, unchanging in meaning and unchanging in value, for generation after generation. It is the glory and the challenge of the great works of art that they have not been fixed, unchanging, inert, but have possessed the power to enter into the life of generation after generation, bringing much—yet much that is different—to each.

The terms "masterpiece" and "classics" are admittedly being used here rather loosely. For purposes of this discussion, it is fortunately not necessary that we agree on a finely drawn definition of these terms. I shall use the term "classics" to apply generally to those literary works of the past that have been traditionally considered a necessary part of the literary training of American high school and college students. (Each of us can make his own more limited selection, with which there would probably be little likelihood of unanimous agreement.) Since I know of no one who seriously advocates a complete diet of contemporary literature, the practical issue before us is whether the emphasis in literature teaching should be preponderantly on the literature of the past, or whether contemporary literature should also be given an important place in the literature program.

Let us face the facts. The majority of our graduates read neither the classics nor admirable contemporary works. They have not learned to turn spontaneously either to the good literature of the past or to the comparable literature of the present. Our central problem, therefore, is not whether we should or should not emphasize the classics in our curricula. The difficulty, indeed, is not that the classics have not been taught in the past, or are not being read in most schools today. The difficulty is rather that they are not being taught and read creatively, selectively, personally.

Thus, it is my thesis that the question of the classics must be viewed in the light of a broader concern: the need to help our students acquire the habit of turning to literature for personal pleasure, broadened horizons, greater insight. That can come about only as we help them to relate to their literary experiences the life from which they turn, and to which they must bring any enrichment or clarification that the works of the past may offer. We shall be able to solve our problem only as we include within its purview both the literature of the present and the literature of the past.

If there is abroad in the land today a certain skepticism about the revered works—literary or otherwise—of the past; if young people balk at accepting docilely the literary enthusiasms of even their immediate elders, that is not matter for lamentation. Rather it is one of many symptoms of the fact that in this era of world crisis our society is engaged in the momentous process of seeking some valid pattern for living, some freshly grasped central image of man's relationship to man. We are being forced to become conscious of our basic assumptions, to think out their implications, to accept or reject them—in short, to build up a new synthesis, a new, or at least consistent, system of values. This will flower from, not a rejection, but a re-evaluation, of the past in the light of a new vision of the potentialities of man's life.

We have glimpsed the strenuous possibility of a renaissance as seminal and all embracing as that of five centuries or more ago. Yet we are aware, too, of the danger that we may still be too much under the domination of certain strongly entrenched social mechanisms and deeply rooted habits of thought that may lead us to retrogression and degeneration. If that happens, probably the great works of the past *and* present, as in Nazi Germany, will be almost totally rejected, and there will be no problem of the classics as such.

In such a portentous setting this matter of the literature of the past presents itself. If the classics are to have value for us today, they must be proved meaningful for our present lives; they must illuminate the dilemmas before us, they must clarify, not obscure, the vision of a way of life better than any that the scarred history of the past reveals. Traditions are, indeed, the very stuff of our lives—but there are baleful and inhumane traditions, as well as those worthy of reverence. Many of the elements that make up the very fabric of the past, and that are reflected in its literature—war, superstition, poverty, disease, fixed-class distinction, autocratic power—are coming, at least in this country, to be looked upon as unnecessary, condemnable, and—without extreme utopianism—eradicable. In the realm of literature, as in all of life, we are confronted with the necessity for discrimination between that in the past that is worth of preservation, and that which is no longer valid for life and its rich potentialities as we now, even in this tragic moment, understand them.

Precisely because we live in an age of change, some are urging that we restrict our concern in school and college to the "time-tested masterpieces." The works of the present are to be shunned, since we have not yet had time to "gain perspective" on them. This desire to escape into the imaginary security and stability of the past seems to me to reflect a fear of what the insecurity of the present age may bring forth, rather than a willingness to assume the burden of laboring to create a better way of life for all men. Here, however, I wish merely to point out the unarticulated assumption concerning literature teaching upon which that position rests: namely, that when we as teachers present a literary work to the young, we are indicating that here is something which they can accept unquestioningly and in its entirety as "good." It is my contention that we should present *neither* the literature of the present nor the literature of the past to our students with the idea that they are being offered pre-tested, pre-evaluated views of life or models of literary excellence.

Time, unfortunately, cannot do any definitive "testing" for us or for our students. If certain works have survived from age to age, it is because in each age men and women of discrimination experienced them anew, reinterpreted them in terms of the life about them, derived from them new insights applicable to their own contemporary society. They kept the classics alive simply because they themselves were alive in the truest sense, not cut off from the world about them, but aware of the conflicting currents of thought and feeling, the unsolved problems, the new visions struggling to be born. Moreover, a study of the reading of many of those who have helped to build our literary traditions and heritage reveals that they often derived stimulation and insight from contemporary works no less valuable to them because they are no longer read by us. We shirk our responsibility as teachers unless we seek to help our students to live as fully and fruitfully in their age as did the creative spirits in the past. Our task is thus to seek to develop in our students a similar discrimination in terms of an awareness and understanding of their own life today.

Instead of passive exposure to works which they are to accept as already definitively pronounced "good" ("good" for whom and under what circumstances? I venture to ask), the youth needs to be helped to achieve the ability intelligently to question, to challenge, to appreciate. Thus he may acquire the sensitivities and the reasoned system of values that will make him not only proof against the appeal of the shoddy and the sensational, but also receptive to the sound and the humane in all that he reads, whether of the past or present. Those who feel that there is much that is confused, hasty, distorted, in contemporary literature, should all the more be eager to help their students to develop such powers of judgment, through approaching the classic and the contemporary side by side, in the same spirit of intelligent challenge and discrimination.

Sound standards, a reasoned system of values, cannot be legislated, imparted from above, by the teacher or adult, no matter how well intentioned. To be valid and operative, such power of judgment must be achieved by each individual for himself, through the long and slow process of countless experiences reflected upon, through repeated opportunities for seeing relationships and implications in ever wider and more consistent contexts, through learning ever more willingly to reject the easier and lesser satisfaction as the greater and more demanding one is perceived. The teacher can aid, advise, guide him in this quest for a personal set of standards, but cannot present him with such standards, ready-made. The development of the power to discriminate, to accept what is good and to reject what is valueless in literature and in life, is frustrated by any view which sets up a body of works as "time-tested classics," hence passively to be accepted as *ipse facto* valuable, without the necessary struggle to perceive values in terms of life and literature as the student himself experiences them. As George Santayana says in *Three Philosophical Poets*,

> The sole advantage in possessing great works of literature lies in what they can help us to become. In themselves, as feats performed by their authors, they would have forfeited none of their truth or greatness if they had perished before our day. We can neither take away nor add to their past value or inherent dignity. It is only they, insofar as they are appropriate food and not poison for us, that can add to the present value and dignity of our minds. . . . Even native classics have to be reapprehended by every reader. It is this continual digestion of the substance supplied by the past that alone renders the insights of the past still potent in the present and for the future.[1]

But whether what is one man's meat will be another man's poison depends on the digestive apparatus each brings to it. What do we mean by understanding or appreciating a book, if not that the experience offered by the book has been related to, assimilated into, our already accumulated fund of experience, knowledge, insight, and that out of this has come a readjustment, a broadening of sensitivities and a better ordering of values? The reader, young or old, comes to the book from life. He turns for a moment from his direct concern with the various problems and satisfactions of his own life. He will resume his preoccupation with them when the book is closed. There is every reason to believe that as he reads, these concerns are guiding factors in his response to some things, and

1. Cambridge, Harvard University Press, 1922, p. 3.

obtuseness to others, in the book. If the images and the ideas presented by the work have no apparent relevance to past experiences or present emotional needs of the reader, to the questions that face him concerning himself as a personality or his relations to others in the society of his own time, his response to the book will be only feeble, inadequate, or negative.

Feeble, inadequate, or negative, unfortunately, is the response of most students to the literature taught as "the classics" in our schools. Often, evidently, the student functions on two planes. He learns what the teacher says *about* the work, and then has his own private opinion of it. This leads to the feeling that literature is something remote, academic, something to be approached with all the decorum of the classroom. We all know the student who says, "But I have *had* Shakespeare," as though it were something to suffer through and to forget, like the measles. Cut off from the living value that good literature may have for him, the student turns to the more facile satisfactions of the popular magazine and cheap novel.

If we are merely custodians of antiquities, if we use the classics to perpetuate an unthinking ancestor-worship, we are not worthy of being trustees of the great literary heritage which is ours to pass on. But how can we be more than mere antiquarians, unless our attention is focused on both elements in the literary process: on the student as well as on the literary work? Our teaching materials are not only literary works but also the problems, preoccupations, sensitivities and insensitivities, anxieties and aspirations, which our students bring to the literary work. An understanding of the way of life, the emotional conflicts, the personal and social perplexities of the age in which we and our students are living, is as essential for the teacher as the usual apparatus of scholarly training.

When we envisage our task as of helping the student to understand and to evaluate his own responses to books, to become aware of and critical of his own sense of what is important and unimportant in life and literature, we shall make of literature a medium of enjoyment and insight rather than an object of academic study. If we are solving that problem adequately, we need not, indeed, be troubled about the fallacious opposition between the classics and the much-dreaded contemporary writings. We shall be ranging freely with our students through the whole golden realm of literature—of which contemporary literature is an integral part—bringing a challenging receptivity to it and deriving a joyous discriminating enlightenment from it.

The greatness of a work of art, we may maintain, lies in its intensity or breadth of vision, its inner integrity, its power to give us a sense of dominating for the time being the fragmentary, inchoate, multiple diversity of human life. We like to speak of the" permanent" and "traditional" human values which have caused the great works to survive. Yet the warp and woof from which this basic design, these basic values, emerge is, after all, the language, the images of behavior, the habits of emotional response, the customary idea of human relationships, the social arrangements, the inarticulate and unquestioned assumptions, which made up the cultural pattern and intellectual estimate of the author's own day.

Surely, many of the works that we speak of as "things that every person should have read" offer powerful reinforcement to emotional attitudes and assumptions concerning human nature and society that our contemporary life and contemporary science have discarded as inhumane or false. We must at least feel the responsibility for estimating the possible influence of a steady diet of literature emerging out of social systems and moral codes very different from those valued by upright and thinking men in a democracy. Ideas concerning the relations between man and woman, employer and employee, between the citizen and the state, even between man and the universe, as they are reflected in much of our past literature, might, unless approached with such discrimination as I have been urging, reinforce in the minds of our students ideas and attitudes which the person of average enlightenment today considers reactionary or fallacious. To what extent, one may legitimately ask, is such literary study in the schools contributing to the persistent hold of habits of thought and images of behavior no longer appropriate to our present-day knowledge and our aspirations for a more democratic way of life?

The classics merely present our basic problem to us in heightened form. It is easy to understand why they have too often become objects of study instead of media of enjoyment and illumination for the pupil. Much of the reading of the classics tends to become largely an effort to recapture the past, its vocabulary, its view of the world, its customs, its social relationships. Surely, we argue, this is a valuable thing. An important part of education is historical perspective, a liberation from the provincialism of our own time, a knowledge of the extraordinary diversity of ways of life, social codes, philosophic systems, that man has created.

But must we not often seem to our students to be playing a strange adult game, in which one tries to become a contemporary of Chaucer or Shakespeare, Goldsmith or Scott? I am reminded of the remark that even though a man were to reproduce exactly, down to the slightest detail, an eighteenth-century home, there would still remain in it one anachronism—himself. How much more true this is for literature, since the literary work is recreated within the mind and personality of each reader. Historical perspective is valuable, but the idea of perspective implies that the observer of the human scene has himself some fixed location. The modern reader's standpoint must inevitably be the present and its implications for the future.

As we recreate the "background" of the classic for our students, are we not also implicitly or explicitly providing the necessity for acceptance or rejection of the images of life, the moral attitudes, the social arrangements, which those works present, and which may merely be the ephemeral materials through which the author presented some more basic insight? Should we not feel the responsibility for making our students seek to understand what elements in a play of Shakespeare, for example, are peculiar to the time in which it was written, in order that we may disengage those elements which are still relevant to our life today? *Hamlet*, read as a mere revenge story, reflecting the code of an eye for an eye, a tooth for a tooth, can give little enlightenment. As a vibrant image of a sensitive, thoughtful, impulsive personality faced with a world more sinister, more confused, more demanding of drastic decision and action than he had dreamed possible, we can feel its impact in personal and twentieth-century terms. But careful differentiation of these elements from the more ephemeral ones is essential. And does it not follow that the reader must have the sense that he, too lives in a world "out of joint," that he, too, is constantly faced with alternatives none of which satisfy the potentialities of his own nature or of his own sense of possible better ways of life?

All of this brings with it the necessity not only for understanding the works of the past in light of all that we may know about the past, but also for comparison, acceptance and rejection, in terms of all that is best in the thought and aspirations of the present. The classics will remain remote, meaningless, inoperative, unless we lead our students to them in this spirit of clear-sighted discrimination.

## II

It would be absurd and harmful, we have said, to propose to cut off the youth from the literature of the past, for knowledge of the past is an essential part of his equipment for living in and understanding the present. But do not the preceding considerations suggest that it is equally absurd and harmful to restrict our students entirely to the works of the past, to leave them in ignorance, or without power of discrimination, concerning the literature of the present? Just as the fact that a book was written in the past is no guarantee of its worth, so a book's contemporaneity is no guarantee. Still, the great stream of literary expression knows no academic dams and barriers. There is much in the mass of work produced today that represents the areas of growing insight and aspiration of our own age, as did the writings of the past for theirs. We can leave to posterity the problem of deciding what works in our age will still be meaningful for *them*. We shall, however, intellectually cripple the youth of the present if we deprive him of the opportunity for awareness of contemporary tendencies, contemporary problems and hopes, not only as he meets them in his day-to-day living, but as they are pondered on and given thoughtful expression by sensitive writers of his time.

Only as the student encounters these expressions of contemporary life in conjunction with his experience of the literature of the past, will he acquire an understanding of the continued reality, in terms of our age, of the basic problems of man's life that the great writers of the past have wrestled with. Like Milton, men in the present are struggling with the problem of evil in the world. Like him, they are achieving his ultimate insight, that human acts have human consequences, that if man is to possess Paradise, he must strive to dominate himself, to achieve that inner paradise of the reasoning, sensitive spirit. Will not Milton's work become operative in the present only as our students see it in relation to contemporary life and literature? Will not the tragically won wisdom of Lear have present meaning and impact as the student sees in contemporary works, too, the egocentric man of power, bringing ruin and suffering upon himself and others through lack of understanding and concern for them as separate human beings? We shall be defeated in our aim to develop sensitivity and discrimination toward the life and literature of the past, unless we feel the need also for developing a similar sensitivity and discrimination toward the life and literature of the present.

A respect for the dignity of the human being, a desire to enable each individual to develop to his fullest capacities while acting in harmonious cooperation with his fellowmen—values such as these are not to be fostered through mere exposure to the literature of the past. Not from the works in themselves, but from lively interaction with them, may flower heightened sensitivities and powers of judgment based on an ever more humane scale of values.

## III

Thus the valid test of what books should be read by youth is, not what adults or critics of the past have found "good," but what is "good," meaningful, effective, for this particular young human being at this stage of his emotional and intellectual development; "good" in that it offers him human experiences to which he is able to respond intimately and with understanding; "good" in that it enables him to exercise his powers of judgment, to understand in terms of the life he knows, the implications of the personal and emotional choices represented; "good" in that it helps him make the longest possible step forward to greater sensitivity than he now possesses. We need not trouble concerning the value of the book *sub specie aeternitatis*, for only through such growth can he gain the power to respond more fully to ever richer and subtler values in literature and in life. Sometimes a work of the past, a classic—even a "masterpiece"! —will be the "best" book according to our definition of good. Sometimes, and perhaps often, a work of the present will speak more directly and more constructively to him than some much "greater" work of the past. Let us not be distressed by this. The desire to run the whole repertory of the classics down the throats of unresponsive students implies admission of defeat, the assumption that once out of our influence, they will turn no more to good literature. We need not fear the persistence of our present low cultural level, however, if we concentrate, not or forced-feeding of the classics, but on the nourishing of a personal awareness of the joys of literature, and a capacity for critical judgment. We shall then send forth from our schools and colleges men and women eager to turn spontaneously to literature, as their own life creates the need, able to distinguish and to assimilate the good and great, wherever it manifests itself, in the literature of the past and of the present.

We have little real faith in the power and worth of the classics if we fear that they cannot withstand such a challenge. Instead of embalming them in the aura of ancestor-worship, let us make possible for those still meaningful works of the past that life beyond life which Milton envisaged. In place of the dead hand of the past, let us recover for our students the warm clasp of human companionship. Let us lead them to the literature of the past *and* of the present, as to the words of fellow men. From each we shall seek a work of art that will illuminate the question about "man's relation to the world he lives in, man's relation with the men among whom he lives, and, finally, man's relation to himself," which like Maugham's Philip Carey, so many young people today have come to see as the lot of each of us to strive to answer anew.[2]

---

2. I have not here attempted to deal with the implications concerning the development of sensitivity to the so-called formal, or purely esthetic, elements in literature. The first half of my book, *Literature as Exploration* (D. Appleton-Century Co., 1938), treats the relationship between insight and esthetic sensitivity.

Chapter Ten

# The Writer's Dilemma: A Case History and a Critique

So accustomed are we to thinking of Victorian writers as being cabined, cribbed, and confined within the limits of Victorian prudery that there seems to be little point in singling out any one writer's plight for consideration. Particularly is this true of Robert Louis Stevenson, whose genius seemed so blithely to flower in ways congenial to his public, which in return whole-heartedly idolized him. Yet the truth of the matter is that Stevenson felt the pinch of Victorian repression as much as any of his contemporaries. Only recently, since the publication of George S. Hellman's article in the *Century* in 1922, and of his book in 1925, has the official and popular image of the martyred champion of optimism and morality, the somewhat saintly prophet of cheerfulness and resignation, been replaced by the image of a full-blooded man, who in his eagerness for life had experienced and approved much that would have horrified and scandalized the far-flung thousands of his idolators. But, as we have said, the disclosure that even the popular "R. L. S." had been irked by Mrs. Grundy would not in itself seem so amazing. The reason for our singling him out from his fellow-sufferers is the peculiar *modus vivendi* he worked out for himself, the special and self-conscious compromise he arrived at between his own nature and his need of a wide-reading public that would also be a generous patron. An understanding of Stevenson's case may, moreover, throw some light upon the problem of the relation between writer and public today.

Stevenson began to write at a time when for a half-century the English reading public had been increasing in numbers at an extraordinary rate. The spread of literacy and the increase in the solid middle classes had since early in the century made the great reading public—through its representative, the publisher—the patron of literature. This change, from the outset, had aroused the vigilance of the dominant class. What sort of literature was it safe to publish, since it was to be read by the great public that was gaining political power with such alarming rapidity? What ideas about life was it proper to give to that great dependent class, the weaker sex? The novelist, particularly, felt the pressure of these questions. He was confronted constantly, as a survey of the periodicals of the second half of the century shows, with sententious and dogmatic discourses on the duties and province of the novelist. The nineteenth-century reviewer, when he was not warning his readers that novel-reading was essentially a frivolous pastime in which it was not wise to overindulge, was ever ready to point out that the novel must have a "conscious moral purpose." This meant, of course, that the novelist must set out to uphold and reinforce the current moral attitudes. Nor was the reviewer slow to denounce with the utmost virulence any offense against the current prudishness that might somehow have slipped past the vigilance of publishers. Not even George Eliot or Thackeray, to say nothing of such later writers as Hardy or Meredith, had been safe from the accusation of impropriety. Obscure or famous, writer of "three-decker" novels for the ladies' circulating libraries, or author of realistic studies, the novelist found it necessary to make some conscious adjustment to that great and heterogeneous army of patrons, the English reading public.

One of the most curious adjustments, as we have said, was that arrived at by Robert Louis Stevenson. For, contrary to the still popular notion of him, he was fundamentally out of sympathy with his public's sense of the duties and aims of the novelist. It is amazing how many times, in his essays and letters and conversation, Stevenson uttered opinions on the writer's function that were identical with those of the literary rebels of the second half of the century, particularly those writers with whom the attitude of art for art's sake is usually associated, such as George Moore, Henry James, Walter Pater, or even Oscar Wilde.

First of all, Stevenson at various points revealed his hatred of the Victorian dogma as to the "moral purpose" of art. In his essay on *Fontainebleau*, for instance, he says, "Here, in England, too many painters and writers dwell dispersed, unshielded, among the intelligent bourgeois. These, when they are not merely indifferent, prate to him about the lofty aims and moral influence of art." And this insistence on a definite moral purpose is "the ruin" of the artist, Stevenson declares. He goes so far as to maintain that, for him, the essential impulse of the writer is the creation of a beautiful form, or pattern, not the promulgation of ideas or teaching of lessons.

> The love of words and not a desire to publish new discoveries, the love of form and not a novel reading of historical events, mark the vocation of the writer and the painter. The arabesque, properly speaking, and even in literature, is the first fancy of the artist; he first plays with his material as a child plays with a kaleidoscope; and he is already in a second stage when he begins to use his pretty counters for the end of representation . . . it is only the few who will really grow beyond it, and go forward, fully equipped, to do the business of real art—to give life to abstractions and significance and charm to facts.

One would not have expected this almost sanctified writer *virginibus puerisque* to assume the attitudes usually associated with a Walter Pater, a

George Moore, or an Oscar Wilde. Yet are not the above dicta merely another assertion of the essential importance of form in art, such as Walter Pater made in *The Art of Giorgione* and in other essays? Stevenson's remark about the arabesque is curiously like Wilde's contention that "the real artist is he who proceeds, not from feeling to form, but from form to thought and passion." Henry James had demanded, in *The Art of Fiction*, that the novel be judged, not by the unique standard of its didactic usefulness, but for its execution, the art with which the novelist sets forth his vision of life; Stevenson paralleled this with the comment in his essay on Burns, "There is, indeed, only one merit worth considering in a man of letters—that he should write well; and only one damning fault—that he should write ill." Nothing could be farther from the popular Victorian point of view, for which not even the greatest artistry might condone a breach of the conventions.

Undoubtedly, in Stevenson's case, as in that of James and many others of their generation, this jealous and exaggerated vindication of form as the prime concern of the artist was provoked by the contemporary moralistic blindness to aesthetic values, and was in large part reinforced by an impulse derived from nineteenth-century French literature. Between 1874 and 1879 Stevenson spent much of his time in France; one needs neither Stevenson's reminiscences in *The Wrecker* and *Fontainebleau*, nor his biographers' data to see in his defense of the artist a reflection of the aesthetic theories of Flaubert, Baudelaire, and their followers—theories which were, as Stevenson remarked, "in the very air of France" at that time.

With this sense of the artist's responsibility to his ideal of form Stevenson associated also the belief of Flaubert and his followers in the writer's responsibility to his sense of the truth. Stevenson had written in 1881 in *The Morality of the Profession of Letters*:

> Man is imperfect; yet in his literature he must express his own views and preferences; for to do anything else is to do a far more perilous thing than to risk being immoral; it is to be sure of being untrue. . . . To conceal a sentiment, if you are sure you hold it, is to take a liberty with the truth.

Similarly, Henry James, in *The Art of Fiction*, had maintained that an *artistic* morality—the responsibility of the novelist to his subject matter, to life itself as he saw it—transcended all "conscious moral purpose" or loyalty to convention and Sunday-school formulas. Only complete liberty to choose his subject matter and to treat it honestly, James had contended, would enable the novelist to create really serious art. Like James, or George Moore, or Gissing, to mention only a few of the English crusaders for literary freedom, Stevenson also resented the prudish, narrow-minded, timid restrictions placed upon the English novelist by contemporary conventions. Repeatedly, in letters and in conversation, Stevenson lamented the fate of the novelist in "this Anglo-Saxon world." Not even Gissing surpassed the bitterness of Stevenson's remark, quoted by his stepson, Lloyd Osbourne: "The *bourgeoisie's* weapon is starvation. If as a writer or artist you run counter to their narrow notions, they simply and silently withdraw your means of subsistence. I sometimes wonder how many people of talent are executed in this way every year."

Such resentment against English prudishness, combined as it was with a fervent belief in the writer's duty toward the truth, had as its usual concomitant an uncompromising disdain of the public. But Stevenson's contemporary success would in itself be sufficient proof that his attitude was more complex than that. The problem is, rather, how he nevertheless became the idol of the late Victorians.

The answer lies precisely in the clarity of Stevenson's perception that "the *bourgeoisie's* weapon is starvation." His reaction to this was not, however, always one of resentment. In *A Letter to a Young Gentleman Who Proposes To Embrace the Career of Art* he pointed out that he considered writing a trade, a profession. And as in any trade, the worker must satisfy his master, the one who pays. The writer's first duty, Stevenson says, is to earn his living, and the good bourgeois who holds the purse cannot be expected to pay for things that he does not like or that shock him. Until he has earned his living, the writer "must pay assiduous court to the bourgeois who pays him."

Nothing could be more janglingly out of harmony with the ideals set up by Stevenson in the essays mentioned above. Both his English and French brothers in the love of art for its own sake would have said to the young gentleman, "Starve if necessary, but do not compromise your artistic ideas, your sense of beauty and of truth!"

When Stevenson wrote *A Letter to a Young Gentleman* he evidently was in a mood reminiscent of his Scotch middle-class background, as he was when he called art a less "manly" way of life than, for instance, building lighthouses as his father and grandfather had done. And, despite Stevenson's exposition of the tenets of art for art's sake, this practical acceptance of bourgeois realities was no passing mood. The circumstances of Stevenson's marriage, his dependence during the early years of his marriage on his religious and rigidly moralistic father, his desire to be financially independent, to support a family, and to maintain a certain generous manner of living, did not permit Stevenson to forget the necessity of pleasing whoever held the purse. Stevenson's biographers have made it clear that certainly Mrs. Stevenson never forgot that the public should be given what it wanted. She watched over Stevenson unremittingly, read his books before publication, that he might not destroy or blur the impression of him that the public so enthusiastically cherished. Even after his death she resisted the publication of anything that might shock or disturb the thousands of readers who turned to him so eagerly and confidently for edification, encouragement, and entertainment.

Yet here again Stevenson did not follow simply and unequivocally the point of view he espoused. Others before him had felt that it was the writer's duty to give the public what it wanted. Dickens, for instance, had also believed that the most important thing was to please the public, to gain their sympathy and suffrage. He had been willing frankly and ungrudgingly to modify or suppress anything that might seem disagreeable or immoral to his public, whether or not he fully agreed with their prejudices. Discussing the idea that he might show Walter Gay in *Dombey and Son* declining into dissipation and ruin, Dickens asks, "Do you think it may be done, without making people angry?" He did not do it, and he undoubtedly felt no pangs of conscience at thus belying his sense of what would be most true to life. Completely identified with his public, Dickens felt no other responsibility than to please his readers, and as many readers as possible.

Therein lies the difference between Dickens' and Stevenson's attitudes. Dickens' conscience was free, Stevenson's was not. The writer, for Stevenson, had responsibilities toward art and life as well as toward his public. Stevenson had been inoculated with the contemporary French worship of art, the ideals of perfect form and uncompromising truth. He could no longer, like Dickens, with untroubled conscience alter his vision of reality.

And to seek a large public, in the Victorian era, meant inevitably to make such concessions. Careful as Stevenson was, even his *The Beach of Falesá*, in which a trader marries a native Samoan by means of a false certificate but later makes her legally his wife, was objected to as immoral, and his sprightly *The Treasure of Franchard* was refused as improper for a family magazine!

Concessions were necessary, for the simple reason that Stevenson did not share the moral values of his public, as, fundamentally, Dickens did. Stevenson, in his essays, revealed a concern for conduct, a preoccupation with the moral side of life, and a hatred of the scientific pessimism of the times, which explain in part why his essays were so sympathetic to the English public. But his Victorian readers seem not to have noticed that his gospel of energy and optimism was not always in harmony with their own conventional morality. Though he rejected the pessimism of his "decadent" contemporaries, Stevenson was still in agreement with their condemnation of the narrowness of Victorian morality. In *Pulvis et Umbra*, for example, there is an implicit criticism of the bourgeois moral code, with its rigid conception of right and wrong. Victorian optimism was sustained only by shutting the eyes to much in life; Stevenson evidently believed that one might look at all of life, the bad and the good, and still remain optimistic.

Stevenson in his youth had sought those experiences that most obviously signified revolt from the rigid conventions. His poem of the eighties (first published in 1916 by the Boston Bibliophile Society), which opens

Hail! childish slaves of social rules

reflects the simple terms in which this revolt expressed itself:

O fine, religious decent folk,
In Virtue's flaunting gold and scarlet,
I sneer between two puffs of smoke,—
Give me the publican and harlot.

Even in his settled maturity there lingered an unorthodox sympathy with those brave enough to cast convention aside and live in terms of their fundamental humanity. As for the particular bugbear of the Victorians, nothing could be less

Victorian than Stevenson's reply to a question concerning *Dr. Jekyll and Mr. Hyde* (in a letter to J. P. Bocock, referred to in the *New York Sun*, January 1, 1888, and quoted by G. S. Hellman in *The True Stevenson*):

> There is . . . no harm whatsoever in what prurient fools call "immorality." The harm was in Jekyll, because he was a hypocrite—not because he was fond of women; he says so himself; but people are so filled full of folly and inverted lust, that they think of nothing but sexuality. The Hypocrite let out the beast Hyde—who is no more sexual than another, but who is the essence of cruelty and malice and selfishness and cowardice, and these are the diabolic in man—not this poor wish to love a woman that they make such a cry about.

Both the youthful poem and the mature statement possess a certain excessiveness that is the unfortunate earmark of reaction against an equally excessive prudery. Yet what matters to us is the evidence that Stevenson was fundamentally unsympathetic toward the moral timidity of his contemporaries.

This, then, was Stevenson's dilemma: either to render faithfully his sense of life, and suffer the fate of all non-conformists, or to cast his work in the accepted molds, and violate his artistic honor.

A stronger or more courageous man, or one less encumbered with domestic responsibilities, would not have hesitated. The young rebels in France, a generation before, and some among Stevenson's own English contemporaries, had seen the dilemma, and had chosen to make a virtue out of the necessary poverty and neglect that accompanied a disregard for entrenched ways of thinking. But Stevenson lacked either the singleness of purpose of a Flaubert or the naïve sense of identification with his public of a Dickens. For Stevenson neither path was open.

Stevenson escaped into neutral territory. Perhaps the most important clue to the man and his attitude toward his work is the casual and unremarked passage in *A Gossip on Romance*, published in 1882:

> There is a vast deal in life and letters both which is not immoral, but simply non-moral; which either does not regard the human will at all, or deals with it in obvious and healthy relations; where the interest turns, not upon what a man shall choose to do, but on how he manages to do it; not on the passionate slips and hesitations of the conscience, but on the problems of the body and of the practical intelligence, in clean, open-air adventure, the shock of arms or the diplomacy of life. With such material as this it is impossible to build a play, for the serious theatre exists solely on moral grounds, and is a standing proof of the dissemination of the human conscience. But it is possible to build, upon this ground, the most joyous of verses, and the most lively, beautiful, and buoyant tales.

Here is the secret of Stevenson's evasion of his dilemma. To deal with ordinary life in his stories and novels, to treat men and women meeting the usual problems of life, and yet to please his public, would have required a falsification of life as he knew it, a conformity to standards he felt to be outworn. Stevenson recognized this, and chose to confine himself to those spheres in which, if he could not tell the whole truth about life, at least he need have no so-called "moral purpose" and need perpetrate no direct falsifications. Other writers, such as George Moore or Henry James, had declared that all of life was the legitimate province of art, that art had its own ethic, and that the subject matter of literature was outside the jurisdiction of practical Victorian morality. Stevenson could not bring himself to make this challenge. Only thus, by restricting himself to neutral, "non-moral" territory, could he devote himself to the solution of purely artistic problems and yet avoid outraging the moral timidity of his public.

Stevenson was quite self-conscious and articulate about his desire to skirt the moral "No Man's Land" of his day. In *A Humble Remonstrance* of 1884, for instance, he defends the right of the novelist to depart from ordinary life, and places the novel of adventure on a par with the novel of character or emotion.

> In this elementary novel of adventure, the characters need to be presented with but one class of qualities—the warlike and the formidable. . . . Danger is the matter with which this class of novel deals; fear, the passion with which it idly trifles; and the characters are portrayed only so far as they realize the sense of danger and provoke the sympathy of fear. To add more traits, to be too clever, to start the hare of moral or intellectual interest while we are running the fox of material interest, is not to enrich but to stultify your tale. The stupid reader will only be offended, and the clever reader lose the scent.

"Romance" is, by definition, then, that enchanted realm in which the writer need never meet the challenge of a moral issue; in which, indeed, to avoid moral choices is an artistic merit. One might bravely fight the pirates, or take all manner of chances on the heather with David Balfour and Alan Breck, or roam the world with the Master of Ballantrae—and beneath all the fun of the adventure one might feel the security of morally neutral ground in a bigoted world. There is something about all this "adventure" of Stevenson's that is, alas, pathetically unadventurous.

The stultifying effect of his compromise seems immeasurable. One may see the results of it, for instance, in Stevenson's discussion of how he planned *The Master of Ballantrae*. Most of his attention is devoted to the externals, to such matters as the ingenious working-out of devices for carrying the story into three continents. Relatively little discussion is devoted to the situation from which the action springs—a situation that might, indeed, have been worked out most powerfully, among the four people concerned, within four walls— provided, that is, that one wished to hazard such concentration on human ambitions and passions. Hence it is that in the book itself Stevenson gives us only rare glimpses into the inner life of the intense and stormy characters whose involved adventures we follow. Only in Stevenson's last, unfinished work, *Weir of Hermiston*, did he give promise of consistently accepting the challenge of the rich human implications of his story.

If Stevenson had had no other leanings we should gratefully have accepted his charming and entertaining romances, and have asked no more from him than he could give. Certainly, one part of Stevenson's nature, nourished on Scotch legend, delighted in the breezy pursuit of adventure and the making of "lively, beautiful, and buoyant tales." But the evidence indicates that Stevenson did at heart aspire to a more direct grasp on life. George Moore had said of him, "If any man living in this end of the century needed freedom of expression for the distinct development of his genius, that man is R. L. Stevenson." The paradoxical truth seems to be that if Stevenson had given free rein to his artistic interests and highly sensuous temperament, he might have written in a daringly realistic vein. He wrote to Sidney Colvin in May, 1892:

> With all my romance, I am a realist and a prosaist, and a most fanatical lover of plain physical sensations plainly and expressly rendered; hence my perils. To do love in the same spirit as I did (for instance) D. Balfour's fatigue in the heather; my dear sir, there were grossness, ready made! And hence, how to sugar?

Since Stevenson preferred not "to sugar," we have seen what line of escape he usually took. Yet evidently not without certain regrets and lapses, since G. S. Hellman tells of the manuscript of a realistic novel dealing with the life of a prostitute. Stevenson probably planned to draw upon his own experiences. In his student days he had frequented the low resorts of Edinburgh and had been deeply in love with a young prostitute—the Claire, evidently, of the poems edited by Professor W. P. Trent and George S. Hellman in 1921, and the mother of the unborn child of the poem, "God Gave to Me a Child in Part" (in G. S. Hellman's 1916 edition of Stevenson's unpublished poems). Though it is unlikely that Stevenson would have slavishly imitated the Goncourts or Zola, he might have turned their realistic approach to his own use, as Moore did in *Esther Waters*. Stevenson's realistic aspirations and sense of divergence from the French, as well as his feeling of frustration, are touched on in his remarks to his stepson:

> How the French misuse their freedom; see nothing worth writing about save the eternal triangle; while we, who are muzzled like dogs, but who are infinitely wider in our outlook, are condemned to avoid half the life that passes us by. What books Dickens could have written had he been permitted! Think of Thackeray as unfettered as Flaubert or Balzac! What books I might have written myself! But they give us a little box of toys, and say to us, "You mustn't play with anything but these."

Stevenson may have approached his novel with some such belief that he could contribute a profounder note to the realistic method. But the distress and disapproval of Mrs. Stevenson, her fear that Stevenson's reputation would be wrecked and his thousands of readers alienated, are said to have led Stevenson in a moment of despair to destroy the manuscript of his novel. (Mr. Hellman claims that Henry James's *The Author of Beltraffio* was based on this episode.) The first version of *Dr. Jekyll and Mr. Hyde* suffered a similar fate. Poor Stevenson found it in the long run wiser not to venture at all outside the realms of "Romance."

In declaring romance to be the twilight zone of morality, Stevenson was, of course, overstating his case. Not even in his special kind of romance could one escape moral implications. (It is conceivable, for instance, that controversies might, in another age, have raged about whether David Balfour should have helped Alan Breck in *Kidnapped*.) The magical protection of Stevenson's "Romance" lay, not in the absence of all moral choices, but in the absence of those particular moral choices about which Victorian society was most intensely concerned.

Stevenson himself, in a letter to Colvin in February, 1892, touched the sore spot directly. He exclaims, "This is a poison bad world for the romancer, this Anglo-Saxon world: *I usually get out of it by not having any women in it at all* . . ." It was not enough to withdraw into "Romance"; he restricted his range still further; he sought to eliminate women entirely, for only thus could he avoid the necessity to "sugar." In other words, he attempted to avoid precisely those subjects about which the society of his time had the keenest prejudices. The parts of life into which Stevenson withdrew were not, as he claimed, "non-moral"; they were "non-controversial." Behind the image of Stevenson, the lover of romance, the celebrator of the joy of "twopence colored" illusion, there lurks the distressing image of the writer who sought out precisely those moral regions about which his public cared least.

It is shocking to the contemporary mind to think of a writer, a master of technique, deliberately cutting himself off from almost all the most significant and most profound materials of human life, consciously restricting himself to those aspects of experience which were safe precisely because of their lack of moral significance for his time. We do not, of course, feel that to write a realistic novel about a prostitute is the height of the artist's felicity. Rather, just as the young Stevenson's sallies into the dissipated life of the underworld were a sad product of too puritanical a discipline, so Stevenson's impulse to make such subject matter the symbol of artistic freedom was another unfortunate result of Victorian social bigotry. Since even to write about normally respectable people in an honest manner would have been attacked as immoral, it was natural that the early realists, in their reaction, should have chosen the most *outré* of subjects as a sign of complete emancipation. The responsibility lies with the society that made it necessary for the novelist to react so violently, or, as in the case of Stevenson, to seek a conscious escape from vital problems and moral choices into safe neutrality.

We cannot dismiss this revelation of Stevenson's sad compromise as merely another illustration of the disastrous effects of Victorian prudery.

Stevenson's plight has a broader significance. The Victorians, to be sure, resisted any departure from the conventionalized and sentimentalized version of sex. They probably felt that once the passionate undercurrents of life were frankly recognized, down would tumble the whole structure of bourgeois respectabilities—the very basis of a stable petty capitalist society. But Victorian society was merely running true to its own pattern of culture, as every society does. Every society has its taboos, its tissue of dogma, to question which seems to threaten the very social fabric. In Victorian society, the first barrier, the bulwark against further challenge happened to be erected at the point of the relations between man and woman. In other societies the primary defenses may be erected at other levels; the taboo may fall elsewhere, on religious, political, economic, or other social attitudes.

The writer in our present-day society does not entirely escape Stevenson's dilemma. The problem today is at once clarified and complicated by the fact that the writer does not attempt to reach so broad a cross-section of the reading public as Stevenson did. So tremendous has the public become that there are many separate strata of readers to which a writer may choose to address himself. Still, for the writer of Stevenson's literary pretensions the problem remains. We are living in an age when in some countries the artist is subjected to an active censorship more drastic than any mere pecuniary or critical chastising administered by Victorian society. And can we be sure that the democratic countries, in those matters vitally important to them, are more liberal than the Victorians?

To point to the extraordinary freedom in the treatment of sex accorded the writer at present, to say that Stevenson today would have had no difficulties, is to evade the question. The realm of taboo has changed since Stevenson's time. Paradoxically enough, the writer who now seeks neutral, "non-moral" territory may find it precisely in the fields forbidden to Stevenson. To deal with sex, with personal relations, is one way of escape for the novelist today. For, as in the days of the landed aristocracy, the vested interests in our society are no longer firmly interwoven with sex restrictions. Whether we like it or not, the pressure of changing economic and social conditions, the values for which the masses as well as the masters are striving, the things that vitally matter to the society as a whole, tend to make sex increasingly a personal, less a group, matter. Thus the liberalism about sex, the preponderance of works dealing with sex, reflect what from one point of view might be considered as indifference; society seems to be less and less concerned with the individual's ordering of his personal life.

Now that the bad effects of the violent reaction from Victorian pruriency are wearing off, we can be grateful for this liberalism and honesty. The writer may treat the relations between man and woman frankly, he need no longer cast a rosy glamour about the Family, with the father as a stern but benevolent minor deity and the mother a cross between saint and upper servant. The writer may be as honest as he wishes—as long as he confines himself to purely personal matters. But if his genius happens to lead him into other, broader fields, more vitally important to society at this moment, can he be so certain of tolerance? The writers whose temperament leads them naturally to deal with the individual purely as an individual are, perhaps, fortunate; but those whose interests lead them to place the individual frankly against his social and economic background, to present, as Stevenson did in the case of sex, a dissenting point of view on social or economic aspects of life, may find themselves in Stevenson's dilemma. His remark that "the *bourgeoisie's* weapon is starvation" remains just as true today.

Stevenson's concept of "non-moral" or neutral subjects—those which society unconsciously feels not to be fundamental to its structure—should give pause. How many of the writers today who so boldly offer us the anatomy of love, or who so realistically study the pathology of emotion, are merely finding an escape as Stevenson did? and perhaps without the saving grace of Stevenson's honest admission of his plight?

We do not mean that the artist should always be in revolt against the dominant attitudes of his time. The ideal is, rather, a rational society with which the artist might be completely sympathetic, and in which he would function normally as an integral member. Nor do we wish to set up a hierarchy of approved subjects for art. We feel, for instance, that romance is an entirely legitimate field of artistic creation, and that the subtle study of individual psychology is part of the permanently important material of art—but not, however, as an escape, a substitute for the materials the artist fundamentally desires to treat, and dare not. For the artist who also possesses the temperament of the rebel there is, of course, no problem. But how many such rebels are there, and what price must they pay? As Santayana has said, "to defy the world is a serious business, and requires the greatest courage." The only guarantee against the necessity for the artist's flight from the most vital materials of his time is an aggressive public sense of the artist's right to tread seemingly dangerous ground, and a willingness on the part of the reading public to have its fundamental prejudices and presumptions challenged. Only under such circumstances could we feel sure that art might flourish with complete honesty and the writer seek out the materials entirely congenial to his mind and talent.

Such propitious conditions will be created only when we become conscious of the automatic tendencies of our culture, when we see what taboos are imposed upon the artist, what intellectual barriers set up, and when we seek to counteract those automatic pressures. Otherwise, as we saw in the case of the Victorian attitude toward sex, excess and irrationality in one direction will stifle the free play of mind, and inevitably bring an equally excessive and irrational reaction. Hence, it is important for the welfare of the culture, as well as for the healthy flowering of the artist's own genius, that each artistic temperament should be free to find its own medium, its own materials. Like most ideals, such a completely self-critical society may probably never, it is true, be fully attained. What our self-consciousness may, at least, accomplish is a less smug assumption that our society offers the height of tolerance and freedom of expression, and an increased realization of the importance for art of a social atmosphere that welcomes challenge. For, as Henry James said, "no one can ever have made a seriously artistic attempt without becoming conscious of an immense increase—a kind of revelation—of freedom. One perceives, in that case . . . that the province of art is all life, all feeling, all observation, all vision."

# Chapter Eleven

# The Genesis of Pater's
## *Marius the Epicurean*

T.S. Eliot has declared the "true importance" of Walter Pater's *Marius the Epicurean* to be simply "as a document of one moment in the history of thought and sensibility in the nineteenth century."[1] Readers who do not share Eliot's orthodoxy will find the book's amalgam of humanistic rationalism with religious emotion still meaningful in the face of the eternal enigmas. Moreover, a case could be made for the book's literary importance both for the author's contemporaries and for later writers such as Virginia Woolf or Proust or James Joyce—with Pater viewed not only as a critic or stylist, but also as one seeking to develop a fictional method in his series of "imaginary portraits." *His Sensations and Ideas*—the subtitle of *Marius*—surely could apply to much twentieth-century fiction. Hence the work maintains interest both as a document in the history of ideas and as a work of literature.

Published in 1885, this portrait of a sensitive young patrician in the entourage of Marcus Aurelius embodied Pater's own intellectual autobiography. Marius, after a childhood pervaded with the charm of traditional religious observances, becomes a skeptic. He passes through a phase of intense aestheticism, then derives from the literature and philosophies of the ancient world an aesthetically and morally elevated Epicureanism. At the court, he encounters the exalted morality of Marcus Aurelius, but the Stoic philosopher lacks the warm humanity, the gracious hopefulness, which Marius finally discovers in the Christian community at Rome. Although he remains an agnostic, he meets his death by taking the place of his Christian friend in a time of persecution. Throughout, we are aware of a modern sensibility and of modern parallels for the philosophic conflicts.

Kenneth Allott's proposed explanation of Pater's choice of setting for his essentially nineteenth-century hero revived for me an earlier interest in the

---

1. "The Place of Pater," in *The Eighteen-Eighties*, ed. Walter de la Mare (Cambridge, 1930), p. 106; reprinted as "Arnold and Pater" in *Selected Essays* (London, 1932).

sources of *Marius*, and my inquiry soon broadened into concern with various possible springs of inspiration for the work. The following discussion seeks to make explicit the rationale of choice among these alternatives, and to present implications of such a study in the logic of influences for the work both as a document in intellectual history and as a work of art.

"It seems highly probable," Allott writes, that "the germ of *Marius the Epicurean*"[2] is to be found in Matthew Arnold's "Marcus Aurelius," which Pater could have read in 1863 in the *Victoria Magazine* and in 1865 in Arnold's *Essays in Criticism*. Arnold speaks of Aurelius as "a man like ourselves" living "in an epoch akin to our own."[3] Allott suggests that from this essay Pater gathered "the notion of a parallel between Victorian England and Antonine Rome with Marcus Aurelius as a typical 'modern man,'" that Arnold's discussion of Lucretius in "On the Modern Element in Literature" might have reminded Pater of this again in 1869, and that the publication of W.W. Capes' *The Roman Empire of the Second Century* in 1876 would have provided "detailed material for making use of Arnold's comparison."[4] We know that Pater echoed, reinforced, and adapted to his own temperamental mode many of the notes first struck by Arnold.[5] To think of Arnold's words in "Marcus Aurelius" as the germ of Pater's book is thus not only plausible but also satisfying, since it adds another link in the close and intricate relationship between the two writers. Why, then, cavil at this suggestion?

Allott's phrasing reminds us of Henry James' efforts to recapture "the productive germ"[6] for each of his novels. Especially suggestive is James' remark in the preface to "The Aspern Papers," that "the seeking fabulist . . . *comes upon the interesting thing as Columbus came upon the isle of San Salvador, because he had moved in the right direction for it.*"[7] He "finds" the germinating idea

---

2. Kenneth Allott, "Pater and Arnold," *Essays in Criticism*, II (1952), 219.

3. Matthew Arnold, *Works* (London, 1903), III, 389. Arnold praises the translator, Long, for treating Aurelius' writings "as documents with a side of modern applicability and living interest." Perhaps the influence of the translator should be seen as in part the source of the interest in Marcus Aurelius to be pointed out below.

4. Allott, *loc, cit*. I agree with Allott's views on the suggestions made by R.V. Osbourn in "*Marius the Epicurean*," *Essays in Criticism*, I (1951), 387–403. Osbourn argues that the choice of setting appears to have been prompted by *The Roman Empire of the Second Century* by W. W. Capes, who had been Pater's tutor. Allott objects that, although Pater undoubtedly used this book, there is little in it to provide the initial suggestion for a comparison between Victorian and late Roman times. Nor, as Allott says, is this point met by Osbourn's remarks concerning the numerous "Victorian comparisons of contemporary life with the life of Greece and Rome," or his passing reference to a vogue for historical novels dealing with Christianity in an ancient setting, such as Kingsley's *Hypatia* (1853) and Newman's *Callista* (1856).

5. Louise Rosenblatt, *L'Idée de l'art pour l'art dans la littérature anglaise pendant la période victorienne* (Paris, 1931), pp. 172, 182, 186 f., 265; T.S. Eliot, "The Place of Pater," in *The Eighteen-Eighties*, ed. W. de la Mare, pp. 93–106; Geoffrey Tillotson, "*Criticism and the Nineteenth Century* (London, 1951), Chap. IV.

6. Henry James, *The Art of the Novel* (New York, 1948), p. 79.

7. *Ibid.*, p. 159.

because he is prepared for an "alert recognition" of its potentialities. Hence, at least as important as the author's exposure to a given "germ" is his readiness at that time to respond, his state of receptivity. In the case of *Marius*, this state of receptivity arose about 1878. James' account of the genesis of *The Portrait of a Lady*, with only the substitution of "young man" for "young woman" in the passage that I have italicized, applies as well to Pater in 1878:

> Trying to recover here, for recognition, the germ of my idea, I see that it must have consisted not at all in any conceit of a "plot," nefarious name, in any flash, upon the fancy, of a set of relations, or in any one of those situations that, by a logic of their own, immediately fall, for the fabulist, into movement . . . but altogether *in the sense of a single character, the character and aspect of a particularly engaging young woman, to which all the usual elements of a "subject," certainly of a setting, were to need to be super-added.*[8]

Pater had early sought indirect expression for his autobiographical impulse. When in 1873 he had spoken out in his own person in the conclusion to his essays on the Renaissance, espousing a rarefied Epicureanism—"To burn always with this hard, gemlike flame . . ."—he had been attacked by moralists and misunderstood by disciples. He had then turned to the indirect method of the "imaginary portrait" in a modern setting. The first of these, that tender remembrance of things past, "The Child in the House," was published in 1878.[9] Its autobiographical character and its resemblance to the childhood of Marius have often been noted. "Imaginary Portrait 2. An English Poet,"[10] found in Pater's unpublished papers, represents another stage in the evolution of this nineteenth-century alter ego, withdrawn, contemplative, sensitive to beauty, aspiring to an ideal way of life. But, as the novelist Mary Arnold Ward, Pater's Oxford neighbor and friend, remarked in her review of *Marius*, Pater had obviously broken off this vein because it was too patently autobiographical.[11] Thus, after 1878, Pater had his idealized alter ego, his—to use James' phrase—"particularly engaging" young man; he had his "subject," the quest for a philosophy of life. The setting was yet to be "super-added," a setting sufficiently remote to mask the personal source, yet sufficiently similar to his own epoch to permit him to convey contemporary implications.

The paucity of Pater's publications from 1878 until the appearance of *Marius* has led to the assumption that he began working on it in that year. In 1880, he resigned his tutorship at Brasenose College in order to devote himself more fully to writing. The dates on the final page of *Marius* are "1881–1884"; it was not until 1882 that he went to Rome, evidently to make studies for this book.[12] Hence the late 1870s, and especially the years 1878 to

---

8. *Ibid.*, p. 42.
9. "Imaginary Portraits: I. The Child in the House," *Macmillan's*, XXXVIII (1878), 313.
10. Ed. May Ottley, *Fortnightly Review*, CXXIX (1931), 433–448.
11. *Macmillan's*, LII (1885), 133.
12. William Sharp, *Papers Critical and Reminiscent* (London, 1912), p. 212.

1881, represent the period of receptivity, when Pater was "moving in the direction" of his novel, and would have been especially "alert" to suggestions concerning a remote setting with modern traits. In this period Pater may have recalled Arnold's essay of 1863, with its analogy between the age of Marcus Aurelius and the nineteenth century. But the hypothesis of a single influence operating *in vacuo*, so to speak, for a decade and a half is somewhat oversimplified.

A pluralistic hypothesis seems to be required, especially for a writer as alert to contemporary intellectual currents and as eclectic as Pater.[13] In *Marius*, his readers found Pater's own effort at a selection and synthesis among various philosophical positions with which they were familiar. The disillusion with orthodox religion, the positivism of Mill or Comte, the theories of Darwin and Spencer, the epistemology of Kant, the Hegelian view of history, Goethe's quest for universality, and the philosophy of Spinoza are some of the current interests reflected in his work. Similarly, in selecting second-century Rome as the setting for these themes, Pater was using an idea not unfamiliar to contemporary readers. In the late 1870s, periodicals such as *The Fortnightly Review* or *Macmillan's Magazine*, to both of which he himself contributed, and various current books provided reminders of the modernity of the age of Marcus Aurelius, and pointed the analogy between contemporary philosophic tensions and the relations of Epicureanism, Stoicism, and Christianity in the second century. In the *Fortnightly Review* for May 1, 1882, Frederic W.H. Myers even felt it necessary to apologize for such a "well worn" subject as Marcus Aurelius. "Few characters in history," he wrote, "have been oftener or more clearly discussed during the present age. . . . The subject has lost, no doubt, its literary freshness, but . . . even an increased interest, indeed, may be felt at the present time . . ."—and he emphasized its modern significance.[14]

Among the works which Myers may have had in mind, in addition to the Matthew Arnold essay, are W.W. Story's "A Conversation with Marcus Aurelius" in the *Fortnightly Review* for February 1, 1873[15] and Frederick Pollock's "Marcus Aurelius and the Stoic Philosophy" in the January 1879 issue of *Mind*, both of which stress Aurelius' modernity. Even Capes' history of the Antonines need not stand alone as a source of historical details. The *London Quarterly Review* for October 1874 reviews the "valuable" social history of the Antonines by Forbiger. This German work used the device of a narrator, a young Greek, who, like Marius, became a secretary of the emperor and had "the privilege of beholding Aurelius in public and private."[16] Capes himself in

---

13. Helen Hawthorne Young, *The Writings of Walter Pater: A Reflection of British Philosophical Opinion from 1860 to 1890* (Lancaster, Pa. 1933).

14. XXXVII (1882), 565.

15. XIX (1873), 188. Young, p. 100, notes passages anticipating ideas in *Marius*.

16. "'Hellas und Rom' [A Popular View of the Public and Private Life of the Greeks and Romans. Part I. Rome under the Antonines] von Dr. Albert Forbiger," *London Quarterly Review*, XLIII (1874), 125.

1880 added a volume on *Stoicism*, which contains a chapter on Marcus Aurelius and discusses the contemporary implications of his philosophy.[17]

Also in 1880 there appeared a companion to Capes' *Stoicism*, a book on *Epicureanism* by William Wallace, like Pater a fellow and tutor at Oxford.[18] The first sentence of Wallace's book singles out the period of Marcus Aurelius as one in which four schools were dividing the best thought of the time. In the course of the book, analogies are drawn between ancient and modern philosophies, and Jeremy Bentham and Auguste Comte are described as modern analogues of Epicurus.[19] Pater surely owed something to Wallace's sympathetic presentation of Epicureanism, yet here again we encounter other possibilities. In 1879 he might have read in English periodicals[20] long discussions of J. M. Guyau's *La Morale d'Epicure, et ses rapports avéc les doctrines contemporaines* (Paris, 1878), which treated Epicureanism mainly as the forerunner of modern utilitarian and hedonistic theories.

Two other examples of the recurrent idea of the modernity of the second century are also rather curious anticipations of *Marius*. Pater devotes Chapter X, "The Golden Book," to Apuleius and introduces him as a character in Chapter XX. "The Golden Ass of Apuleius" by W.H. Mallock, in *Fraser's Magazine* for September 1876, praises the work as a source of knowledge about second-century Rome and cites modern literary analogues for various aspects of the tale. Especially in the discussion of Apuleius' treatment of the Cupid and Psyche story, "its wayward humor, its Keats-like poetry," Mallock foreshadows Pater's retelling of it in *Marius*.[21] A month after the publication of the Mallock article, there appeared in *Fraser's* what might be considered a companion article, "Lucian," by J.A.F. (James Anthony Froude?). Lucian, we are told, enables us to see the life of his times and, moreover, offers helpful counsel for the present, which, like the second century, is "once more in a cycle of analogous doubts."[22] The article ends with a translation of one of Lucian's dialogues. Again, we note that Pater uses a quotation from Lucian as the epigraph of *Marius*,[23] quotes from his work in Chapter XX, [24] and introduces Lucian as a character participating in one of his own dialogues, the *Hermotimus*, in Chapter XXIV, "A Conversation Not Imaginary."

17. W.W. Capes, *Stoicism* (London, 1880), pp. 220–229, 249.

18. R.W. Macan, "Oxford in the 'Seventies," in *The Eighteen-Seventies*, ed. Harley Granville-Barker (New York, 1929), p. 235.

19. Wallace, *Epicureanism* (London, 1880), pp. 1 f., 14, 224, 264 f., et passim.

20. *Athenaeum*, Aug. 30, 1879, no. 2705, p. 266; H. Sidgwick, *Mind*, IV (1879), 582.

21. N.S., XIV (1876), 373.

22. *Ibid.*, p. 425.

23. *Lucian*, with an English translation by A. M. Harmon (London, 1921), III, 231. Pater would, of course, have been acquainted with Apuleius and Lucian; our concern here is with emphasis on their modernity.

24. *Marius the Epicurean: His Sensations and Ideas* (London, 1910), II, 83 f. Unless the first edition is indicated, all references are to this more easily available Library Edition, which follows the final text of the third edition.

By the late 1870s and early 1880s, then, when Pater was moving toward his book, the idea of a parallelism between contemporary and Antonine times was very much in the air. Hence, chronological priority is not a guarantee that we can pinpoint Arnold's essay as the single germ of *Marius*. Pater's actual choice of the second century for the setting of his novel may have been crystallized by any of a number of publications later than Arnold's essay of 1863. At the very least, Arnold's brief remarks must have been repeatedly reinforced by such frequent references to second-century Rome as we have noted. We have been reminded that, *when a parallelism exists, we need to ask how the date of its encounter relates to the period of the author's readiness to respond. And we need to place even the most likely single source in the context of possible alternatives or reinforcing influences operating at the time of the probable inception of the work.*

The suggestion of an English germ has focused our attention thus far mainly on English publications at the probable time of the genesis of *Marius*. But our pluralistic hypothesis and Pater's interest in foreign literatures must lead us further afield. The first volume of Arnold's *Essays in Criticism*, which contained the study of Marcus Aurelius, is undoubtedly important in Pater's career, but primarily as a precedent for critical attention to foreign literatures, ancient and modern.[25] The Pater of the late 1870s was accustomed to turn for intellectual sustenance and literary subjects to the classical world, to Italy, to Germany, to France, as well as to England.[26] His continuing interest in German thought is reflected in his work of this period; over his Greek studies broods the spirit of Winckelmann, of Goethe, of Schiller; Hegel's aesthetics, an early inspiration, provides a "critical instrument"; the repeated references to *Wilhelm Meister* may not be without significance in Pater's desire to write a *Bildungsroman*. His interest in French literature is equally manifest: his debt in theory and practice to Flaubert, his knowledge of Baudelaire and Gautier, his admiration for, among others, Balzac, Stendhal, the Goncourts, Hugo, George Sand, Sainte-Beuve, and Mérimée. Any study of possible sources for Pater's work should recognize his cosmopolitan interests. Discussions of *Marius* have, however, tended to ignore certain French affinities and possible sources of this work. Some years ago I published a preliminary study of French sources;[27] the problem is here re-examined in a broader context, in the light of additional evidence, with a closer analysis of fictional methods, and with a deepened concern for such factors as the writer's receptivity.

In turning to the question of French sources, we move from concern simply with statements of an idea—the suggested similarity between the Antonine

25. George Saintsbury, *A History of Criticism* (London, 1949), III, 535.

26. Rosenblatt, *L'Idée de l'art pour l'art*, pp. 186–205. Mr. John Leje of the University of London has informed me that he is preparing a thesis on the German background of Pater's thought, going beyond the work of Bernhard Fehr.

27. "*Marius l'Épicurien* de Walter Pater et ses points de départ français," *RLC*, XV (1935), 97–106. Pater himself claims to speak for both French and English contemporaries: "Let the reader pardon me if here and there I seem to be passing from Marius to his modern representatives—from Rome, to Paris or London" (*Marius*, II, 16).

and Victorian ages—to actual literary parallelisms. Curiously enough, Pater himself provides a clue of the kind usually relished by seekers after sources: a parallelism of character, plot, and philosophic position. In *Macmillan's Magazine* for November 1887 he published a long and laudatory unsigned article on a French work, "M. Lemaitre's *Sérénus* and Other Tales."[28] His extended account of *Sérénus* reads for the most part like a synopsis of *Marius*. The French story "embodies the imaginary confession of a supposed Christian martyr, who was not in reality a Christian at all." Pater describes him in terms applicable to his own Marius: "It is a charming figure, certainly, which Sérénus displays, rich with intellectual endowments, and a heart that, amid all the opportunities for corruption which could beset a fortunate patrician in the days of Domitian, never loses its purity to the last—affectionate, reflective, impressible by pity, with 'the gift of tears.'" Pater remarks on "the varied intellectual interests offered to a reflective mind in that curious, highly educated, wistful age."

> In a few effective but sparing traits Sérénus depicts his intellectual course, through the noble dreams of a chaste Stoicism, through the exquisite material voluptuousness of Epicureanism when the natural reaction had come, until, having exhausted experience, as he fancies, he proposes to die.

At this point, he is introduced to the ceremonies of the Eucharist in a Christian oratory.

> The company, the office for which it was assembled, seemed grave, majestic, touching, and something altogether new. . . . Noting the ardent quality of their faith and its appropriateness to human needs, the needs specially of the poor and suffering, Sérénus could not but feel that the future would be with them. . . . Yet with all his heartfelt admiration for believers, Sérénus is still unable to believe. Like a creature of the nineteenth century, he finds the world absolutely subject to the reign of physical law.[29]

Without faith, but in order to remain with the Christians, Sérénus allows himself to be baptized, looking upon the rites as only a "symbolic formula" for his sympathy. He is arrested with the others in a time of persecution. His death, actually a suicide, is looked upon by the others as a Christian martyrdom. Pater's hero is not baptized, and dies, not a suicide, but of a fever after having permitted himself to be arrested in place of his Christian friend. Yet Lemaitre's

---

28. "M. Lemaitre's *Sérénus* and Other Tales," *Macmillan's*, LVII (1887), 71–80. This article, listed in a review of Pater's *Essays from the 'Guardian'* in the *Athenaeum*, June 12, 1897, and in Thomas Wright, *Life of Walter Pater* (London, 1907), II, 260, is reprinted in Walter Pater, *Sketches and Reviews* (New York, 1919).

29. *Op. cit.*, pp. 77–79.

phrase, "le martyr sans foi,"[30] applies to both Sérénus and Marius. At the end, Marius reflects on "the irony of men's fates," since, "in his case at least, the Martyrdom, as it was called . . . would be but a common execution."[31]

Pater's summary of *Sérénus* actually tends to minimize those elements of tone and treatment which are different from his own work. Lemaitre's long *conte* sketches very briefly the intellectual attitudes and philosophic developments that Pater's novel elaborates in nuanced detail. Lemaitre uses action and violent incident to mark the process of intellectual change. Moreover, after sympathetic presentation of Sérénus' story, he changes his tone and affixes a comically naïve list of "prodigious" miracles performed at the tomb of the supposed martyr when, eight hundred years later, his remains are worshipped in France as Saint Marc le Romain. This satirical, humorous note is foreign to the wistfully pious concluding description of Marius' death. Yet beneath these differences the basic narrative and intellectual resemblances remain.

Pater wrote very few reviews of contemporary works. As George Moore stated, "something personal"[32] seems in most cases to explain his decision to write his reviews—which mainly treat works by his friends or disciples, like Mary Arnold Ward or George Moore, or works of authors like Flaubert, in whom he had found a model for his ideal of the artist and his theory of prose style.[33] The questions naturally arise: What "personal" interest led Pater to write this article on a work in French by Lemaitre? How shall we interpret the striking parallelisms between Lemaitre's *Sérénus* and *Marius the Epicurean*?

The collection of Lemaitre's tales reviewed by Pater was published in 1886,[34] the year following the publication of *Marius*. *Sérénus* was first published separately, however, in the July 14, 1883 issue of *La Revue politique et littéraire de la France et de l'étranger*. This chronology rules out indebtedness of either one to the other for the initial idea for his work (we shall consider later other possible relationships). But the curious parallelisms clearly suggest the next alternative in the logic of "influences," a common source. Lemaitre obligingly leads us to the possibility of a common inspiration in the works of Ernest Renan, whom he acknowledges as the major influence on his

30. Jules Lemaitre, "Mes Souvenirs," *Revue Hebdomadaire*, Feb. 1, 1913, p. 49. (Pierre Moreau points out in *RLC*, XXX (1956), 85, that Lemaitre dispensed with the *accent circomflexe* usually affixed to his name.)

31. II, 214; see also 213: "Yet he was, as we know, no hero, no heroic martyr—had indeed no right to be . . ."

32. George Moore, *Avowals* (New York, 1926), p. 233.

33. In addition to the reviews of works by Mrs. Ward and Edmund Gosse included in *Essays from the 'Guardian,'* see Pater's reviews of works by Arthur Symons (*Guardian*, Nov. 9, 1887, *Pall Mall Gazette*, Mar. 23, 1889), Oscar Wilde (*Bookman*, Nov. 1891), George Moore (*Daily Chronicle*, June 10, 1893), Flaubert (*Pall Mall Gazette*, Aug. 25, 1888; *Athenaeum*, Aug. 3, 1889).

34. *Sérénus: Histoire d'un martyr. Contes d'autrefois et d'aujourd'hui* (Paris, 1886).

own intellectual development.[35] From Renan, he tells us, he first learned "la piété sans foi," and refers to "ce conte vraiment renanien de Sérénus ou le martyr sans foi."[36]

In calling his story "renanien," Lemaitre referred to more than its underlying piety without belief. The central situation, the background, many specific details, as well as the general point of view, of *Sérénus*, are obviously derived from *Les Évangiles*, the fifth volume of Ernest Renan's *Histoire des origines du christianisme*.[37] Lemaitre simply places his imaginary character, Sérénus, beside the figures of the historical Flavius Clemens and his wife, whom Renan describes in terms that might apply equally to Lemaitre's Sérénus and to Pater's Marius:

> Flavius Clemens et Flavia Domitilla ne paraissent pas avoir été de véritables membres de l'Église de Rome. Comme tant d'autres Romains distingués, ils sentaient le vide du culte officiel, l'insuffisance de la loi morale qui sortait du paganisme, la repoussante laideur des mœurs et de la société du temps. Le charme des idées judéo-chrétiennes agit sur eux. Ils reconnurent de ce côté la vie et l'avenir; mais sans doute ils ne furent pas ostensiblement chrétiens. . . . Si les Clemens furent chrétiens, ce furent donc, on l'avouera, des chrétiens bien indécis. [pp. 229–232]

Renan tells how Flavius Clemens' death was attributed to his association with the Christians (p. 296). Lemaitre found the crowning irony for his story tucked away among the details of a scholarly footnote (p. 229). Renan reports that, although the Clemens probably died non-Christians, Flavia became the subject of various saints' legends, and in the Middle Ages Flavius' remains were thought to be those of Saint Clement the Roman. Here, obviously, is the germ of Lemaitre's story.

*Les Évangiles* was published in 1877 when, we have seen, Pater was probably beginning to seek a setting for his *Bildungsroman*. Perhaps it should be noted that the very issue of the *Fortnightly Review* for 1877 that contains Pater's essay, "The School of Giorgione," contains also a twenty-four page article on the newly published *Les Évangiles*.[38] It cannot, of course, be assumed that what is obviously the germ of *Sérénus* is also, obviously, the source of the parallel English work. There is here an extremely tangled web of similarities and differences, to be expected with authors of such decided individuality. Still, like Lemaitre, Pater could have found in *Les Évangiles* the general idea for his story of a Roman patrician at the imperial

35. Jules Lemaitre, *Impressions de théâtre*, 7th series (Paris, 1896), p. 39.

36. "Mes Souvenirs," *loc. cit.*

37. *Les Évangiles et la seconde génération chrétienne* (Paris, 1904). All references in the text will be to this edition.

38. N.S., XXII (1877), 525–538, 485–509.

court who, though not a convert to Christianity, sympathizes and associates with the Christians.[39]

The Clemens live under Domitian, but *Les Évangiles* also includes material on the age of Marcus Aurelius. In the second century, under Aurelius and his predecessors, Renan tells us, there was a moment of equilibrium, when Christianity was faced with the strong competition of practical philosophy, working rationally for the amelioration of human society. "Il y avait décadence intellectuelle, mais amélioration morale, comme cela semble avoir lieu de nos jours dans les classes supérieures de la société française" (p. 410). Here, again, well documented, is the analogy with the nineteenth century.

Renan's fame as a critic of orthodoxy was so great in England in the 1860s and later that, knowing Pater's intellectual history, we hardly need the testimony of his tutor, the Capes who wrote the history of the Antonines, that Pater as an undergraduate, after an early interest in German thought, "was drawn to Renan."[40] His undergraduate mentor, Jowett, master of Balliol, yearned to be able to "write as well as Renan."[41] Matthew Arnold, above all, must have led Pater to Renan. Arnold, throughout his career, sought consciously to play the role of an English Renan, and was constantly citing, imitating, or reacting to the continuing stream of Renan's writings.[42] Moreover, Renan's works were widely reviewed and discussed in the flood of writings on religion and philosophy during that "crisis of doubt" in England.

Even more important, Renan lectured in London in April 1880, and briefly visited Oxford.[43] In his four Hibbert Lectures he drew largely on the already published volumes of his history of the origins of Christianity. On April 16, 1880, he gave a lecture at the Royal Institution, consisting mainly of material drawn from his volume on *Marc-Aurèle et la fin du monde antique*, which was published in the following year. If Pater did not attend the lectures, he could have read the French text of the lecture on Marcus Aurelius the following

---

39. Pater's Cecilia, the wealthy matron who is the widow of the Christian, Cecilius, and the description of the family sepulchre which she has converted into a place of Christian burial and worship (*Marius*, II, 95 ff.) recall Renan's account of the widowhood of Flavia Domitilla and especially his description of the family sepulchre which became a Christian catacomb (*Évangiles*, p. 342 f.). See also references to the Caecillii (*Marc-Aurèle*, pp. 389 ff., 402, 453 f.). Marius and Cornelius, because of their rank, are sent to Rome for trial (*Marius*, II, 212); cf. *Évangiles*, p. 477. Marius takes the place of his Christian friend, whom he has come to value because of his importance for the future (II, 212, 221); Renan tells of those Christians "qui se mirent dans les fers pour délivrer des captifs qu'ils jugeaient plus précieux à Eglise qu'ils n'étaient eux-mêmes" (p. 298).

40. Wright, *op. cit.*, I, 156.

41. R.W. Macan, "Oxford in the 'Seventies," *The Eighteen-Seventies*, p. 230.

42. Lewis Freeman Mott, "Renan and Matthew Arnold," *MLN*, XXXIII (1918); F.L. Wickelgren, "Arnold's Literary Relations with France," *MLR*, XXXIII (1938); F.E. Faverty, *Matthew Arnold, the Ethnologist* (Evanston, 1951).

43. Lewis Freeman Mott, *Ernest Renan* (New York, 1921), p. 339.

month in *Nineteenth Century*.[44] And, within the year, the lectures were published in book form, in French and English.[45] Pater must also have been familiar with the lively comment on them, for example by Saintsbury in his long *Fortnightly Review* article on Renan.[46] Dr. James Martineau, in his address of thanks at the conclusion of the Hibbert Lectures, spoke of "the number of resemblances which they suggested between the age which they depicted and our own. . . . The unsatisfied wants and eager tentatives which found expression in the ethics of the philosophical schools of the Empire are evident again in the anxieties and throughout the conflicts and even behind the levities of contemporary thought."[47]

In 1877 *Les Évangiles* probably helped to turn Pater's thoughts to the "modernity" of the life of a patrician in the second century. Renan's lectures of 1880, especially the "Marc-Aurèle," and his volume of 1881 must have been important, at the least, in confirming the choice of period and the introduction of Aurelius as a character. Madame Duclaux, who had been a friend of Pater at Oxford and in London, and who was a friend and biographer of Renan, was convinced that Pater "drew his inspiration from Renan's magnificent book [on Marcus Aurelius] for his own portrait" of the Stoic emperor.[48]

Despite the fact that Aurelius' self-portrait in his *Meditations* tends to impose a certain uniformity upon all his biographers, Pater's image is closer in some respects to Renan's than to Arnold's in the essay which has been called the germ of *Marius*. Both Renan and Pater, for example, stress the emperor's reluctant acquiescence in certain pagan cruelties and superstitions; Pater echoes Renan's description of Aurelius' impassive conduct—writing or reading, with averted eyes—during the cruel shows in the amphitheater. And both reproach him for his lack of joy in the things of this life, his contempt for the body.[49] Renan's reference to the Antonines as examples of the sober way of life of "the old Roman families" (p. 5) and his account of the childhood and youth

44. "Marc-Aurèle," VII (1880), 742–755. "Notre bon Marc-Aurèle ... devança les sièles ... Comme s'il avait lu la *Critique de la raison pratique*, il vit bien que lorsqu'il s'agit de l'infini aucune formule n'est absolue" (p. 749).

45. Ernest Renan, *Conférences d'Angleterre* (Paris, 1880); *English Conferences*, tr. C. E. Clement (Boston, 1880).

46. N.S., XXVII (1880), 625. See Francis Espinasse, *Life of Renan* (London, 1895), pp. 183 ff., and Henri Tronchon, *Ernest Renan et l'étranger* (Paris, 1928), p. 295, for accounts of the enthusiastic reception given Renan.

47. "Dr. Martineau's Address," in Renan, *Lectures on the Influence of the Institutions, Thought and Culture of Rome on Christianity*, tr. Charles Beard (London, 1884), pp. 210 f.

48. Mary Duclaux, "Souvenirs sur Walter Pater," *Revue de Paris*, Jan. 15, 1925, p. 351. Pater actually refers to Renan in the first edition of *Marius* (London, 1885, II, 134 f.), translating two sentences from Renan's Introduction to *Marc-Aurèle* (p. ii). "The Minor Peace of the Church," in which this direct quotation occurs, clearly reflects both *Marc-Aurèle* and *Les Évangiles*.

49. Cf. *Marc-Aurèle*, pp. 30 f. and *Marius*, I, 239 f.; *Marc-Aurèle*, p. 10, and *Marius*, II, 55. Pater's account of the people's superstitious reaction to the plague and earthquake as the source of violence against the Christians (II, 210 f.) recalls *Marc-Aurèle*, p. 60.

of Aurelius seem also to have influenced Pater's evocation of his own hero's family background and meditative youth. Such echoes appear especially in Marius' early stage of "mystic enjoyment . . . in the abstinence, the strenuous self-control and *ascêsis*" associated with the family religion (I, 25) and in his youthful view of philosophy: "Such manner of life might come even to seem a kind of religion—an inward, visionary, mystic piety or religion . . ." (I, 148).[50]

Although Pater does not have the robustness of Renan and tends to modulate all into a minor key, he reveals strong affinities with Renan's "piété sans foi," his ambivalent, skeptical, yet nostalgic sympathy with man's religious impulses, his determination to regard life as a beautiful and engrossing spectacle. At the end Marius strikes a Renanian note; he sees his life as a success because he has fulfilled his aim of "impassioned contemplation," and has been content with the effort, above all, to *see* clearly, rather than to *have* or *do* (II, 218). Edmund Gosse found that the similarity between Pater's and Renan's spectator-like attitude extended even to certain common mannerisms in conversation.[51] Similarly, according to George Moore, Henry James complained that in the carefully balanced praise for pagan and Christian in *Marius*, Pater "adopted a tone as conciliatory as Renan."[52] Yet, like both Renan and Arnold, Pater also had a sense of a "duty,"[53] as he phrased it, to demonstrate the solutions open to a religious temperament in a naturalistic age.

Renan's works present not simply analogies of ideas, but also literary analogies, embodied in a narrative evoking characters, situations, and events. In *Histoire des origines du christianisme*, Pater was offered not only the congenial ambiguity of "la piété sans foi," not only relevant historical scholarship, but also what Saintsbury called "a picturesque historian."[54] *Marc-Aurèle*, especially, provided the example of a creative imagination playing on scholarly data, original documents, and literary materials. From a few recorded details, Renan evokes a character with its homely traits and circumstances, embodying at the same time a particular philosophic or religious attitude. Behind the narration, through the people and events, we see the interplay of contrasting ideas. This is also Pater's purpose in the portraits of the people—some historical, some imaginary—whom Marius encounters. Pater had been working toward this vein in "Winckelmann" and the Greek studies. Like Renan, he sought to show a philosophic position throught the subjective attitude or, to use his term, the "sentiments" it entailed. Pater's evocation of the character of Flavian as the

50. Cf. *Marc-Aurèle*, p. 9: "La philosophie était alors une sorte de profession religieuse, impliquant des mortifications, des régles presque monastiques. Dès l'âge de douze ans, Marc revêtit le manteau philosophique, apprit â coucher sur la dure et â pratiquer toutes les austérités de l'ascétisme stoïcien."
51. Edmund Gosse, *Critical Kit-Kats* (New York, 1897), pp. 255, 266; Duclaux, *loc. cit.*, p. 345, makes a similar comparison.
52. *Op. cit.*, p. 206.
53. A.C. Benson, *Walter Pater* (New York, 1906), p. 90.
54. *Fortnightly Review*, XXVII, 634.

imaginary author of the *Pervigilium Veneris* (Chapter VI), his introduction of long translations from authors such as Apuleius and Lucian, his portrait of Marcus Aurelius, with the long passages from his *Meditations*, are much closer to Renan's method as a historian than to the method of the conventional nineteenth-century novelist. Pater could have derived inspiration from Renan, not only for setting and philosophic position, but also for certain elements in literary method.

Pater's interest in Lemaitre's story, and its parallelism with his own work, reinforce the probability that they found a common inspiration in Renan's writings. Pater, however, does not share Lemaitre's direct, literal, and obvious indebtedness to Renan for the specific details of his plot, many of them elaborations from the briefest hints. We are confronted with the paradoxical fact that in many specific ways Pater's work is closer to Lemaitre's story than to its source. Have we, then, adequately explained Pater's selection of Lemaitre's volume as the subject of one of his rare reviews, and his overgenerous praise of *Sérénus*? Was his personal reason simply recognition of the curious parallels with his own work, and interest in a fellow-disciple of Renan? A stronger motive seems likely.

*Sérénus*, we have noted, was published in *La Revue politique et littéraire de la France et de l'étranger* in July 1883. Pater could have seen the magazine in London or Oxford,[55] or during his visit to the continent that summer.[56] In July 1883 he wrote to Viola Paget ("Vernon Lee"): "I have hopes of completing one half of my present chief work—an Imaginary Portrait of a peculiar type of mind in the time of Marcus Aurelius, by the end of this vacation."[57] William Sharp, a personal friend, tells us that "*Marius* had been begun, and in part written, long before Pater went to Rome in 1882 . . . but it was not until the summer of 1883 that he wrote it as it now stands—wrote and rewrote, with infinite loving care. . . ."[58]

What, then, might he have derived from *Sérénus* at that stage of the writing of *Marius*? In his article, Pater himself provides a clue:

> M. Jules Lemaitre is before all things an artist, showing in these pieces, the longest of which attains no more than sixty pages, that self-possession and sustained sense of design which anticipates the end in the commencement, and never loses sight of it—that gift of literary structure which lends so monumental an air to even the shortest of Flaubert's pieces.[59]

Pater overstresses here the quality which he himself lacked in writing *Marius* and his other imaginary portraits—the anticipation of "the end in the commencement," a structure of external events, of what Percy Lubbock terms "drama."

55. I have searched unsuccessfully for a copy of this issue at the Bodleian, Taylorian, and Brasenose libraries; but the magazine was known in England.
56. Wright, *op. cit.*, II, 59.
57. Benson, pp. 59 f.
58. *Loc. cit.*
59. *Op. cit.*, p. 71.

Indeed, Lubbock remarks that "in *Marius* . . . the art of drama is renounced as thoroughly as it has ever occurred to a novelist to dispense with it."[60] Even Pater's most enthusiastic admirer, George Moore, concedes that "Pater, knowing himself not to be altogether a story-teller, never plunged into story, but remained always a little outside, on the eve, as it were."[61] Preoccupied with Marius' "sensations and ideas," Pater does evoke, in Charles Du Bos' phrase, "a chamber music of the inner life."[62] He creates a cumulative effect through seemingly disconnected and static moments of insight, as his meditative hero looks within or gazes upon some scene or personality or work of art. In saying that Pater lacks Lemaitre's gift as a story teller, we are not unaware of his compensatory virtues. Indeed, the tale by Lemaitre reads at points like a scenario or sketch for the leisurely, richly nuanced, reflective work by Pater. Still, for many readers, the English work lacks forward movement and external incident.

Given the character of his hero, Pater's method finally creates a problem. An impasse seems to be reached. Marius has come to know the Christian community, and admires the Christians' sensitivity to human suffering, their gracious fellowship, their blithe hopefulness. He recognizes that the future lies with them. Yet—if he is also to be true to his implicit Victorian role—he cannot share their unquestioning faith. Pater wrote in 1883, concerning *Marius*: "I think that there is a . . . sort of religious phase possible for the modern mind the conditions of which phase it is the main object of my design to convey."[63] Clearly, this did not include Marius' full conversion to Christianity (an ending that some readers have nevertheless wishfully read into the book). Marius could continue indefinitely in this complex state of mind. From the point of view of narrative structure, this indecisive final position is unsatisfactory. More even for Pater's contemporaries than for us post-Joyceans, some resolution was needed.

In the death of Sérénus as a "martyr sans foi," Pater could have found a dénouement both technically and philosophically appropriate—a decisive dramatic action which yet symbolizes the ambivalent state of mind of his hero. This is not the simple killing off of the hero which is the weak novelist's last resort. Marius' death in his Christian friend's place transforms into positive affirmation an extremely complex state of mind which might otherwise seem merely vacillating. Without accepting the supernatural sanctions and doctrines of Christianity as more than an expression for him of a mystic mood or a yearned-for "possibility," Marius still acts in the spirit of Christian self-sacrifice. Marius' death, Sharp even claimed, can also fulfill Epicurus' picture of his ideal man as one who will die for his friend.[64] The martyrdom without faith

60. Percy Lubbock, *The Craft of Fiction* (London, 1921), p. 195.

61. *Op. cit.*, p. 209.

62. ". . . une musique de chambre de la vie intérieure." Charles du Bos, *Approximations*. IV (Paris, 1930), pp. 10 f.

63. Benson, *loc. cit.*

64. William Sharp interpreted the death of Marius entirely in Epicurean terms. Pater commented that he preferred not to limit himself to any "parti pris." Sharp, *op. cit.*, pp. 213, 233.

becomes thus symbolic of the "religious phase" possible for the modern mind; nineteenth-century man, depending only on reason and experience, can yet derive the highest morality and elevation of spirit from a fusion of pagan and Christian inspiration.

Pater, in his account of *Sérénus*, had stressed irony as Lemaitre's main trait, and had phrased his "philosophy of life" as imposing, on the one hand, a recognition of the irony of nature and circumstance, and, on the other, an obligation to promote a mood of kindliness, "like Sérénus, with a great pity for people, a great indulgence"[65] In his own book, Pater underlines the irony of Marius' end, an irony that reminds us of Sérénus' account of his feelings before death. "Yet Marius was, as we know, no hero, no heroic martyr—had indeed no right to be. . . . Had there been one to listen just then, there would have come, from the very depth of his desolation, an eloquent utterance at last, on the irony of men's fates, on the singular accidents of life and death" (II, 213–214). Yet this mood gives way to a more peaceful acceptance, a kind of optimistic agnosticism (II, 220).

Internal evidence confirms the view that Pater's ending was suggested to him midway in the writing of this book. Lemaitre's story, which opens as the bodies of Sérénus and the other martyrs are being removed from prison, is built around the idea of the "martyr sans foi." In Pater's work there clearly had not been such an anticipation of "the end in the commencement." (That he composed in this way—even starting publication of a work without a clear view of its end—is suggested by his unfinished novel *Gaston de Latour*.[66]) The final chapters of *Marius* represent in various ways a break with the method of the rest of the book.

The number of traditional and sensational elements of plot crowded into these final chapters has occasioned surprisingly little comment. The last chapter alone contains an outbreak of the plague, an earthquake which precipitates mob violence against the Christians, the arrest of Marius and his friend, the forced march of the prisoners toward Rome, the strategem for Cornelius' release, the illness and death of Marius. And, contrary to Benson's remark that "there is no hint from first to last of the distracting element of love,"[67] Pater suddenly introduces late in the book Marius' contemplation of the idea of marriage with Cecilia, the Christian widow. The page devoted to this dwells, it is true, mainly on his reasons for retreat from involvement with "any too disturbing passion," among these the Christian prohibition of second marriages (II, 187). Evidently the desire to hint a further love motive (in the form of a

---

65. *Op. cit.*, p. 80. A similar note of pity and sympathy is struck at the end of *Marius* (II, 217 f.), and is the theme of chap. XXV, "Sunt Lacrimae Rerum."

66. Charles L. Shadwell, Pater's close friend, in his preface to the posthumous edition of *Gaston de Latour*, indicates "that Pater was himself dissatisfied with the framework which he had begun, and that he deliberately abandoned it." Benson, p. 146, says: "The difficulty is to comprehend what was to be the issue."

67. *Op. cit.*, p. 91.

Sydney Carton situation) led Pater to forget this when explaining Marius' self-sacrifice: "Marius believed that Cornelius was to be the husband of Cecilia; and that, perhaps strangely, had but added to the desire to get him away safely" (II, 212). Rather wraithlike, but a love story nonetheless.

Pater's sudden change in method and pace is cushioned for the reader by the consistency of tone, the continuing "harmonious murmur" of his style, and the presentation of even the more violent and dramatic events mainly by refraction, as it were, through the meditative personality of Marius. Yet Pater himself evidently felt it necessary to prepare the reader for the break in method. In the opening paragraph of the final chapter, he seems almost to be discussing his technical problem with the reader when he has Marius reflect that his life had lacked "movement and adventure."

> Actually, as circumstances had determined, all its movement had been inward; movement of observation only, or even of pure meditation; in part, perhaps, because throughout it had been something of a *meditatio mortis*, ever facing towards the act of final detachment. Death, however, as he reflected, must be for everyone nothing less than the fifth or last act of a drama, and, as such, was likely to have something of the stirring character of a *dénouement*. And, in fact, it was in form tragic enough that his end not long afterwards came to him.

The awkward concluding sentence reveals that Pater has been preparing the way for the sudden shift to "stirring" external incident.

A similar excrescence appears early in the book in another curiously amateurish reference to the final development. We have just been told how the boy Marius had derived from the religious atmosphere of his home a feeling of responsibility toward the world. There is nothing, however, in this "religion of usages and sentiment" that would suggest the idea of martyrdom. Yet we are informed that this devoutness "made him anticipate all his life long as a thing towards which he must carefully train himself, some great occasion of self-devotion, such as really came, that should consecrate his life, and, it might be, its memory with others, as the early Christian looked forward to martyrdom as the end of his course, as a seal of worth upon it" (I, 18). The reference to Christian martyrdom seems especially arbitrary at this point. Does this suggest something introduced during the 1883 period of writing and revision, a rather forced linking up of the end with the beginning?

That Lemaitre's story provided a solution when Pater had reached an impasse concerning the outcome of his own novel seems the best explanation of Pater's final chapters and switch in narrative pace. It is very unlikely that Pater shared Lemaitre's indebtedness to Renan for the idea of using the martyrdom without belief; the important resemblances are between Pater's handling of Marius' death and what Lemaitre made of Renan's hints concerning the Flavius Clemens family. Renan's remarks on Clemens' death (p. 296) stress mainly the political implications, and we can hardly be sure that Pater read the few sentences about the pseudo-martyrdom embedded in the fine print toward the end of an involved, page-long footnote about other matters (note 3, pp. 228–229). Pater's debt to Lemaitre for his dénouement would also explain his singling out Lemaitre for special attention and his emphasis on Lemaitre's handling of narrative.

Since, as Sharp indicated, Pater undoubtedly revised his work considerably after the summer of 1883, the many other parallelisms between *Sérénus* and *Marius* may reflect a similar influence. In addition to the already-noted resemblances between the heroes, we find, for example, the similarities in the descriptions of Séréna and Cecilia; the similar roles played by Séréna and Cornelius in relation to the heroes; their introduction to Christianity without doctrinal preparation, through attendance at a Eucharistic service; their attitude as sympathetic spectators within the Christian community; their thoughts concerning the Christians and the future. But, without such reinforcement as the internal evidence provides in the case of Pater's dénouement, the precise extent of Pater's indebtedness to Lemaitre must remain problematic. In the intricate triadic relationship of Pater, Renan, and Lemaitre, the latter's influence is more likely to have been toward strengthening the narrative and fictional elements in Pater's "imaginary portrait," as he called it in 1883, to the point that permitted it to be considered a novel.

For general philosophic attitudes, what may be directly due to Renan merges also with Arnold's pervasive influence. *Marius* is often viewed as a development from Arnold's religious position. In turn, Arnold, it must be recalled, from 1859 on imitated Renan's style and echoed or adapted many of his interests. Pater ultimately approached more closely to the tone and temper of Renan, yet still followed the path opened by Arnold. Similarly, the part that Renan's work played in crystallizing Pater's choice of setting and method in *Marius* was prepared for by the intellectual climate created by Arnold and other English writers. As Pater said, "Producers of great literature do not live in isolation, but catch light and heat from each other's thought." Even when the writers are less than great, the study of this process yields insights for literary history, the history of ideas, and critical interpretation.[68]

---

68. A shorter version of this paper was presented in the Comparative Literature Section of the Modern Language Association of America at the 1957 annual meeting at the University of Wisconsin.

# Chapter Twelve

# Whitman's *Democratic Vistas* and The New "Ethnicity"

One aspect of contemporary America—the emergence of the new "ethnicity"—might at first glance seem incommensurate with Whitman's vision of an "ideal American nationality." Whitman bases his whole vision of democracy on the autonomous worth and uniqueness of the individual human being. In *Democratic Vistas* (1871), he speaks of

> the idea of that Something a man is . . . standing apart from all else, divine in his own right, and a woman in hers, sole and untouchable by any canons of authority, or any rule derived from precedent, state-safety, the acts of legislatures, or even from what is called religion, modesty, or art. [*The Prose Works 1892*, II, ed. Floyd Stovall, New York University Press, 1964, p. 374]

Again and again Whitman phrases his central concern:

> Even for the treatment of the universal, in politics, in metaphysics, or anything, sooner or later we come down to one single, solitary soul.
> There is, in sanest hours, a consciousness, a thought that rises, lifted out from all else, like the stars, shining eternal. This is the thought of identity—yours for you, as mine for me. [393–94]

He sees the nation as an aggregate of individuals—indeed, he tends mainly to use the word *aggregate* to denote the nation, the society, the country.

Throughout his efforts in *Democratic Vistas* to peer into the future—and he is willing to think in centuries—Whitman's thought reverberates between the pole of individualism (or personalism as he calls his particular mystic sense of the individual), and the pole of the aggregate or the nation. Thus, as he looks at the world around him, he sees with unblinking clarity the pressure toward bigness, aggregation. He castigates the forces "everywhere turning out the generations of humanity like uniform iron castings" (424). He opposes to this the "indispensable and unyielding" principle of individuality, "the pride and centripetal isolation of a human being in himself—identity—personalism." In this sense of the absolute worth of the individual human being Whitman sees "the compensating balance-wheel of the successful working machinery of aggregate America" (391f.).

Whitman, we must recall, had only a few years before lived through the agony of the Civil War and had whole-heartedly shared Lincoln's belief in the overwhelming importance of the Union. Perhaps Whitman's emphasis on individual separatism is even more surprising than the fact that at times he pauses to swing to the other pole, the side of a common bond. Thus he admits that as he thinks of the United States, "the fear of conflicting and irreconcilable interiors, and the lack of a common skeleton, knitting all close, continually haunts me" (368).

For Whitman, the vision of free, flourishing, fully developed human beings with "identified individualities" requires the accompanying vision of a unified society which provides the conditions for their flowering. "This idea of perfect individualism it is indeed," he says, "that deepest tinges and gives character to the idea of the aggregate. For it is mainly or altogether to serve independent separatism that we favor a strong generalization, consolidation" (374). Hence the proof of Democracy, he maintains, is "in its personalities rich, luxuriant, varied." Thus, Whitman explains, if in his great poetic work, *Leaves of Grass*, he had intended "the song of a great composite *democratic individual*, male or female," he sought in his following works to utter the chant "of an aggregated, inseparable, unprecedented, vast, composite *democratic nationality*."

Whitman had a vision, but he was not a visionary. Democracy, he felt, was in embryonic condition, its history yet to be enacted. He had no illusions about the contemporary state of affairs. His outraged denunciations of contemporary political corruption make our indignation at Watergate seem pale. He condemns "the depravity of the business classes," with their one sole object, pecuniary gain. "Our New World democracy, however great a success in uplifting the masses out of their sloughs, in materialistic development, products, and in a certain highly deceptive superficial popular intellectuality, is, so far, an almost complete failure in its social aspects, and in really grand religious, moral, literary, and esthetic results" (370). Indeed, we who are so keenly aware of contemporary political and economic woes may feel that the primary applicability of *Democratic Vistas* for today lies in its vigorous attacks on the weaknesses and vices that Whitman saw in American society. Yet Whitman did not give way to a facile pessimism. He fervently believed that, underneath it all, the potentialities existed for the creation of a truly great democratic society.

Nor did he undervalue the importance of the political and economic foundations of such a society. His Jeffersonian suspicion of great economic contrasts of wealth and poverty were not at all inconsistent with a zestful pleasure in the stupendous labors and great material productivity of the country, in the oceanic amplitude and rush of its great cities, its many-threaded wealth and industries.

Similarly, Whitman does not let his contempt for corrupt self-interested politicians and narrow-minded party hacks blur his sense of the importance of democratic political institutions. He advises every young man, studying these things, who may be disillusioned with "the antics of parties and their leaders, these half-brain'd nominees, the many ignorant ballots, and the many elected failures and blatherers," not to fall into the error of shirking his political duty. "To practically enter into politics is an important part of American personalism," he declares (399).

And if he addresses himself here to the young men, *Democratic Vistas* is not without prophetic thought to the political participation of women; and beyond, to their present egalitarian demands. Throughout Whitman's concern for the individual, he again and again makes clear his view that men cannot become whole until women too are given the opportunity and the impetus to live wholly from their own centers, and to fulfill themselves not only through a nobler motherhood but also through all the roles of work and thought and creativity open to men.

However, in the political and economic life of the nation Whitman sees only the frame within which the true greatness of a society may flourish—its esthetic, and above all, its moral life. In any model of personality, the essential is "the simple, unsophisticated Conscience, the moral element." "Offsetting the material civilization of our race, our nationality, its wealth, territories, factories, population, products, trade and military and naval strength, and breathing breath of life into all of these, and more, must be its moral civilization" (414).

Whitman had a very strong sense of how such a moral civilization can come into being. Despite the political innovations and economic achievements of this nation, he felt that the ideas and attitudes governing men's and women's day-to-day lives were largely those inherited from the Old World. Those cultures had been great in their time, and they have bequeathed us great monuments of literature and art. Whitman does not wish us to completely reject these, but rather to make them serve as a means of attaining insight into "ourselves, our own present, and our own far grander, different, future history, religion, social customs, etc." Whitman reminds us that this cultural heritage was produced mainly for people living under feudal and oriental institutions and religions, to which the democratic ideal of the common man is foreign. "The great poems, Shakespeare included, are poisonous to the idea of the pride and dignity of the common people." None of our writers or thinkers, he declares, has yet "created a single image-making work for them, or absorbed the central spirit and the idiosyncrasies which are theirs" (388).

Whitman used the word "Literatus" to cover the wide gamut of those who, through their words, their writings, their learning, would foster a healthy moral substratum for our national life, permeating the American mentality. The poet or imaginative writer would play an especially important role in this, since he possesses the "image-making" capacity in its highest form. "The literature, songs, esthetics, etc., of a country are of importance principally because they furnish the materials and suggestions of personality for the women and men of that country and enforce them in a thousand effective ways" (392). In calling for a literature that would have its roots in the lives of the people—the laborers, the farmers, the factory workers, the small homeowners and businessmen, in complaining that no image of woman in her fullest development as a person had yet appeared, Whitman was pointing to the subject that awaited the pen of the "Literatuses"—the poets and scientists and writers and thinkers—who would be the inspiration of the true democracy of identified individuals.

Whitman was not calling for a preachy, didactic literature. Indeed, he explicitly sets up esthetic criteria and sees literature exerting its influence "by curious removes, indirections" on personality and moral attitudes through the power of suggestion and through the unconscious absorption of ideas and attitudes (419). Individual men or women are to be liberated from old irrelevant images, in order to live freely and fully and nobly from their own centers.

How relevant, then, is this conception of the democratic idea, and this view of the humanistic writer, a century or more later? We might, of course, cite as a major difference the fantastic dimensions of our present-day concerns and problems—though Whitman was not at all niggardly of imagination, predicting fifty states (included among them Canada and Cuba), and elatedly offering prophetic glimpses of "stupendous labors" and vast enterprises. Despite the great changes in our material life, the size and complexity of our nation, I believe that the broad principles he enunciates are relevant today. We draw in a similar way on the Declaration of Independence and the Constitution, seeing beneath the changing specifics their continuing meaning for our contemporary society. Actually, many of Whitman's broad principles are more widely capable of application today than when he enunciated them: his emphasis on the worth and dignity of the individual, regardless of economic or social or intellectual status; his concern for the autonomy of the individual against the forces of uniformity and conformity; his attack on the sexist view of women and his call for their full equality in politics, in work, in intellectual life, with motherhood as an additional and honored fulfillment; his appeals for political and social morality (especially meaningful in this post-Watergate time); his rejection of extremes of wealth and poverty; his secular religion, which transcends the dogmas of individual creeds; his sense of man's life in and through nature, a fit ancestor of our current ecological concerns. I could continue the list of Whitman's exemplifications of the meaning of democracy, and of their applicability to our present world. On the whole, these ideas are more widely accepted today than when Whitman expounded them. When we draw back from our immersion in present-day moods, and look through Whitman's eyes at the alienation and disillusionment expressed by an influential segment of our youth, our writers and intellectuals, we see that their very disillusionment stems in large part from widespread acceptance of the kinds of ideals Whitman promulgated, and their anguish at the extent to which these still remain unfulfilled. The very real social and economic advances that have been made in this past century have only made more urgent the pressures toward a fully realized democracy.

Yet there is one development during this past century that might seem less clearly provided for in Whitman's view of democracy. As we look back over the century, one of the primary phenomena is the tremendous influx of peoples from many parts of the globe. The diversification of the population in the years between colonial days and Whitman's time was already notable. But think of the further diversity in this past century, the different national or cultural origins of the men and women on farms and in cities, the laborers and lumberjacks and miners and clerks and factory workers and bus drivers and sailors whom Whitman saw as making up "the people" when he quoted Lincoln's "this government of the people, by the people, and for the people" in *Democratic Vistas.*

We have noted that Whitman felt some reasonable concern, after the ordeal of the Civil War, about the necessity for unifying the country, for finding common bonds, a common skeleton, to link its diversities. Surely a similar concern motivated in part the efforts known as the Americanization movement that developed after 1890 in response to the arrival on these shores of the millions of immigrants from farflung lands and dissimilar societies. The pressure was to make these newcomers into "Americans" as soon as possible—at least so far as their integration into the economic life of the nation was concerned, and, perhaps with less urgency, into its political life.

The metaphor for that Americanization process was "the melting pot." But, we must recall, it was assumed that the White Anglo-Saxon Protestant image would color the whole homogenized social mass. Had not the WASPs, as they came to be designated, founded the democracy that opened its doors to all comers? Politically and economically established, they provided the model for assimilation. The story, not only of the immigrants, but also of their second- and third-generation descendants, is the story of external economic and social pressures reinforcing internal drives to merge with that dominant image. Among the instruments for fostering such assimilation, the schools were considered especially important. The tendency for the generations to move upward on the economic ladder also constituted a powerful influence in that direction.

There was an ugly underside to this willingness to give to all comers, in exchange for Americanization, the opportunity to become part of the American success story. Even in the 1840s, early in Whitman's career as a journalist, he had had to speak out against the nativists' fear and hostility toward the differentness of the newcomers from other lands, with other languages and mores. The Know-Nothing Party and, after the Civil War, the Ku Klux Klan were among the most extreme expressions of this ignorant, fearful, bigoted reaction. But perhaps the quiet assertion of the dominant group's superiority and their assumption of the inferiority of the newer immigrant groups exacted an even heavier economic, social, and psychological toll. The newcomers naturally tended to gravitate toward their own ethnic groups for support, settling in the same cities, pioneering in the same regions, engaging in the same lines of work. This undoubtedly helped to keep alive group consciousness, despite the effects of upward economic mobility and the increasing trend toward assimilation from generation to generation. Probably another reason for the preservation of a sense of ethnic identification was a counterreaction against overt and covert discrimination, which continued despite the efforts of those who, like Whitman, sought to fight such prejudice.

These reminders of past history may serve as background for a new and often dramatic development that has occurred during the last two decades. Partly because of the limitations on immigration and partly because of the maturing of second and third generations, the numbers and proportions of assimilated, native-born Americans had tremendously increased. Moreover, civil rights legislation opened the doors wider to all groups. Yet along with the widely supported official rejection of discrimination against any individuals for reasons of race, creed, color, sex, or national origin has come a kind of renaissance of group consciousness, even among some of those who had most completely grown away from their ethnic origins.

The sources of this development are very complex and the phenomenon is so striking that a new term— "ethnicity"—has been added to the vocabulary of the sociologists and historians and psychologists who are seeking to describe, understand, and evaluate it. Emphasis on the element of "ethnic pride" especially explains the need for a new terminology. The blacks have provided the most clearcut model of this phenomenon. At the point when the highest courts of the land and national and state legislatures insisted, finally, on their integration into various aspects of American life, many blacks felt the necessity to draw more closely together and to assert pride in their ethnic origins. Chicanos and Puerto Ricans—and in even more extreme terms, American Indians—have similarly demanded recognition of their ethnic identity and rights. Other groups, the Italians and the Poles, the Irish and the Slovaks—have their spokesmen; Michael Novak has called them "the unmeltable ethnics" (more, I suppose, in repudiation of the melting pot than as accurate description, since as more recent newcomers they may not be "unmeltable" but simply may as a group be less far along the general road to outward assimilation). Many Jews, for various historic reasons, also have manifested such intensification of sentiments linking them to their ethnic origins.

The rise of ethnicity had economic sources in part, but it was generated also by wider cultural and social pressures, among them disillusionment with the dehumanizing tendencies of our industrialized society and the impersonality and atomism of the great cities. Was there also the realization that all of us, including those of Anglo-Saxon derivation, who by 1960 made up only about 35 percent of the population, are today members of minority groups?

One symptom of this upsurge of awareness of ethnic identity is the demand that the schools qualify their melting-pot role and recognize the pluralistic nature of our society. For example, American history texts have been revised to do greater justice to the black experience and contribution, and similar demands are being made for other ethnic or minority groups. This has sometimes taken the form of special Black or Jewish or Puerto Rican or Women's "Studies" in the colleges and schools, and materials concerning minority groups have been introduced at appropriate points into the regular curriculum in history, literature, sociology, and political science. The English classroom, for example, has traditionally been concerned with providing a common language and a common literary heritage, drawn from English and "mainstream" American literature. Recently, the National Council of Teachers of English has developed materials and set up committees and conferences to study the problem of introducing multi-ethnic materials into the curriculum in language and literature. A recent bibliography, *The Image of Pluralism in American Literature* (Babette F. Inglehart and Anthony R. Mangione, New York, 1974), lists literary works, largely novels and biographies, that depict the experience of eleven groups of Americans of European ethnic derivation. Familiar names such as William Saroyan (Armenian-American), David Cornel deJong (Dutch-American), Bess Streeter Aldrich, Theodore Dreiser, Conrad Richter (German-American), August Derleth (Hungarian-American), Stephen Crane, James T. Farrell, Eugene O'Neill (Irish-American), Pietro DiDonato (Italian-American), Sholem Asch, Saul Bellow, Bernard Malamud (Jewish-American) are in the list, together with many other writers selected for their expression of what is both unique and universal in the lives of those who, uprooted from their traditional environments, came to make a new life in this land. The proliferation of many similar bibliographies and anthologies devoted to black literature, the literature of the Indians, and of other minorities reflects the new pluralistic emphasis in education.

Needless to say, parallel to this affirmation of the multicultural character of our society is the insistence on elimination of the old demeaning ethnic stereotypes from the mass media and the casting out of denigrating labels and epithets from our language. In the schools, there is also a growing effort to honor the intrinsic dignity of the child's home dialect or language. The National Council of Teachers of English has recently published a rather extreme manifesto of this position, entitled "The Students' Right to Their Own Language." In various parts of the country bilingualism has been introduced into the schools, to help the child bridge the transition from the speech of the home environment to participation in the mainstream language and life.

What, then, is the relation to all this of Whitman's *Democractic Vistas*? First of all, we can start with the premise that Whitman welcomed the diversity of America's people:

> These States are the amplest poem,
> Here is not merely a nation but a teeming Nation of nations

We know, too, that he rejected not only slavery but also any class or caste discriminations.

The great word Solidarity has arisen. Of all dangers to a nation, as things exist in our day, there can be no greater one than having certain portions of the people set off by a line drawn—they not privileged as others, but degraded, humiliated, made of no account. [382]

The year after the publication of *Democractic Vistas*, he wrote of the United States as "the modern composite nation, form'd from all, with room for all, welcoming all immigrants— . . . not the man's nation only, but the woman's nation."

It becomes necessary, however, to ask, is there room for the new ethnicity in Whitman's view of the state as an aggregate whose prime justification is that it creates the stable environment within which the individual can freely and fully develop? Does he see the individual American, like a newborn Adam in his own divine selfhood, free of the past, ethnic and otherwise, reaching out from his personal center to a mystic union with other such individual "Children of Adam," as he calls them in *Leaves of Grass*? In his insistence that the individual man and woman slough off all that is external, imposed, adventitious, does he not imply a freeing of the individual from all ethnic bonds? Does his concern for individuals joined in the solidarity of American nationality rule out the current quest for a narrower solidarity based on ethnic roots and ethnic memories? Paradoxically, Whitman's intense individualism seems to me both to support affirmation of the importance of ethnic roots, and to qualify it.

The man who had written "There was a child went forth" would not fail to understand all the subtle ways in which family and early home environment shape personality, nor would he ignore the legacies of temperament and values from generation to generation:

There was a child went forth every day,
And the first object he look'd upon, that object
    he became . . .
His own parents, he that had father'd him and she that
    had conceiv'd him in her wornb and birth'd him,
They gave this child more of themselves than that,
They gave him afterward every day, they became part
    of him . . .
The family usages, the language, the company, the
    furniture, the yearning and swelling heart,
Affection that will not be gainsay'd, the sense of
    what is real, the thought if after all it should
    prove unreal . . .
These became part of that child who went forth every
    day, and who now goes, and will always go
    forth every day.

In *Democratic Vistas* Whitman suggests that all literary works, even foreign ones, "touch a man closest . . . in their expression through autochthonic lights and shades, flavors, fondnesses, aversions, specific incidents, illustrations, out of his own nationality, geography, surroundings, antecedents, &c." Whitman speaks of something "rooted in the invisible roots, the profoundest meanings of that place, race, or nationality" (411).

To repress one's ethnic awareness, to hide or be ashamed of one's inheritance or early environment, would be to violate a part of one's inner self. It could be done only by shutting one's ears to Whitman's call for self-pride and self-reliance. One can imagine Whitman, with his broad-brimmed hat and flannel shirt open at the throat, smiling in sympathy with those youths who today seek by dress, stance, or idiom to announce their proud membership in some hitherto scorned ethnic or social group.

Whitman's insistence on the equality of all human souls rules out also any notion of any intrinsic ethnic (or sex or other) superiorities or inferiorities. As for specific WASP pretensions, we hardly need the further confirmation of Whitman's own pointed remarks about the contributions to our nationality by people of other "widely different" antecedents besides the British and the German. Or, again, his statement:

> I like well our polyglot construction-stamp, and the retention thereof, in the broad, the tolerating, the many-sided, the collective. All nations here—a home for every race on earth. British, German, Scandinavian, Spanish, French, Italian—papers published, plays acted, speeches made, in all languages—on our shores the crowning resultant of those distillations, decantations, compactions of humanity, that have been going on, on trial, over the earth so long. [540]

But such praise of diversity has its qualifications. Recall, for example, that although Whitman accepts the perennial, universal elements derived from earlier literatures, he again and again reminds us that these older cultures embody much that is alien to, and inimical to, the ideal of democracy. Thus, he enjoins upon us an active selectivity, a testing, a rejection of all derived from our ancestry that is alien to the special needs of a free society, all that cramps and confines the individual.

Through this aspect of his vision Whitman warns us against a possible danger in the new ethnicity, the danger that membership in the group may impose its own kind of rigid conformity upon the individual. Some of the developments in student groups in our colleges in these past years, for example, demonstrate the positive value of ethnic identification, but also the tendency of the group to dictate to the individual member, to be jealous of his other affiliations or his participation in the mainstream. Whitman would strengthen him to resist such group dictation. We want respect for ethnic traits, for the ethnic group as the support and the source of richly endowed individuals. But the individual, Whitman could help us to remember, is more than his ethnic label. He must be free to make his own choices, to seek out his own friends, to enter freely into other associations, other groups.

In our populous land, individuals naturally gravitate toward others with whom they have affinities. These affinities may be other, and sometimes even stronger, than ethnic similarities. Think of the comings-together because of work or professions, or economic interests, or sport, or concern with schools and children, or religion, or political philosophy. Part of our democratic freedom is expressed in this multiplicity of associations open to us. And these are associations that often transcend or cut across ethnic or sex or religious or other groupings and associations of the individual. Whitman shows us the man and woman, accepting themselves in all their uniqueness, honoring their own roots, but free to reach out in all directions to their fellow humans.

The desire or need to maintain ties with an ethnic past may also become a barrier to change and growth. Whitman makes us elatedly aware of the special unprecedented conditions and opportunities in our country for the development of a nation of more liberated, more fully self-disciplined, more fully "identified" democratic personalities.

> Our America today I consider in many respects but indeed a vast seeth-
> ing mass of *materials*, ampler, better, (worse also) than previously
> known—eligible to be used to carry towards its crowning stages . . .
> the great ideal nationality of the future. [460]

As he looked into the coming centuries, he saw any one period as a stage in the process of building an ideal society. It would be a sad descent from such a dynamic ideal if the current ethnicity, along with its positive achievement of acceptance of ethnic differences, congealed into a static society of closed sub-cultures. In this country, we already in many ways exemplify the intermingling of cultural strands, the diversity within unity, that is Whitman's—and the American—idea. Each group already has produced individuals who have enriched not only their own group, but the lives of other groups and the whole nation. For example, the bibliography of the image of pluralism in American literature that I cited earlier classifies writers according to the ethnic group depicted, not the author's derivation. It is important that the authors be thought of as American authors, bringing their special contributions to American liter-ature. Any separatist contention that, for example, only blacks can produce or understand literature dealing with the black experience, or Jews with the Jew-ish, women with women's, and so on, is not only self-defeating but contrary to the very nature of the literary imagination. Whitman reminds us that, much as we honor the uniqueness of Homer, Shakespeare, or Cervantes, their greatest value lies in their permitting us to transcend our limitations of time and place and ancestry, and to participate in the common life of humanity.

Hence the relevance of Whitman's other fundamental principle of democ-racy—the need for unity, for an American identity that, though composite, plu-ralistic, including multitudes, still creates the solidarity which makes possible the freedom of each segment, and of each individual within it. Here, again, Whitman can help us perceive potential dangers in the new ethnicity. For in the aggressive withdrawal into groups lies the danger of an intensification of differences, the danger of competition, of separatism, of conflict. We can understand resentment of discriminations imposed by a dominant group; but our society has seen, and is, alas, currently seeing, the effects of prejudice directed by one minority or ethnic group against another, of conflict between them in the upward struggle for economic and social status. Whitman understood the need for allegiance to an overarching generalized national ethos, and for collective adherence to the political ways of a democracy. Thus all together could create and preserve the free society that would ensure the equality of all its diverse component groups. In a nation in which all at one point or another are members of a minority, all would be equally protected against weaknesses of that minority position.

Whitman's vision projects a living, organic whole, a nation based, it is true, on unique individuals, on groups with their special ethnic or other bond of association, but a nation equally imbued with the sense of fraternity, with a vision of a collective interdependence. Whitman says of the religion of democracy

> it alone can bind, and ever seeks to bind, all nations, all men, of however various and distant lands, into a brotherhood, a family. . . . Not that half only, individualism, which isolates. There is another half, which is adhesiveness or love, that fuses, ties and aggregates, making the races comrades, and fraternizing all. [381]

As we look about us today, it seems essential for survival that, step by step with the recognition of the worth and dignity of all individuals, and recognition of the rights and contributions of all ethnic groups or all minorities, should go the propagation of Whitman's fervid sense of a religion of democratic brotherhood, of the equality and unity of all in a free society.

As early as 1915, the philosopher Horace Kallen had given the name "cultural pluralism" to his view of the place of the ethnic group in American society. He sought to substitute for the metaphor of the melting pot the metaphor of the orchestra, with each instrument likened to a cultural group making its special contribution to the symphony of civilization. "With this difference: a musical symphony is written before it is played; in the symphony of civilization, the playing is the writing." Kallen affirms the positive role of the various cultural or ethnic groups while stressing the primary importance of the individual. Thus his symphonic "cultural pluralism" is more consonant with Whitman's ideas than are some of the separatist tendencies in the new ethnicity.

In a letter to Kallen (31 March 1915), his fellow-philosopher John Dewey underlined the harmonizing implications of Kallen's metaphor:

> I quite agree with your orchestra idea, but upon condition we really get a symphony and not a lot of different instruments playing simultaneously. I want to see this country American and that means the English tradition reduced to a strain along with the others . . . genuine assimilation to one

another—not to Anglo-Saxondom—seems to be essential to an America. That each cultural section should maintain its distinctive literary and artistic traditions seems to be most desirable, but in order that it might have the more to contribute to others.

Perhaps an even better musical analogue for the role of ethnic groups in American society may be Ralph Ellison's description of jazz, "that embodiment of a superior democracy in which each individual cultivated his uniqueness yet did not clash with his neighbors."

We read Whitman's *Democratic Vistas* at a time of great economic uncertainty. We are acutely aware of the possibilities for corruption of our democratic institutions and of how far we are from realization of democratic ideals of economic and social equity. Yet Whitman can be listened to because he, too, looked squarely at the distortions and defections of the society about him, and nevertheless could predict the ability of our democratic institutions to surmount them, to persist, and to advance. His vistas extend far beyond the century that separates us from him. To America he says, "If you would have greatness, know that you must conquer it through ages, centuries" (423). Precisely in such times of self-questioning as the present lie the need and the potentiality for "the subtle and tremendous force-infusion" of active purpose that he saw as essential to real change and real progress. We can catch fire from Whitman's sense of democracy as still in process of becoming, of slowly rising above the obstacles to "a truly grand nationality."

Whitman's declaration of the importance of "the Literatuses"—the "image-makers" and thinkers of all kinds—also articulates our present-day need for writers, scholars, scientists, professional people, and political leaders, who will do more than express our disillusionments, intensify our alienation, or dwell on our separateness. Whitman calls equally on each of us to be ready to listen to those who, sharing his faith in the democratic idea, and refusing either complacency or despair, would seek to inspire us to create the symphony of a society of free, varied, mutually respecting men and women.

The following notes were prepared for the essay, but were eliminated, because the Yale Review did not publish notes.

# Notes

This paper was presented at the Walt Whitman Colloquium on *Democratic Vistas*, sponsored by the Walt Whitman Birthplace Association and the English Department of the State University at Stony Brook, N.Y., on April 5, 1975.

1. *The Prose Works 1892*, II, ed. Floyd Stovall (New York: New York University Press, 1964), 374. Subsequent references to this work will be indicated by page numbers in parentheses within the text.

2. "Preface, 1872, to 'As a Strong Bird on Pinions Free,' " Prose Works 1892, II, 463.

3. Israel Zangwill's play, *The Melting Pot*, which opened in Washington, D.C. on October 5, 1908, was the source, although Zangwill may have had a less simplistic view of the process than the one generally associated with his metaphor. See Neil Larry Shumsky, "Zangwill's *The Melting Pot*: Ethnic Tensions on Stage," *American Quarterly*, 27, (March 1975), 29–41.

4. Oscar Handlin, *The Uprooted*, 2nd ed. (New York: Little Brown and Co., 1973); John Higham, *Strangers in the Land: Patterns of American Nativism*, rev. ed. (New York: Athenaeum, 1963). Announced for publication in 1975: Leonard Dinnerstein and David M. Riemers, *Ethnic Americans: A History of Immigration and Assimilation* (New York: Dodd, Mead and Co.).

5. See references below to Horace M. Kallen. After World War II, there was a backlash against racism. Some educators attempted to introduce "intergroup education" into the schools. E.g., the present writer edited the June, 1946, issue of the *English Journal*, the official publication of the National Council of Teachers of English, which was devoted to the subject of intergroup relations, with contributions from Thomas Mann, Ruth Benedict, Ernst Kris, James T. Farrell, Alain Locke, and others.

6. Nathan Glazer and Daniel P. Moynihan, "Why Ethnicity?," *Commentary*, 58, (October, 1974), 33; see also Handlin, *op. cit.*, Chapter Thirteen.

7. Michael Novak, *The Rise of the Unmeltable Ethnics* (New York: Macmillan, 1972). This usage of "ethnics" as a noun also reflects the developments of the sixties: "To say that someone is a member of an ethnic group is implicitly to say that one is describing only one of his characteristics. To say that he is an ethnic is to imply that this is the most important characteristic about him, the determining characteristic. . . ." Henry Fairlie, "The Language of Politics," *The Atlantic Monthly*, (January, 1975), 27.

8. Ben J. Wattenberg in collaboration with Richard M. Scammon, *This U.S.A.* (New York, 1965), p. 45.

9. Babette F. Inglehart and Anthony R. Mangione, *The Image of Pluralism in American Literature: The American Experience of European Ethnic Groups* (New York: Institute on Pluralism and Group Identity of the American Jewish Committee, 1974).

10. *Leaves of Grass*, ed. Harold W. Blodgett and Sculley Bradley (New York: New York University Press, 1965), p. 343.

11. "Preface, 1872," *Prose Works 1892*, II, 461.

12. *Leaves of Grass*, pp. 364–366.

13. "The Spanish Element in Our Nationality," *Prose Works 1892*, II, 552.

14. "The Last Collective Compaction," *Prose Works 1892*, II, 540.

15. *Prose Works 1892*, II, 460.

16. Horace M. Kallen, *Culture and Democracy in the United States* (New York: Boni and Liveright, 1924), p. 125; see also Kallen, *Cultural Pluralism and the American Idea* (Philadelphia: University of Pennsylvania Press, 1956).